In neglecting maritime and naval matters, students of the reign of Charles I have missed or misunderstood important elements in the sickness of the early Stuart polity. The crisis of the monarchy at that time was bound up with the failure of the nation's sea forces in the wars of the 1620s and with Charles's efforts to reform and strengthen the navy by means of ship money. The studies of the shipping industry, shipowning, mutiny and one particular seaman's experience in the transatlantic servants' trade explore the economic and social aspects of seafaring, especially the relations between owners, masters and men at a time of rapid growth and change in the merchant marine.

But the relations between the merchant marine and the Royal Navy were so close that the two should be studied together. The essays on Sir Kenelm Digby's privateering venture in the Mediterranean, on ship money (the longest and most central), on the expedition against the Sallee rovers and on the Parliamentary Navy demonstrate in different ways how naval policy, naval finance and naval enterprise were linked with the problems and the interests of the private sector, which actually took over the Navy in 1642, with not altogether savoury results. This novel juxtaposition of topics will, it is hoped, stimulate new thinking about Caroline society and politics.

SHIPS, MONEY AND POLITICS

SHIPS, MONEY AND POLITICS

SEAFARING AND NAVAL ENTERPRISE IN THE
REIGN OF CHARLES I

KENNETH R. ANDREWS

*Emeritus Professor of History,
University of Hull*

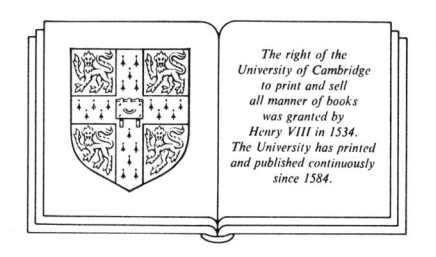

CAMBRIDGE UNIVERSITY PRESS
CAMBRIDGE
NEW YORK   PORT CHESTER   MELBOURNE   SYDNEY

Published by the Press Syndicate of the University of Cambridge
The Pitt Building, Trumpington Street, Cambridge CB2 1RP
40 West 20th Street, New York, NY 10011, USA
10 Stamford Road, Oakleigh, Melbourne 3166, Australia

© Cambridge University Press 1991

First published 1991

Printed in Great Britain at the
University Press, Cambridge

British Library cataloguing in publication data
Andrews, Kenneth R.
Ships, money and politics: seafaring and naval enterprise
in the reign of Charles I
1. English seafaring, history
I. Title
910.45

Library of Congress cataloguing in publication data
Andrews, Kenneth R.
Ships, money, and politics: seafaring and naval enterprise in the reign of Charles I /
Kenneth R. Andrews.
p. cm.
Includes bibliographical references and index.
ISBN 0 521 40116 X
1. Great Britain – History, Naval – 17th century. 2. Great Britain – Politics and
government – 1625–1649. 3. Great Britain – History – Charles I, 1625–1649. 4. Merchant
marine – Great Britain – History – 17th century. 5. Seafaring life – Great Britain – History
– 17th century. 6. Shipping – Great Britain – History – 17th century. I. Title.
DA86.A74 1991
359'.00941 – dc20   90-40407   CIP

ISBN 0 521 40116 X hardback

CONTENTS

Preface		*page* ix
Note on the text		x
Introduction		1
1	The growth of the shipping industry	16
2	The shipowners	34
3	Seamen and mutiny	62
4	Anthony's account	84
5	Digby at Scanderoon	106
6	Ship money: its purposes and uses	128
7	William Rainborowe and the Sallee rovers	160
8	Parliamentary naval enterprise	184
	Appendix A The shipping returns of 1582 and 1629	203
	Appendix B The Trinity House certificates, 1626–1638	210
	Appendix C Charter-parties	215
	Appendix D The 1582 and 1629 returns of seamen	221
Bibliography		225
Index		234

PREFACE

Rather than a general and potentially boring account of Caroline maritime enterprise, I have chosen to make studies of certain topics or episodes which interest me and, I trust, form a meaningful cluster. But while this is not a comprehensive history it does attempt to comprehend the different dimensions of maritime history – economic, naval and political – for it is my main intention to stimulate thought about their relationship and to break down the walls of specialization between them. If students of political history, for example, pick up this book, I hope they will read more than the chapters on ship money and the Parliamentary Navy; and I hope students of economic and social history will get beyond the first three or four chapters. Since my aim is to open up rather than to close down inquiry, the book does not end with conclusions, but it has an introduction putting the particulars into some sort of pattern and perspective.

I wish to thank the Leverhulme Trust for their Emeritus Fellowship award in 1986–7, which enabled me to undertake extensive research on this project at that time. The chapter on mutiny has benefited from exposure to seminars in the Department of History at Hull and in the Department of History at King's College, London (under the auspices of the British Committee of the International Commission on Maritime History), and I am grateful for the helpful comments made on those occasions. Brian Dietz and Leslie Price have been generous with their expertise on specific matters and I am indebted to Howell Lloyd, Geoffrey Scammell, Donald Woodward and Leonard Hebblewhite for their encouragement. In addition to these, I would like to convey special thanks to John Appleby, with whom I have discussed this period of maritime history in many long and fruitful sessions over the years. Finally, for her patient listening and constant support and for helping me to understand my own ideas I am more than grateful to my wife, Otti.

Cottingham, Yorks. March 1990

NOTE ON THE TEXT

The spelling and punctuation in quotations from contemporary sources have, with a few exceptions, been modernized.

Unless otherwise noted, dates herein are rendered in the Old (English) Style, the year being shown also in modern style (according to the Gregorian calendar) for dates from 1 January to 24 March: e.g. 3 February, 1634/5.

For full titles and publication details of works cited in the footnotes see Bibliography.

INTRODUCTION

AFTER THE ignominious retreat of the English fleet from Cadiz in October 1625 the word ran from Spain to Morocco that 'there were now no more Drakes in England, all were hens',[1] and two years later Captain Richard Gifford, in his proposals for naval reform, concurred: in Queen Elizabeth's time, he said, the nobility, gentry and merchants 'did apply themselves much to sea affairs...but we have no such shipping nor such affection to sea affairs; neither have we such seamen to put in execution, and few that know the right way to perform any royal service'.[2] The last notable event in the history of Charles I's Navy before Parliament took it over was M. H. Tromp's rout of a Spanish armada in the Downs, when Admiral Sir John Pennington, commanding an English fleet but powerless to intervene, looked on with mixed feelings. There is indeed little to celebrate in the nation's seafaring activities during the second quarter of the seventeenth century, when its naval forces were finally reduced to fighting each other, though spending rather more time and effort capturing the other side's merchantmen. The only victories it could boast were Rainborowe's at Sallee, which owed much to the alliance of a powerful local marabout, and Digby's at Scanderoon, where the defeated were neutrals.[3] For ships' commanders it was a dismal era, when mutiny, formerly an occasional symptom of bad management, became a habit in merchantmen and king's ships alike, a habit which thenceforth persisted for many generations.[4] No maritime discoveries or great feats of navigation redeem the depressing record. The new colonial trade across the Atlantic produced, apart from a short-lived boom in tobacco, a disproportionate loss of life and shipping.[5] The pressing of seamen for the king's ships and of merchantmen for royal service embittered relations between the merchant marine and the Royal Navy, while the

[1] Castries, *Angleterre*, III, 31.   [2] SP16/54, fols. 14–30.   [3] Chapters 5 and 7 below.
[4] Chapter 3 below.   [5] Shilton and Holworthy, *Examinations, passim*.

old antagonism between gentlemen and tarpaulins festered into a general and debilitating resentment: 'they hate all gentlemen', exclaimed one of Charles's young commanders, and reported that the masters of English merchantmen were more loath than any foreigner to show deference by lowering their topsails in the presence of a royal ship.[6]

The impression of general failure, universal incompetence and unmitigated disaster created by some historians is nevertheless unwarranted by the known facts. The contrast between Elizabethan success and Caroline disgrace, which may have served rhetorical purposes well enough to heap discredit upon the duke of Buckingham and other luckless servants of a devious and unpopular monarch, was and has since been overdrawn. Oppenheim's remark that the Cadiz fiasco was 'an indictment against the government of James I, which had allowed the seamanship of Elizabeth [sic] to die out in this generation' was an unfortunate lapse by the grandfather of English naval history.[7] Seamanship, consisting in the skill, courage and endurance of thousands of men in what were acknowledged abroad as the most formidable men-of-war of that time, and in the great trades to the Mediterranean, the Indian Ocean, the Arctic and the Caribbean, as well as those no less difficult and dangerous trades nearer home, had not declined but improved. Masters and ships' officers were now better equipped in navigation and the handling of relatively large ships than they had been in the queen's time, as the art of navigation was systematically propagated and shipwrights multiplied at least eightfold the handful of large ships (of 200 tons and over) available to Elizabethan sailors.[8] The new long-distance trades demanded and brought forth a generation of masters of nautical capacity and entrepreneurial initiative well beyond the competence of the vast majority of Elizabeth's commanders, while even in the royal ships professional standards were probably higher in the ship-money fleets than they had been in the fleet which faced the Spanish armada in 1588.

Even so, it is not surprising that historians have neglected this phase of maritime history. Not only does it lack the appeal of more heroic or adventurous times, it presents special difficulties to the investigator. The history of commercial shipping is, by comparison with the period after 1660, poorly documented, as is evident even in Davis's eminent masterpiece.[9] Naval affairs, on the other hand, are plentifully documented but particularly hard to interpret. Naval finance in the

[6] SP16/222/13.   [7] Oppenheim, *Administration*, p. 221.
[8] Waters, *Art of Navigation*. On shipping see Chapter 1 below.   [9] Davis, *Shipping Industry*.

early seventeenth century is a baffling subject and naval corruption in Charles I's reign is less visible, perhaps because less rife (though we cannot know) than in his predecessor's. But the main problem arises from the convergence of naval, commercial and political affairs in a period of crisis and revolution. Neither the state Navy nor the merchant marine can be treated separately, for they were far more closely related than in later times, so that anything deeper than mere narrative or superficial description must embrace them both, an embrace few if any naval or economic historians have ever seriously contemplated. Worse still, both had political implications, becoming entangled in the crisis of the monarchy and caught up in the civil conflict which finally overwhelmed it, but whereas an earlier generation of writers recognized this, their descendants have evidently lost interest, leaving naval and maritime matters to the specialists. Simply to juxtapose studies of shipping, seafaring society and naval politics may, it is hoped, stimulate thinking about the connections as well as the spaces between them, but better understanding of the whole complex requires also some attempt to place these phenomena in a larger historical setting, combining, so to speak, the telescope with the microscope.

While England in the reign of Charles I endured the turmoil of a political revolution, another kind of revolution, profound in its consequences for Europe and the world, was at work. The maritime revolution of modern times, which began before 1500, had already by the later seventeenth century transformed international trade and merchant shipping and had also changed the character and dimensions of sea power and naval armament. That developments in the scale and technology of warfare and in the power and machinery of the major European states interacted in varying ways with varying results in the early-modern era is a historical cliché, but it is not often applied to the English case. Here the relationship was constructive later, as Brewer has recently shown,[10] but in the decades before 1650 it was essentially destructive. This is not to say, crudely, that the demands of war caused the collapse of the old régime; but to neglect their impact, or even to accept it without further analysis, is to miss a major factor in the sickness of the early Stuart polity. The question concerns not simply, as might be thought, the financing, or failure to finance, an adequate state Navy, but also the particular character of the kingdom's naval forces and their special relationship with commercial shipping. Naval technology and the requirements of sea power were changing fast in the early seventeenth century, especially after the outbreak of the Thirty

[10] Brewer, *Sinews of Power*.

Years War, and simultaneously the scope and content of England's overseas trade and the structure of her merchant marine changed substantially. How were the government, the naval administration, the shipping world of merchants and masters, as well as Parliament and the public, to react to such a complex of problems, blinkered as they were for the most part by the misleading tradition of Elizabethan glory, and divided in any case by religion and political attitude? It would be pretentious to claim that these studies provide the answer to this multiple question or to the many others implied by it, but they have been designed to shed light on such issues, provided always the reader will take them together, leaping the mental barriers between economic, naval and political history which have been erected inadvertently in the course of specialization.

The term 'commercial revolution' has been applied, justifiably enough, to the growth and re-orientation of England's overseas trade in the century following the Restoration, but this process was in fact a development of the European commercial revolution which dated from the Renaissance. The powerful surge of the European economy in the 'long sixteenth century', that great boom of population, agriculture, trade and industry from the 1470s to the 1610s, brought with it the integration of the Mediterranean, the Atlantic seaboard and the Baltic together with their central-European hinterlands, and was accompanied by the dramatic rise of the valuable trades of Portugal and Spain across the oceans, already by 1600 linking China with Peru and both with Europe. These developments were not so remote from Tudor England as our insular histories seem to imply. The country's prosperity under the early Tudors reflected the prosperity of her European markets, just as the rapid growth of her cloth industry aggravated her social problems. But it was in the later sixteenth century that English shipping began in earnest to grasp the opportunities that European economic expansion had created. The first breakthrough came with the opening of the White Sea trade in the 1550s, but much more valuable in terms of commodities and employment of shipping was England's re-entry into the Mediterranean in the 1570s. From that decade onwards the range and size of the nation's merchantmen advanced with the privateering boom of the nineties, the founding of the East India Company in 1600 and the long-delayed rise of the transatlantic trades after that.

In commercial value these new trades did not equal England's old and manifold exchange with the Continent, but in their pace of growth they far outstripped it and in terms of shipping they were especially

INTRODUCTION

important. Not only were they responsible for much of the striking increase in the nation's tonnage, but to a large extent they employed ships of substantial size and strength, the so-called 'defensible' merchantmen characteristic of the Mediterranean, African and East India trades, ships generously equipped with men and guns even in their normal voyages and deemed suitable for war service when the need arose. But alongside these powerful vessels now appeared increasing numbers of vulnerable ships great and small, principally the huge fleet of east-coast colliers and the numerous West Country craft frequenting the Newfoundland fishery. The English merchant marine was thus not only growing at an unprecedented rate, but acquiring a different shape, posing new problems and changing the terms of sea warfare and sea power.

Charles's subjects generally cherished the legend of a triumphant Elizabethan war upon Spain, won primarily at sea by the sea-dogs who commanded and manned the queen's ships as well as their own, promoting combined fleets of royal men-of-war and privateers in a continuous campaign of plunder against the plate fleets and the silver-bearing colonies of the Papist tyrant. This richly embroidered version of history was not entirely fictitious, for Elizabethan sea power, though far from capable of winning the war or even striking the enemy a crippling blow, did consist in the combined efforts of the queen's ships and the much more numerous voluntary ships of her subjects, among whom shipowning merchants, and especially Londoners, contributed most. Moreover this national, if somewhat motley, maritime force could devote most of its attention to enemy (and not seldom neutral) shipping because it had no great commerce of its own to defend. Before the end of the war, however, the development of Dunkirk privateering against England's lesser merchantmen and fishing fleets had already upset that comfortable scene, which was to be further disrupted by the rising menace of the Barbary corsairs and the resumption of Dunkirk raiding in 1625, by which time British waters teemed with easy prey.

On the other hand, England by then had also accumulated a far more impressive array of strong merchantmen, which in practice exercised a kind of sea power on the trade routes they frequented. Only twice before 1650 did the Crown send its own ships past Gibraltar: once to parley with the Algerines and once ostensibly to discipline private English men-of-war whose indiscriminate depredations were arousing a chorus of protest.[11] In fact the English *bertoni* in the Inland Sea were well able to fend for themselves and in certain parts, such as the

[11] Andrews, 'Cecil and Mediterranean'.

neighbourhood of the Gulf of Corinth, achieved at times a dominant presence.[12] This was likewise the case in the East India and West African trades and above all in the West Indies, where the maritime presence was associated with the planting of the island tobacco colonies in the 1620s. What part was this great reserve of maritime force to play in time of war? In 1588 a then much smaller and less powerful reserve had rallied (though not with all the enthusiasm the government wished to see) to support the Royal Navy in protecting the realm, and for the rest of that war the armed traders and privateers had either collaborated with the queen's ships in joint-stock enterprise or had set forth, singly or in petty squadrons, on voyages of plunder or ventures combining plunder with trade. In short, they had pursued the sea war much as they pleased, without being called upon to bear the brunt of unrewarding duties such as military transportation, convoying and patrolling the Narrow Seas.

But when war with Spain broke out again in 1625, soon to be followed by war with France, conflicting views about the conduct of the war at sea quickly emerged. No longer seriously worried by threats of invasion and uninterested in military intervention in the Continental struggle, the political nation responded eagerly to Buckingham's talk of a profitable war, with letters of marque denied to none and 'propositions of venturing whither you yourselves may go and shall have the honey of the business'.[13] Maritime and colonial ambitions fortified Puritan hostility to Spain, memories of Elizabethan privateering were evoked and Sir Walter Ralegh's notion of breaking that great empire in pieces was revived, along with the story of Drake's first raids on Panama.[14] Proposals for an English West India Company were floated and it was suggested in Parliament that a great joint-stock company should be formed to undertake offensive operations while the Royal Navy should protect the coasts, which meant of course protecting commercial shipping in home waters as well. Such a division of labour would have served the interests of the London shipowning merchants and their friends admirably and emanated from a group of MPs associated with Robert Rich, second earl of Warwick. Chief promoter of the Bermuda colony, privateering magnate and shipowner, with wide-ranging interests in transatlantic enterprise, Warwick was to lead the Providence Company in a private war on Spain in the West Indies and would eventually become the Parliamentary Lord High Admiral. A patron of Puritans and an outspoken opponent of ship

[12] See Chapter 5 below for example. [13] Lockyer, *Buckingham*, p. 265.
[14] Drake, *Sir Francis Drake Revived*.

INTRODUCTION

money, he advocated and actively pursued a strategy of maritime enterprise in an Elizabethan tradition generally perceived to be at odds with the main direction of early Stuart policy.[15]

For, in spite of Buckingham's honeyed rhetoric, events soon showed that the Royal Navy could not cope with the tasks of war in home and neighbouring waters without large-scale assistance from the merchant marine. Elizabeth's Navy, supreme in its day, had under her successor decayed for fifteen years and then, from 1618, recovered some semblance of its former strength, but now faced rivals far more powerful and demands far more onerous than any Drake and Hawkins had known. With the advent of the Thirty Years War the long naval revolution of early-modern times moved up a gear. Change in the size, fire-power and numbers of warships, which technical innovation had rapidly propelled in the decades around 1500, had slowed in the later sixteenth century, but now gathered pace once more. The race for sea power became urgent as Spain with the Spanish Netherlands on the one hand and the United Provinces on the other, with the later help of France, fought for control of the Narrow Seas and the vital sea-link between Spain and Dunkirk. These wealthy and strong states, which had each laboured under severe disadvantage as naval powers in the late sixteenth century, built up formidable navies in the following decades, particularly from 1620 under the spur of a war of attrition. Their capital warships, prototypes of the ships of the line, those floating gun platforms soon to dominate the sea, were supplemented by numerous light men-of-war combining quick manœuvre and striking force, some state owned, some privateersmen.

England lost her lead, and by the 1630s found she could no longer match the naval forces exercised by either side in the intensive conflict waged for the sea-lanes of western Europe. Formidable war machines though the king's great ships certainly were, they were few in number, notoriously sluggish, unwieldy and leaky, and so expensive to operate that it was a matter of policy to use them as little as possible. Yet the king possessed very few light warships either, and most of those, notably the ten 180-ton Lion's Whelps hastily built in 1627–8 to meet desperate need, spent far too much time in dock under repair, and when at sea found themselves too often outsailed by the speedy and nimble raiders of Dunkirk and quite incapable of catching corsairs in open water. In 1618 a royal commission of inquiry into abuses in the Navy had found the ships deplorably decayed and the administration

---

[15] Warwick still awaits an adequate biography. On the West India Company proposals, see Appleby, 'West Indies'.

wasteful and corrupt. It had instituted substantial reform and greatly improved the administration in the years that followed, but the principal object of its worthy chief, Sir John Coke, was financial retrenchment. The Navy was to be restored to something like its Elizabethan strength, but at cut price, as the architect of Jacobean reform, Lord Treasurer Cranfield, demanded, and as royal policy, inherited by James from Elizabeth herself, dictated. The sinews of state power, dependent as they were on taxation and the voluntary collaboration of the landed and commercial élites which largely owned and managed the realm, could not sustain re-armament on the scale required to wage successful war in the 1620s.

The Crown's prime interests and concerns lay in Europe. Apart from the dynastic involvement of the early Stuarts in the fate of the Palatinate, the safety of the British Isles and British seas and relations with the states bordering the Atlantic necessarily governed the disposition of the Crown's forces, just as they had in Elizabeth's time. Charles's priorities were broadly similar to hers in this respect, but to meet them he needed a more powerful Navy, which could not have been created at short notice when war came in 1625, nor in the few years following, even had Parliament consented to finance it. A principal reason for the popularity of a diffuse, commerce-raiding strategy was its cheapness, but, although much of the cost of Elizabeth's sea war had taken the form of private investment in joint-stock expeditions great and small, the notion that her Navy paid its way in Spanish silver was a myth. Even with Parliamentary subsidies more valuable and more often granted to her than to her successors, she could not maintain her wars without ruining the financial health of the régime and undermining its political strength. After 1603 the escalation of the nation's maritime commerce, of European naval forces and of the needs of increasingly sophisticated warships so inflated costs that even the routine operations of sea warfare were expensive, and anything more ambitious became exorbitantly so. Thus the Cadiz expedition of 1625 was reckoned to have cost half a million sterling: more, that is, than Elizabeth's gross yearly income in the 1590s.[16]

Faced with the rising price of sea power, the government might and did expect Parliament to do its duty, but that did not extend to readying the state for war before it happened – nor even, as it transpired in 1625, when it happened. Charles, unable to obtain adequate supply from Parliament, tried to raise the funds he required by other means

---

[16] Oppenheim, *Administration*, p. 225; Dietz, *Public Finance*, pp. 109, 227; Andrews, *Trade, Plunder and Settlement*, p. 228.

and ran into widespread resistance he could not overcome. A succession of disasters abroad, partial breakdown of civil government at home and open conflict between king and Commons virtually forced the termination of the wars with France and Spain. Such a bald and unilateral account of the onset of the crisis of the monarchy obviously fails to do justice to the complexity of its causes and features,[17] but it may serve as a reminder that the crisis was, at least immediately, about money and power, and more particularly the cost — as well as the character and conduct — of what was essentially a sea war. The miserable course of that war was responsible, however, not only for the political crisis of 1629 and Charles's recourse to personal rule, but also for a change in naval thinking which afterwards bore bitter fruit.

In these five years of sea war the government could make up for the deficiencies of the Royal Navy only by engaging the services of merchant auxiliaries on an unprecedented scale for the naval expeditions and other operations it found necessary. They proved unwilling and ineffective partners. Owners grudged endangering their ships and waiting months or years for payment, masters resented subordination to the captains set over them, seamen rounded up by the hated press were mutinous and quick to desert. Many of the owners would have preferred to employ their ships in trade or privateering, many no doubt wanted a different kind of war, sentiments endorsed by masters and men. Their war experience did nothing to endear the seafaring community to the royal service and left a legacy of suspicion and dislike on both sides. On the side of authority, disgust with the performance of the merchantmen contributed to discussion of proposals for expansion of the Navy, brought forward in 1627, providing especially for large numbers of lighter men-of-war and pinnaces to replace most of the merchant auxiliaries. Little was done to implement these plans, but in 1628 acute financial stress prompted the government to initiate a new and radical scheme of ship money, by means of which the entire country was to subscribe money (not ships, as the ports and maritime parts had formerly) to meet the Crown's naval expenditure.[18] This demand, though abandoned within days, anticipated in essentials the ship-money levies of 1635 and subsequent years. Although it cannot be maintained that the 1628 scheme was designed to finance a programme of naval development, the two concepts at least coexisted and would in due course come together, for good and ill, in the shape of royal fleets funded directly by the nation.

[17] A good recent discussion is the introduction to Cust and Hughes, *Conflict*.
[18] Swales, 'Ship money levy'; Chapter 6 below.

SHIPS, MONEY AND POLITICS

This is not to say that the purpose of the ship-money levies of the 1630s was simply naval re-armament. Nor, however, was it simply to impose general taxation without representation, nor yet by some wicked plot to provide the king of Spain with a fleet to crush his Protestant enemies. The motivation of ship money was complex and – thanks partly to disingenuous presentation and partly to hostile comment then and later – obscure.[19] But the argument for a more efficient and effective state Navy became unanswerable in that decade. Barbary piracy was mounting again, after a lull in the late twenties, into an intolerable scourge and the West Country fishing interest cried out for protection. English merchantmen, as the chief neutral carriers, suffered increasing interference from the belligerents in the Thirty Years War – Dunkirkers, Biscayners, Hollanders and, from 1635, Frenchmen. Naval power was essential to the protection and assertion of English interests abroad, as the doctrine of the Sovereignty of the Sea emphatically declared in 1634. The terms of that declaration may sound chauvinistic, but its intention was fundamentally defensive in the context of the dangerous overspill of the fierce maritime war then being waged by Dutchmen and Dunkirkers in British and nearby seas.[20] Moreover, the Navy was the only considerable lever the king had at his disposal to exert any real influence in Europe or to make his diplomatic moves at all meaningful. Whatever the intentions underlying those moves may have been – and they were perhaps not so unarguably damnable as his critics supposed – Charles needed sea power to pursue a credible foreign policy, and such a policy had to include maritime security as a principal concern. Ship money was in fact as central to his reasonable and responsible aims and interests in the years of peace, prosperity and apparent success as it was to his undoing.

The greatest benefit ship money conferred upon the Royal Navy was the continuity achieved by yearly summer and winter guards. The recent wars had shown that without regular exercise the Navy was likely to be ill led, ill managed and ill manned chiefly for want of experience of war conditions. The readying of ships for active service, always a cumbrous business, was so slow as to elicit constant complaint from frustrated commanders, and the performance of both ships and men was frequently unsatisfactory. The inefficiencies and abuses rooted in the service were of course compounded in those wars by lack of money, but they recurred in 1635 and 1636 when there was no such

---

[19] Chapter 6 below.
[20] Fulton, *Sovereignty of Sea*, saw it as a bombastic excuse for raising ship money.

INTRODUCTION

lack. The earl of Northumberland's criticism of naval abuses, which has usually been cited to the discredit of the ship-money fleets in general, was made in the second of their seven years of operations, the succession of which alone made it possible to identify and tackle the problems. Nor did those fleets deserve the scorn poured upon them by Whig historians. On the whole their service was useful. Since the country was not at war it could hardly have been glorious, and to blame the earl of Lindsey, for example, for chasing up and down the Channel without actually engaging the French or the Dutch is unfair, particularly because his movements had the desired effect of preventing the junction of those fleets. The Navy by its regular presence and steady work did much to ensure the extraordinary prosperity of England's merchant shipping in those years. The forces ship money financed were inferior in strength to those set forth by the warring powers at this time, but their weight in the balance was respected abroad and gave Charles some influence until 1639, when the Scottish wars began his downfall.

In the long run, moreover, the ship-money years hold a significant place in the history of the Navy, marking as they do a distinct step forward in the evolution of a professional state Navy out of the Elizabethan amalgam of royal and private enterprise. Merchant men-of-war played but a small part in the ship-money fleets, being integrated in a unified royal force staffed increasingly by career officers. Though the fleets were not powerful or flexible enough to reverse the tide of disorder and hostilities in home waters, the sources, when fairly examined, show that they did their best in difficult circumstances, hampered though they sometimes were by their master's political ineptitude. Their generally humdrum record includes Rainborowe's well-conducted operation at Sallee and is seriously marred only by failures for which the king personally, not his Navy, was to blame. For Charles took a strong personal interest in his ships and his captains and intervened to direct their operations when he thought fit. Furthermore, in referring to ship money as 'the king's great business' his ministers pointed to the fact, which can have been no secret, that he personally supervised its planning, presentation, administration and vigorous enforcement.

This intense royal concern would in any case have lent a certain political significance to naval affairs in Charles's reign, but what made them centrally important in the crisis of the monarchy was their place in public finance on the one hand and foreign policy on the other. Foreign affairs in this period have for a long time – until quite recently – been out of fashion among historians, who have paid little attention either to public finance. Better understanding of the crisis of the monarchy and the origins of the civil war will surely depend in future upon renewed inquiry into such matters of central policy, neglected unduly as they have been in favour of inconclusive speculation about social change and the minutiae of local history. This is not to say that social change can be ruled out of the account altogether – indeed it was discernible and politically relevant in the seafaring world – nor that local history is beside the point. The key to the régime's power structure lay precisely in that mesh of central and local interests upon which early Stuart policies and local resistance to them imposed increasing strain. But here again the struggle over ship money, perhaps the severest strain in the later 1630s, brings shipping and naval business once more to the heart of politics. This set of studies is not intended to suggest a new interpretation of Caroline politics or to enter into the continuing debate thereon, but those concerned should not overlook the attention paid to maritime affairs in official and political circles throughout Charles's reign. Historians cannot but be aware how large these matters loom in the state papers, nor can they afford to ignore what seemed important to contemporaries.

To the king, as Clarendon makes clear, the loss of his Navy to Parliament in 1642 came as an unexpected blow. That this instrument, the key to his foreign and domestic designs, which he had not merely inherited but laboriously nursed, should pass so easily into his opponents' hands was hard to bear. It was by no means inevitable, but must have come as less of a surprise to others than to Charles. For the merchants, masters and mariners who constituted the seafaring community had ample reason, as we have seen, to dislike the king's service. Though few radicals were to be found in their ranks even in the late forties, politically they belonged to the City of London and Parliament, and once Parliament possessed the fleet the natural leaders of the merchant marine took over its entire management. These were the rising men whose skill and luck had enabled them to exploit the expansion of trade and shipping. Some were rich merchants and members of Parliament like Samuel Vassall and Alexander Bence, both of whom had a strong interest in shipping. Some were those élite masters of the great merchantmen in the rich trades beyond Europe: Thomas Trenchfield, Roger Twiddy, Richard Cranley and others. These too were shipowners, becoming merchant owners as their fortunes progressed. Whether merchants coming from trade into shipping or masters moving from shipping into trade, they formed together a close network bound by business and family ties, an

INTRODUCTION

important interest group influential in the City and commmanding its own special corporation, the Trinity House of Deptford.[21]

It was this London-based element, already dominant in the seafaring business (though each provincial port had a little shipowning élite of its own), which assumed control of the Navy in 1642, under the leadership of the earl of Warwick. A largely Presbyterian clique of shipowning merchants and Trinity House Elders, they staffed the Admiralty and Navy committees and monopolized the naval administration, while the commanders of Parliament's ships were selected from their friends and business associates, the foremost captains of merchantmen. Merchantmen were now engaged in large numbers for Parliament's service and privateers worked closely with the state's forces. Naval operations were for the most part diffuse, consisting not so much in fighting the enemy as in intercepting his supplies, stopping up his ports and helping others to resist the king. Parliament's naval forces thus differed markedly in character from the ship-money fleets, resembling more, in their composition and conduct, Elizabeth's hybrid Navy. They made a useful contribution to the winning of the civil war and doubtless also to the pockets of such well-placed men as the Bence brothers, the Swanley brothers and that ubiquitous entrepreneur, Maurice Thompson. How well these served the cause and how well the cause served them it is impossible now to determine, but without question the service was reciprocal.[22]

What of the men who worked the merchantmen great and small, the privateers and the king's fighting ships? Indifferently called seamen, sailors, mariners, they are reckoned to have numbered only some 20,000–25,000 in 1629[23] though increasing fast in the next two decades. No distinction can be made between those who served in the Royal Navy and those who sailed in merchant ventures: they were the same, though the conditions of work, discipline and pay they found in the two contexts were not. These facts of sea-life of course bred discontent. Bad victuals, arrears of pay, the injustices of the press system and the brutality of punishments in the royal service drove seamen repeatedly to desperate riot during the wars with France and Spain. Not that all was sweetness and light in the merchantmen, as the harrowing reports of disease in Anthony's last voyage and Digby's cruise illustrate.[24] The great majority of serving seamen were less than thirty years of age.[25] At

[21] Chapter 2 below describes shipowning merchants and masters in detail.
[22] See Chapter 8 on the Parliamentary Navy.   [23] Appendix D below.
[24] Chapters 4 and 5 below.
[25] Seamen's ages are given in some of the returns discussed in Appendix D below.

a time when the frontiers of trade were expanding dramatically, life aboard may well have been nastier, more brutish and briefer than in the days of smaller ships and shorter voyages. Piracy had not for generations been so common or so cruel as when it became, in the early seventeenth century, a highly organized and widespread trade in men.

Seamen were not so anonymous as might be supposed. In fact names, ages, places of origin and residence and details of their lives aboard and in port are to be found in plenty in the records of the High Court of Admiralty. In one particular case a purser's business and personal accounts enable us even to assemble a patchy picture of his last years and pathetic end.[26] The wealth of evidence in the sailors' depositions could be used to create a vivid mosaic of sea-life in the second quarter of the seventeenth century, but the picture would in many respects doubtless apply to the previous and succeeding eras of sail. There is no reason to suppose that seamen were worse treated by their owners and masters or more exploited by them at this time than earlier or later. Although the Admiralty Court records do contain some convincing accounts of violent, vindictive or fraudulent masters, much of the evidence in disputes between seamen and their masters or owners was patently exaggerated for the sake of effect and absolutely contradicted by the other side. Gross overstatement in such cases was perfectly normal. Yet there are good reasons to conclude that this reign saw a marked increase in the frequency of mutiny, not only in the king's service, but also in merchantmen, where it often took the form of a strike. Moreover it is now clear that this type of collective action remained a common feature of seafaring in traders and warships alike for many generations after this.

Does this mean that the reign of Charles I saw the onset of that 'class war' in shipping which has been propounded for a later era? It seems unlikely.[27] Highly misleading though it would be to depict the sailor's life in glowing colours, the relations between masters and men were not especially bad at this time. The trust and collaboration necessary in the running of a ship could break down for many reasons, as the law and custom of the sea had long acknowledged, but in the early seventeenth century the traditional elements of common interest and common culture in that relationship had not been eroded so far as to cause general strife. Indeed, one of the remarkable features of the period was a substantial advance in seamen's wages, which surely reflected the

---

[26] Chapter 4 below.
[27] Rediker, *Between*, referring to the period from about 1690 to about 1750, offers a Marxist analysis which has aroused controversy: see Rediker et al. 'Roundtable'.

INTRODUCTION

unusually sustained and heavy demand for their labour. Naval development and commercial growth combined at this juncture (internationally as well as nationally) to promote employment and so improved seamen's bargaining power. Mutiny in the king's service may have been an act of desperation, but in commercial seafaring it signified rather a certain confidence in collective muscle, confidence reinforced by the general and apparent weakness of authority. This was particularly marked in merchantmen and privateers, but even commanders of the king's ships frequently lacked the effective power to impose order and obedience. Did not Charles himself have a similar problem?

CHAPTER 1

THE GROWTH OF THE SHIPPING INDUSTRY

THAT ENGLAND'S shipping resources grew vigorously in the first half of the seventeenth century despite a setback in the late 1620s has long been recognized in general terms.[1] The detailed breakdown of the 1582 and 1629 national surveys in Appendix A below now permits a rather more analytical account of that growth even though the evidence is not good enough to warrant precise and firm conclusions. Allowing for the adjustments there itemized, the total tonnage of the realm appears to have increased in those forty-seven years from about 71,000 to about 121,000, an advance of 70 per cent. The figures suggest, however, that this advance was entirely due to a rise in the number and tonnage of larger vessels, above 99 tons in burden. For with the putative additions the tonnage of lesser vessels in 1582 (approximately 46,000) actually exceeds that in 1629 (43,000), whereas the larger vessels more than tripled their total tonnage – from about 25,000 to 78,000. The figures for shipping of the lesser sort are of course less reliable than those concerning the larger vessels, in which the authorities were more interested. They were especially suspect in 1629, when London and Ipswich, which far outdistanced any other ports in their shipping, returned very few lesser vessels and undoubtedly understated their resources in that respect, as did some other substantial ports. The decline in the tonnage of minor shipping may well therefore be illusory. On the other hand, since we have no reason to postulate any considerable growth, it is safe to conclude that the rise in the total national tonnage was indeed due more or less entirely to the remarkable advance in the total tonnage of the larger ships. Equally striking, however, is the rise in the average tonnage of the larger vessels from 138 tons in 1582 to 194 tons in 1629. Thus the rise in the number of such ships from 180 to 403 (124 per cent) was less impressive than the increase in their total tonnage (222 per cent).

[1] Davis, *Shipping Industry*, pp. 7–11.

THE GROWTH OF THE SHIPPING INDUSTRY

These trends are even more pronounced in the case of London. There the total tonnage increased 163 per cent (from 12,298 to 32,255) and London's share of the nation's shipping rose from 17 per cent in 1582 to 27 per cent in 1629. But the capital's stock of larger ships rose much faster—by 278 per cent (from 8,280 to 31,320 tons)—while its share in the national stock of larger shipping, already one third in 1582 (8,280 out of 24,765 tons), rose to 40 per cent in 1629 (31,320 out of 78,030 tons). At the same time the average burden of the larger Londoners increased from 138 tons to 275 tons—far more than did the national average for such ships—while their actual number rose by only 90 per cent (from 60 to 114). These figures show London rather less dominant in late Tudor times than outport complaints and contemporary opinion generally suggested, though rapidly advancing to realize the fears they commonly expressed.

Yet the East Anglian ports maintained a considerably greater volume of shipping than London did. Their share of national tonnage in 1582 was 28 per cent (20,181 tons), rising to 30 per cent (some 37,000 tons) in 1629. Their stock of larger ships (over 99 tons) advanced faster than London's—by 345 per cent (from 6,290 to 28,010 tons)—and their number of such vessels tripled (from 52 to 156). Conversely, however, the average tonnage of those vessels increased by only 50 per cent (from 121 to 180 tons). Thus, while London and East Anglia both multiplied their tonnage of substantial vessels, London achieved this mainly by increasing their burden, whereas East Anglia did so rather by increasing their numbers. But London and East Anglia were so closely related and mutually complementary in respect of shipping that they deserve joint consideration. Together they accounted for 46 per cent (32,479 tons) of the national tonnage in 1582 and about 57 per cent thereof in 1629. With respect to substantial ships of over 99 tons, they accounted for 60 per cent of the national tonnage in 1582 (14,570 out of 24,285 tons) and 76 per cent of it in 1629 (59,330 out of 78,030), while 69 per cent of the nation's vessels in that class belonged to this combined region.

Behind these figures lay the fact of a commercial revolution in progress. The old structure of the nation's trade, with its heavy dependence on the export of cloth to northern and central Europe, the structure characteristic of the Tudor period, was giving way to a new, more diversified pattern, in which shipping played a greater role. The change, which may be dated back to the middle of the sixteenth century and the beginning of the Muscovy trade, gathered momentum with the re-entry of English ships into the Mediterranean in the 1570s and the opening of the Turkey trade in 1580. The Straits thus became the gateway to England's commercial growth, a prospering trade, despite all the risks and violence, to Italy, the Greek islands and the Ottoman Empire, a trade which employed increasing numbers of strong ships, Londoners for the most part, though the Suffolk ports and Yarmouth also contributed, especially to the Italian trade. With the new century came the founding of the East India Company, which soon became the leading employer of great ships. Although the 1629 return attributed only eight ships, totalling 5,700 tons, to the company, its records show that it dispatched no less than 131 ships in the first thirty years of the century, a total of 57,189 tons, and 37, amounting to 19,986 tons, in the next decade.[2] In fact the company's difficulties were at their very worst in 1629, and that year's survey does scant justice to its contribution to shipping over the period as a whole.

The ending of the Elizabethan war with Spain in 1603 brought on a powerful surge in Anglo-Iberian trade, which continued to flourish until the war of 1625–30. This branch of England's overseas trade, which was responsible (like the Mediterranean and East India trades) for an expanding and increasingly valuable flow of imports, employed numerous ships of middling burden from London and the outports, especially those of the West Country, though East Anglian shipping also played its part. The new Spanish war of course reduced this trade to an illicit trickle, so that once again the 1629 survey fails adequately to register the rising trend, which was renewed with increased vigour after the war, as we shall see. Along with the Peninsula trade, that of the Atlantic islands prospered also, especially the wine trade of the Canaries, which, unlike the young and precarious West African trade, seems to have suffered little from the wars with France and Spain. Both used sizeable ships – of 100 tons or so for the Canary Islands and more powerful ones for the African mainland.[3] Longer voyages, employing larger vessels for longer periods, gave shipping a more important role in the country's overseas trade than formerly, and a more important place in the national economy. Such was the commercial thrust promoting the rapid advance we have noted in London's shipping and to a minor degree in that of East Anglia as well.

It was the east-coast coal trade, however, which did most to boost East Anglian shipping. London itself, the main market for coal,

[2] Chaudhuri, *East India Company*.
[3] Steckley, *Paige Letters*, p. xxix. Typical ships in the Africa trade were the Londoners *Ark* (300 tons), owned by Nicholas Crispe, William Cloberry and others, *Crispiana* (400 tons), owned by Crispe, Humphrey Slany and others, and Crispe's *Negro Merchant* (110 tons): SP16/17, nos. 104, 28, 95.

contributed little to its carriage, which was handled by east-coast ports, led by Newcastle and Ipswich.[4] Coal shipments from the Tyne and Wear grew at a phenomenal rate in the few decades before 1640. The average coal cargo arriving in London rose from 73 tons in 1606 to 139 tons in 1638, while the colliers of Newcastle multiplied and the recorded tonnage of Ipswich rose from 1,818 in 1582 to 14,100 in 1629. The eastern ports also plied a large and rapidly developing trade in fish, corn and other foodstuffs, especially for the London market.[5] Great Yarmouth, thriving on its Icelandic and North Sea fisheries and strongly engaged in overseas as well as coastwise trade, probably advanced its shipping much more than these surveys suggest,[6] though the progress of Hull, competing with the Dutch in the Baltic, was doubtless slower. Even so, Hull's Baltic traders are reckoned to have doubled in size between 1580 and 1640 and her Baltic imports to have reached a higher level in the 1630s then ever before.[7]

Without doubt the predominance of London and East Anglia was accentuated by the depression of West Country shipping at both the dates of these surveys.[8] In 1582 the western ports from Dorset round to Bristol were just beginning to climb their way out of a deep depression. The returns of that year thus measure their resources at or near a low ebb. Thereafter they flourished as the Newfoundland fishing fleet developed from some 40 or 50 vessels in 1578 to about 250 in 1615, a level maintained until 1624. From 1600 also the West Country trade to France, the Iberian peninsula and Italy, which included re-exports of fish, entered a thriving phase, employing many middling ships of some 30 to 80 tons, while larger vessels plied the triangular trade from the western ports to the American fisheries and thence to the markets of southern Europe. Then, from 1625 to 1629, the wars with France and Spain and the incursions of the Barbary corsairs brought disaster. The main fish markets collapsed, men and ships were stayed wholesale by government orders and the fishing fleet, lacking adequate defence against the Dunkirkers and the 'Turks', dwindled even more from fear of capture than from actual losses. The European trade of Exeter, Dartmouth, Weymouth, Poole and doubtless the other main ports suffered heavily. Poole, for example, reported in 1628 that in the

---

[4] Nef, *Coal Industry*; Willan, *Coasting Trade*.   [5] Willan, *Coasting Trade*, pp. 111–45.
[6] Manship, *History of Yarmouth*, pp. 97, 120.
[7] Davis, *Hull Trade*, pp. 22–3. Hull also had a considerable interest in the coasting trade and northern whaling at this time: *ibid.*, pp. 12–14. Hull's 1626 shipping return has to be rejected as far too low for credibility.
[8] The following account of the West Country fishing trade is based on Cell, *Newfoundland*, pp. 100–7.

previous four years it had lost 20 ships amounting to 1,465 tons and was now reduced to 16 totalling 838 tons. Its contribution to the Newfoundland fishery had declined from 20 ships to 3.[9] Early in 1629 the West Country ships at the Banks were said to number a mere 40.

The 1629 returns for Dorset, South Devon and Cornwall show 356 vessels with a tonnage of 17,953, including 37 of more than 99 tons amounting to 4,970 tons. The 1582 figures, with the addition for Plymouth, Dartmouth and Falmouth suggested in Appendix A, show a total of 12,430 tons, with 23 larger vessels accounting for 2,945 tons. Thus, despite the heavy setback of the wars, this part of the West Country (excluding, that is, Bristol, North Devon and Somerset) still had some 36 per cent more tonnage than in 1582. The increase in the tonnage of larger vessels amounted to 69 per cent, a respectable advance, even if not sufficient to keep pace with London and East Anglia, which could hardly be expected in view of the region's characteristic dependence on small and middling ships. It was not in the upper range that the southwest ports suffered serious war-time loss. Indeed the evidence concerning privateering from Plymouth, Dartmouth and Weymouth in those years suggests that they found employment for many more substantial ships than the 1629 returns admitted.[10] It was of course in the lower range that the effects of predation were severely felt. In ships of under 100 tons the 1629 returns measured an increase of only 27 per cent on the 1582 figure, itself a very low one, and clearly misrepresent the long-term trend, which was quickly resumed after 1629. In 1634 the fishing merchants of the West Country claimed, with what is now considered reasonable accuracy, that the Newfoundland trade alone employed 26,700 tons of their shipping, at which time the triangular and European trades were likewise flourishing once again.[11]

The 1629 figures omit Barnstaple, Bridgwater and their neighbours, which probably fared much the same as the Dorset, South Devon and Cornish ports, but they show Bristol thriving, with more than double its tonnage of 1582 and more than treble its former array of larger ships. In fact Bristol, by a shrewd combination of trade and privateering during the war years, was continuing the impressive resurgence it had

---

[9] *CSPD 1628–9*, p. 103.
[10] Weymouth's privateers of 100 tons and over numbered at least 13 and Plymouth's no less than 32, whereas the returns attributed only 3 such vessels to the former and 7 to the latter. Dartmouth had 22 privateers of this class operating and showed only 15 in 1629. These privateering data are convincingly detailed and the figures cited are the calculated minima as opposed to the possible maxima: Appleby, 'Privateering', II, 308, based on details in II, 81–96, 108–37.   [11] Cell, *Newfoundland*, pp. 110, 118.

achieved since 1600 and was much better equipped with shipping than the 1629 return allowed. In the war years it set forth at least 72 ships with letters of marque, having a total tonnage of 8,054, more than treble that reported in 1582 and some 60 per cent more than that reported in 1629. These included 38 of over 99 tons burden, more than four times as many as the port possessed in 1582.[12] Nor does it seem likely that Bristol in 1629 had only 18 vessels under 100 tons, having had 20 such listed in 1582 and 26 as recently as 1626.[13] The 1629 returns thus certainly underrated Bristol's shipping as well as that of Weymouth, Plymouth and Dartmouth, while reflecting also the sharp but shortlived depression of the southwest fishery ports. The general advance of West Country shipping in the period from 1580 to 1640 was undoubtedly much more impressive than the two national surveys imply.

To this extent the 1629 survey understates the progress of the nation's shipping as a whole, as it does in certain other respects already noted. What followed in the 1630s was not merely recovery but a remarkable shipping boom, the extent of which, however, in terms of increased tonnage, can only be estimated by more or less informed guesswork. There is no evidence that any fresh survey was conducted, but Edward Nicholas, who as Secretary to the Admiralty had been responsible for that of 1629, added a note to two later copies of it, dated 1635, stating the number of larger ships (over 99 tons) built and 'repaired' since 1629. One copy gives 88 and 49 respectively, the other 95 and 52. These notes say nothing about the identity, home ports or tonnage of the individual vessels, nor is it likely that the figures are complete. They may, however, be taken to indicate the minimum of new tonnage added to the national stock between 1629 and 1635. Using as multiplier the average burden (194) of ships over 99 tons in 1629, the new ships would total 17,000 tons and those repaired another 10,000 approximately. Treating this as a minimum and allowing for ships scrapped or otherwise lost in those years, we may put the net increase at perhaps 10,000 tons.[14] To this should be added a fairly substantial figure to represent the increased tonnage of lesser vessels. Dorset, South Devon and Cornwall in 1629 returned 12,983 tons of these, which we may suppose to have doubled with the recovery of the fishing fleet by 1635, so that it seems reasonable to postulate for the country as a whole an

---

[12] Appleby, 'Privateering', II, 308, based on details in II, 145–67.
[13] McGrath, 'Merchant Venturers', pp. 79–80. This 1626 report shows 42 ships with a total tonnage of 3,559, including 16 of over 99 tons.
[14] SP16/282, fols. 270–6; SP16/283, fols. 241–6. These documents, like SP16/270/64 of June 1634, reproduce the 1629 data and so imply that there was no new survey.

advance of at least 15,000 tons in the lower range. In this period, however, English merchants bought many ships abroad, in both parts of the Netherlands, chiefly of the larger size. No fair estimate of their total burden is possible, but it would undoubtedly have exceeded, say, 5,000 tons. In all, therefore, the tonnage of the realm may have risen by some 30,000 in the five years following the wars, to reach an estimated 150,000 in 1635, with some further increase in the later thirties. These calculations must obviously be treated with caution, but they are likely to err on the modest side, making no allowance, for example, for the evident understatements we have noticed in the 1629 returns. In short it would not be unreasonable to conclude that the nation's shipping amounted to well over 150,000 tons by 1640.[15]

The shipping boom of the 1630s is well authenticated. As Kepler and Taylor have shown, English shipping benefited greatly from the neutrality of the country during that phase of the Thirty Years War, when Spain (including the Spanish Netherlands) and the United Provinces, joined in 1635 by France, engaged heavily in sea warfare.[16] In the past the English carrying trade had invariably profited from Dutch difficulties, and once the wars with France and Spain ended it assumed a commanding position in the trade between Dutch and Spanish ports, as it also did between French and Spanish ports from 1635. The heavy dependence of the Iberian countries on imports of raw materials, foodstuffs and manufactures created a great opportunity for English shipowners as large quantities of Dutch, Flemish and French goods were sent to England for re-export in English ships. Dover in particular became a staple for the re-export trade to such an extent that government revenue derived from this trade made no small contribution to Charles I's finances. Having reported 36 vessels in 1629, Dover set forth 47 with re-exports in 1633, 114 in 1636 and 144 in 1638. Though many of these were doubtless Dover ships, some were acquired abroad and some were foreign owned, and it is clear that English builders were unable to meet the heavy demand for shipping during this decade. For English ships now found increasing employment in Spain's American trade, in Lisbon's trade with Brazil, in Portuguese trade in eastern waters, in the contraband trade between Marseille and Barcelona, in carrying troops from Barcelona to Italy, and even came to dominate the port-to-port trade of the Cantabrian coast. From 1635, when the overland route from Italy to Flanders

[15] Cf. Davis, *Shipping Industry*, pp. 11, 15, estimating 150,000 tons in 1640.
[16] Israel, *Dutch Republic*. The following account of England's commercial position in the 1630s is based on Kepler, 'Fiscal aspects', and Taylor, 'Trade, neutrality'.

became difficult and dangerous to use, Spain resorted to employing English ships to transport bullion to Flanders, since England was now the only major neutral power. It was a strategically important and financially very rewarding business. English owners were indeed prospering in these years, when their ships were not only fully employed, but often laded the sorts of outward cargoes which earned them freight, which in normal times they usually failed to obtain, unlike their Dutch rivals. They even found it possible on return voyages from the Mediterranean and Seville or Lisbon to pick up Spanish troops at Cadiz or Coruña for the army of Flanders. Meanwhile, as always when the Dutch were at war, English ships frequented the Baltic in greater numbers, competing more successfully with rivals burdened by high insurance charges.

At the same time English shipping received a powerful stimulus from the development of trade with the West Indies and North America. Before 1630 the colonial trade across the Atlantic had been negligible, but now the tobacco trade to Barbados, St Kitts and Virginia developed apace, while New England also grew steadily as a market. These were typically shipping trades, which employed substantial ships in lengthy voyages, with freight charges constituting a major factor in the final price of the commodity. In the 1630s too the African trade, which had struggled with many difficulties, culminating in serious losses during the war with France, made good progress under the leadership of Nicholas Crispe, Humphrey Slany, William Cloberry and John Wood, owners of the powerful ships required in this high-risk business.[17]

By the end of the decade the general advance of England's trade, and of its carrying trade in particular, inspired Lewes Roberts, in his *Merchants Mappe of Commerce*, published in 1638, to hail London as 'the prime city of trading this day in the world'. He even envisaged England's becoming, 'by the policy and government of the state... either the common emporium and staple of all Europe, or at least wise of all these our neighbouring northern regions'.[18] Another writer in 1641 perceived the earnings of English ships abroad to be of some importance to the balance of trade, since 'Italian, Spaniard, French and Dutch do many times freight English ships, whereby good sums of money are yearly raised by our nation abroad, and may serve to pay for the advance of foreign commodities that we bring in, at least for such a proportion as this freight money imports, which is to a considerable

[17] Porter, 'Crispe family'.   [18] Roberts, *Merchants Mappe*, pp. 234, 257.

value'.[19] Such a prospect would scarcely have been conceivable at any earlier date. Of course this growth of trade and shipping depended upon a fortunate conjuncture which could not and would not endure. As Sir Thomas Roe wisely observed to Parliament in 1641, 'Now it is true, that our great trade depends upon the troubles of our neighbours, and we enjoy almost the trade of Christendom; but if a peace happen betwixt France, Spain and the United Provinces, all these will share what we now possess alone, and therefore we must provide for that day.'[20]

No such provision was made and, as England drifted into civil war and the Dutch–Spanish conflict subsided towards the peace of 1648, English shipowners lost the advantage they had enjoyed in the thirties. It is impossible to trace the fortunes of the nation's shipping industry during the 1640s, since neither official figures nor private estimates survive and the volume of trade seems to have fluctuated heavily. But the climate was now clearly less favourable. As Dutch carriers recovered their supremacy in the Baltic, the English presence there dwindled again. The revolt of Portugal against Spanish rule in 1640 helped the Dutch to regain a place in Iberian trade, especially in Setúbal salt, a vital factor in their maritime economy. Meanwhile the Spanish embargoes on Dutch shipping were progressively dismantled until finally in the summer of 1647 Spain opened her ports wide to the old enemy.[21] Thenceforth the English industry, which had been cushioned by circumstances for almost two decades and assisted by protectionist regulations for longer still, faced the grim prospect of uninhibited Dutch competition.

Although the Trinity House certificates (analysed in Appendix B) cannot be used as a guide to the chronology or geography of shipbuilding for the period they cover (1626–38), they do reveal some leading features. Leaving aside the whole country west of the Solent and north of the Wash, for which the House issued very few certificates, it is the strength of the East Anglian shipbuilding centres which stands out in Table 2. The ports from Leigh to King's Lynn accounted for 96 certificates compared with London's 57, Ipswich being by far the largest single centre, with Yarmouth, its nearest rival, a long way behind. Colchester, Woodbridge and Aldeburgh also made important contributions. In the port of London the north bank, and

---

[19] Robinson, *England's Safety*, p. 50 (cited in Kepler, 'Fiscal aspects', p. 262).
[20] BL, Harleian MSS, 6695, fols. 140–6 (cited in Taylor, 'Trade, neutrality', pp. 239–40).
[21] Israel, *Dutch Republic*, pp. 338–47.

THE GROWTH OF THE SHIPPING INDUSTRY

principally Wapping, predominated over the south, where the chief yards were located at St Saviour's and Horseydown. The only other place of importance was Shoreham on the Sussex coast. The certificates frequently mention not only the place of building, but also the name of the builder. Judging from this evidence, the leading providers of merchant shipping were Robert Tranckmore, who was very active at Shoreham (10 certificates) and at Horseydown (6 certificates), Zephonias Foard at Ipswich (15 certificates), John and Matthew Graves at Limehouse (11 certificates), and Thomas Titfall at Yarmouth (10 certificates). Apart from these major figures, the builders named in 3 or more certificates were: at Ratcliffe, John Taylor (5, with 3 more at Wapping) and Peter Pett (5); at Wapping, John Dearsley (4), Nehemiah Bourne (3) and Thomas Hawkins (3, with one more at St Saviour's); at St Saviour's, John Bright (3); at Blackwall and Deptford, William Stephens (3); at Colchester, John Page (5); at Woodbridge, Thomas Browning (7); at Aldeburgh, Henry Danke (3) and Matthew Figgott (3); at Ipswich, Thomas Wright (8) and John, Jeremy and Robert Cole (6); and at Yarmouth, Thomas Barker (5). It should not be assumed that these figures indicate the output of the various firms, which in most cases if not all would have produced other ships than those mentioned in certificates – perhaps many more. Peter Pett, like his cousin Phineas, was heavily engaged in work for the Crown, which also employed the services of other shipwrights as need arose.[22] Finally, worth noting is the contingent of ships, already significant in number (32 out of 381), bought abroad (24) or acquired as prizes (8). In fact by capture and by purchase the merchant marine imported many foreign vessels between 1625 and 1640.[23]

The dominant characteristics of English merchantmen in those days are familiar enough. Contemporary comment and modern authority alike have described them by contrasting them with their Dutch counterparts.[24] Apart from certain distinct types of small vessels, among which

---

[22] Twelve other London and East Anglian shipbuilders are mentioned in the certificates, including William Castle (twice). Graves, Stephens and Tranckmore are known to have done work for the Crown. Tranckmore, of the parish of St Mary Magdalen, Bermondsey, aged 63 and Master of the Company of Shipwrights in 1637 (Shilton and Holworthy, *Examinations*, nos. 292, 312), headed what was possibly the largest firm at that time, and this may well have been the business which came into the hands of William Castle, also of Bermondsey, aged 48 in 1638 (*ibid.*, no. 601).

[23] Appleby, 'Privateering', I, 260 calculates that at least 737 prizes were taken during the wars with France and Spain. By no means all these would have been incorporated in the English marine, but taking into account the frequent references to purchases abroad, it may be that the proportion of foreign-built vessels was more considerable by 1640 than Davis thought: *Shipping Industry*, p. 47.

[24] Barbour, 'Merchant shipping'; Davis, *Shipping Industry*, pp. 44–57.

hoys and ketches were the most common, English-built ships of over 50 tons or so conformed to a fairly standard design: that of the armed trader. Long rather than round, with a pronounced rake fore and aft and tapering towards the keel, their greatest width was above the water-line at the gun deck, all of which features limited the size of the hold in comparison with the squarish, roomy, almost flat-bottomed *fluits* used by the Dutch in their bulk trades. Stoutly built with heavy timbers, the typical English merchantman was literally a tall ship, her three masts towering above the water and bearing an elaborate array of sail and tackling. The weight of the hull, of the broadside of guns such ships were expected to carry in most if not all of the overseas trades, and of the massive superstructure made them plough deep in the sea, so that they were less easy to handle and probably not much faster than the light Dutch carriers. Of course the Dutch had their 'defensible' ships also, employed in their East Indian, Mediterranean and similar trades, where powerful ships were preferred, but their shipbuilding practice was influenced more by the needs of their great North Sea and Baltic trades, where the risk of attack by hostile craft was small and the bulk cargoes of cheap goods called for economical transport, carriers which could operate at low cost. The *fluit* (*Anglice* 'flyboat') cost little because, with maximized stowage, lighter masting, simpler rig and little or no armament, it required few men in proportion to freight. English ships cost more to build in the first place, added much expense on guns to the capital outlay, and operated with large crews, which were partly necessary to handle such ships and partly provided as manpower for fighting. Since wages and victuals together made up most of the running costs for any ship, the English were usually unable to compete with Dutch freight charges outside those trades – which came to be called the rich trades – where power was more important than cheapness of transport because the dangers were greater and because freight charges mattered less for cargoes of high-value goods such as silks and spices.

English shipbuilders doubtless were less adaptable and enterprising than their Dutch rivals, who were working for a far larger and more sophisticated market. Yet the traditional conservatism of a comparatively small industry does not completely explain its devotion to the 'defensible' merchantman. Indeed there were not many of those in 1582: only 180 of over 99 tons, barely a score of which exceeded 199 tons. The creation of a powerful merchant marine was the work of the next three generations of England's builders, who from the 1580s to the 1630s were responding to specific demands and pressures. In the first place the Elizabethan war with Spain, which lasted eighteen years, was the heyday of English privateering, and promoted, in spite of trade depression throughout, the relatively powerful type of vessel suitable for armed trade and commerce-raiding. Thus 133 ships of over 99 tons, 72 of which were over 199 tons, were provided in the years 1581–97.[25] Meanwhile trade with the Mediterranean, including the Levant, demanded increasing numbers of well-armed traders, ranging from 100 tons or so to great ships like the 500-ton *Sampson* and the 400-ton *William and Ralph*, commanded in those waters in the later twenties by William Rainborowe and Thomas Trenchfield respectively.[26] After 1600 the East India trade created a fresh demand for even more powerful ships. Of the 76 the company acquired between 1600 and 1640, 49 were of 300 tons and over, the great majority of which were built by the company itself. All these were trading men-of-war, comparable to royal ships of similar burden, though carrying less ordnance and much smaller crews. The trades to southern Spain, particularly within the Straits, and the Barbary, West African and Islands trades, all of which were exposed to attack by the Barbary corsairs, required defensible ships also. Above all, with the renewal of the Dutch–Spanish war in 1621 sea traffic became increasingly unsafe even for neutrals. England was herself at war from 1625 to 1630 and suffered severe losses as a consequence, and in the following decade the dangers from piracy and privateering reached such a height as to provide some excuse at least for the ship-money fleets.

These circumstances alone might sufficiently explain the preference of English owners and builders for well-armed and well-manned merchantmen, but they were reinforced by official policy. Throughout the reign of Elizabeth and subsequently down to 1618 bounty was paid to owners of new vessels of 100 tons and upwards at the rate of 5 shillings a ton.[27] The general purpose of the bounty was of course to strengthen the shipping of the realm for purposes of defence, the assumption being that the merchant service must assist the Royal Navy in time of war. More specifically, as the Privy Council noted in 1625,

---

[25] Andrews, *Elizabethan Privateering*, pp. 230–1.
[26] SP16/137; BL, Additional MSS, 37816, fols. 55, 68; Appleby, 'Privateering', II, 51, 63; Bruce, *Journal*. The *Sampson* demonstrated her formidable strength in an encounter with four Maltese galleys in 1628: Strachan, *Roe*, pp. 183–5.
[27] I am indebted to Dr Brian Dietz for a list of bounty payments for the period 1559–1618, which he compiled from the Pell Receipt Books (PRO, E401/1794 *et sqq.*), supplemented by Exchequer Warrants for issue (E404) for the years 1558–65, a file of bonds in HCA 25/1 for 1573–6, a list of payments in SP12/154, fols. 83 *et sqq.*, and the Patent Book (Auditors) E403/2500, which fills gaps in the Receipt Book for the Easter term of 1604 and for Michaelmas and Easter of 1610–11.

the payment of bounties 'made his Majesty part owner of all the serviceable shipping of this realm' and enabled him 'to command all ships to serve him at two shillings the ton and tonnage per month, whereas all other men pay double the price'.[28] Furthermore the Council implied that the bounty system required the builders to produce ships capable of bearing and using ordnance, for it complained that, since the bounty had been 'omitted' (as it evidently had been since 1618) the builders laid their decks so low and close together that they had to be altered, at considerable expense to his Majesty, before the ships could be employed in his service. On this occasion, as the document indicates, the Council was concerned with hiring colliers, which were used extensively as auxiliaries in the next five years of warfare. Without the bounty they would clearly have competed more effectively in the coal-export trade, which was largely carried by foreign ships in the first half of this century. The decision of the Council, recorded at the same time, to revive the bounty system for new ships of 200 tons and over no doubt contributed to the continuing success of the Dutch at Newcastle. In these wars, however, the Crown also relied heavily on the services – in the Narrow Seas especially – of the more powerful armed traders.

The needs of commerce and warfare thus combined, in the decades from 1580 onwards, to shape the character of the ships – at least those of the larger sort – produced in England, where the more important part of the shipbuilding industry became committed overwhelmingly to the 'defensible' merchantman. The 59 charter-parties, dating from 1628 to 1640, summarized in Appendix C below, illustrate the heavy manning and gunning of those ships in detail. The average rate of tons per gun, in those cases where the ordnance is specified, is 13.4, the average rate of tons per man being 7.7. On the other hand, the difference between the northerly trades – to Archangel, Norway, the Baltic and across the North Sea – and the rest is very marked: in the former only two out of nine charter-parties give the number of pieces, while manning averages 13.3 tons per man, ranging from 7.6 in one voyage to 25.0 in another. In the rest, the tons per gun rate is 12.9 and the tons per man rate 6.7. In the Barbary and East Indies trades the manning rate rises to four or five tons per man. Quite evidently English owners and charterers could and did adjust the provision of men and guns to the conditions in particular trades. The charter-party for the *Relief* of Ipswich, 220 tons, even provided for a change of

[28] *APC 1625–6*, pp. 52–3.

circumstances: her owners were to furnish her with ten pieces of ordnance and two 'carriage fowlers' for a voyage 'within or without the Straits' (viz. whatever voyage they chose), and the merchant charterer for his part was to pay and victual fifteen men and a boy as well as the master; but if she sailed south of Lisbon the owners must supply four more pieces and the merchant two, as well as eleven more men.[29]

For most of the first half of the century, however, English builders and owners lacked any strong incentive to produce economical ships and run them at low cost. The Dutch, handicapped by their involvement in war up to 1609 and again from 1621 to 1648, could not in those years unleash the full force of their competition, and when they did the official response was protectionist. Thus in 1614, when the English industry did feel the pinch, the preamble to a new navigation bill attributed the decay of shipping to merchants' preference for foreign vessels built solely for carrying merchandise, prohibited the use of such vessels and ordered that all English ships should be so built as to be capable of bearing ordnance and serving as ships of war in case of necessity. In the following year the government issued a proclamation enforcing the former Navigation Acts restricting the use of foreign ships in overseas trade.[30] Merchants continually complained of the high freights charged by English owners and frequently preferred foreign bottoms, but the shipping industry could always count on the support of government and public opinion for measures to protect the walls of the realm and promote the employment of seamen. Most Englishmen concerned in such matters would have joined Nathaniel Butler in deploring any tendency to man ships 'for thrift sake' as both dangerous for the vessels themselves and inimical to the breeding of sailors for the defence of the realm.[31]

In the light of these attitudes and practices one may well ask what profit, if any, lay in shipping. Could owners expect some considerable return on normal commercial ventures or were profits dependent on special circumstances, windfalls, fortune's favours? Such questions cannot be answered satisfactorily without better evidence than is available for this period, but they must be considered because they have in fact been posed. In his examination of the profitability of English shipping in the decades around 1700, Davis found that the average returns on capital investment were 'lower than those normal in

[29] HCA 15/4.   [30] Friis, *Cockayne Project*, pp. 178–92.
[31] Butler, *Dialogues*, pp. 49–50. For Monson's wholehearted support of bounties, Navigation Acts and strong ships, see *Monson's Tracts*, III, 432–3, and V, 248–9.

commercial operations'.³² Elsewhere he argued that, although the potential profitability of English shipping declined in the course of the seventeenth century as capital outlays rose and running costs and freight earnings both declined, reducing the absolute income, and so the ratio of the return to the capital invested, nevertheless improved efficiency, with more regular employment and fuller holds, probably compensated for such a decline. Over the whole period from the 1630s to the 1760s 'a variety of forces were working in different directions to keep shipping profits from moving far or fast', the main change being that the business became less speculative as it grew in scale and regularity.³³ Shipowners, Davis suggested, may have been willing to tolerate poor average profits for various reasons: merchants who laded goods in their own ships because the convenience they gained thereby was valuable; sleeping partners because shares in ships constituted an investment with limited liability in practice at a time when most forms of investment lacked legal protection; and investors generally because the speculative element loomed large enough to encourage hopes of some great haul. Since these conditions and attitudes might equally well be ascribed to any time between 1500 and 1750 at least, the hypothesis that rates of profit on merchant shipping were normally low in early-modern England appears plausible.

The view advanced more recently by Brulez seems still more pessimistic: 'shipping in early modern times was not a significant source of profit or capital accumulation either in the Netherlands or elsewhere. In itself it was scarcely profitable, and seems to have kept going only because it could often be combined with trading ventures, or because war sometimes created exceptionally favourable conditions.'³⁴ The main thrust of the argument here derives not so much from criticism of more optimistic opinions as from analysis of ships' accounts, a highly relevant but potentially misleading form of material. Account books of this period have survived usually because they were produced in court as evidence; thus the data relating to the voyage in question are unlikely to be typical. Davis was careful to use only accounts covering several voyages, and to omit from his calculations the data concerning the most recent one. Even so, he found that his accounts showed earnings so low that he could not believe them 'altogether normal or typical of the industry as a whole', since 'investment in ships and their operation would not have been continued and enlarged, as it was in these decades, if the financial results

[32] Davis, 'Earnings in English shipping'.   [33] Davis, *Shipping Industry*, pp. 363–87.
[34] Brulez, 'Shipping profits'.

of past investment in them had not been tolerably attractive'. He therefore discounted these findings, counterbalancing them with more optimistic ones reached by an alternative procedure.[35] The problem of why the accounts, even when appropriately censored, yielded results which Davis described as 'incredible' nevertheless remains, and it is in this connection that Brulez's contribution is most interesting. For, although stressing that 'shipping in itself was hardly a profitable activity', he allowed that 'it could offer more favourable returns in combination with trade, privateering or hire for war purposes'. The last two forms of activity certainly could be profitable and cannot be dismissed as unimportant in the seventeenth-century context, but the combination with trade is the most important of the three because it was widely practised in many branches of England's overseas trade during Charles's reign. Apart from sleeping partners, owners were usually merchants or masters with an active interest in trade as well as shipping, and there is sufficient evidence in Admiralty Court cases to suggest that they frequently shipped cargo on their own behalf in their own ships. In some cases the owners' lading made up the entire shipment or a large part of it, though probably in most theirs was a minor share. Part-owning masters certainly traded for themselves and perhaps for their co-owners as well. For owners such trading profits might well make the difference between a saving voyage and a losing one. Brulez's approach is to discount them in order to isolate the 'pure shipping' account and emphasize its generally unsatisfactory outcome. Conversely, however, shipowners and masters, as practical men making a living by hook or by crook in those uncertain times, would have placed their emphasis on the actual value of those incidental or ancillary activities – trade, privateering and war service.

Had it been generally unprofitable, there is no doubt that the shipping industry would have declined. At the bottom of the depression following the Dutch–Spanish truce of 1609, Trinity House reported that 'all men in general are so far from building any new shipping [that] they will hardly repair their old, for the freights that merchants do now give is not able to repair their ships in their tackling and apparel'.[36] In 1616 the Privy Council learned that the recent proclamations against the use of strangers' bottoms had not proved effective because the freight rates offered by merchants were so low that owners and masters

---

[35] To offset ships' accounts as evidence, Davis used miscellaneous data on capital investment, running costs and freight earnings to estimate the potential rates of profit in various types of trading voyage, arriving at an average 20 per cent return on capital, a figure he reduced because it assumed full ladings and regular employment.

[36] BL, Lansdowne MSS, 142, fol. 306.

were 'not able to furnish shipping, as is requisite and expedient'.[37] The Council accordingly took steps to bring the two sides to agree on fair charges, and before long international events put an end to the crisis, but the reactions of the shipping interest had been sufficient to show that builders and owners were accustomed to paying their way. Had they not continued to do so, the impressive expansion of the industry between 1580 and 1640 could not have occurred.

There were of course conditions which tended to depress shipping profits in this period. As Table 3 of Appendix A indicates, few ships lived longer than fifteen years, so that the rate of depreciation of capital was in fact higher than modern authorities have thought. The employment of shipping was leisurely to the point of inefficiency; owners were disinclined to venture their vessels in winter; marked fluctuations in the level of activity accentuated the problem of surplus capacity and under-utilization in times of recession. In the perpetual conflict of interest between the owners and the freighters the latter had the advantages of superior wealth and the option of using foreign vessels, since the market for shipping services was already international and the efforts of government to restrict it were scarcely noticeable except at times of special difficulty. These were, however, the normal, chronic ills of early-modern shipping, which in this period were counterbalanced by conditions especially favourable for relatively powerful merchantmen. In England's own wars of the later 1620s such ships, far from curtailing their ventures, sailed on trading voyages with letters of marque and took the opportunity to earn a super-profit by combining trade and plunder. When England was at peace their strength and their neutrality enabled them to command high freight rates in the carrying trade amid the dangers and disturbances of intensive sea warfare. And with the advent of civil war their services remained much in demand while lesser vessels were often confined to port. Now they might be hired by the state between trading voyages and could always carry cargo in their official expeditions. In effect, the average level of shipping profits, apart from being incalculable, is much less significant than their variation. The greater profitability of the larger, stronger ship also explains the major features we have noted in the growth of the nation's stock.

Shipping was in any case, leaving aside the influence of war conditions, a highly speculative business. Every factor in costs and earnings was subject to varying circumstances, chance and human ability or inability to exploit them. A ship with tackle and furniture

[37] *APC 1615–16*, pp. 468, 611–14.

but without armament, stores or victuals might cost anything from £1 to £7 a ton. Victualling expenses differed from place to place and time to time according to frequently heavy fluctuations in food prices. Manning expenses varied with the type of voyage, as we have seen, but also with the state of demand for seamen's services locally as well as chronologically. Freight charges were not standardized, even in the regular and well-frequented wine trades. In the tobacco trade a master charged what he could and sometimes the rate per pound varied within a given cargo. The sample of charter-parties in Appendix C is not large enough to indicate average freight charges, but it sufficiently illustrates their considerable range. Each contract in fact represents a bargain struck by the parties for a particular venture in particular circumstances: the form was common, but the content unique. And if every venture in its planning was a special case, in performance it was truly an adventure, fraught with uncertainty, hopes and fears. Yet the great majority of owners failed to insure their ships, and those that did seldom covered more than half the value.[38] Although some people may have taken shares in ships because they regarded them as a 'safe' investment, it was not in this frame of mind that owners called upon God to bless their ships, choosing for them so often names like the *Hopewell*, the *Fortune* and the *Blessing of God*. For them average profitability was a remote and practically irrelevant concept; what impressed them rather—and should impress us as more significant historically—was the variability of profits, losses and everything connected with the business of seafaring.

[38] Barbour, 'Marine risks and insurance', pp. 587–90.

CHAPTER 2

THE SHIPOWNERS

PATTERNS OF shipowning in Caroline England, as revealed in the Trinity House certificates, local shipping returns of 1629 and Admiralty Court materials, were changing, becoming more complex as ships grew in size and value, more varied as the difference between larger and smaller vessels developed. Sole ownership, which had not been uncommon in any class of ship in Tudor times, appears rarely in the certificates for the years 1626 to 1638: 7 out of 275 vessels of over 99 tons (2.5 per cent), and 6 out of 41 lesser vessels (15 per cent).[1] These certificates, however, do not adequately represent the shipping of the West Country and the south coast, where sole owners occur more often, especially in connection with small craft. Thus the 1629 return for Kent showed 69 vessels, only 2 of which exceeded 30 tons and only 3 of which had more than one owner, the master being the sole owner in 59 cases. Dorset returned 68 vessels of which 26 (38 per cent) belonged to single owners, including one of the 5 over 99 tons. These figures suggest that the incidence of sole ownership tended to vary inversely with the tonnage. But the Bristol return shows that the tendency was less pronounced there: of the 48 ships listed for that port 12 belonged to single owners (25 per cent), including 5 of the 30 which exceeded 99 tons (17 per cent).[2] These 12 were sizeable ships, ocean-going merchantmen with an average burden of 97 tons, and had only 8 owners altogether.

The strong element of sole ownership in Bristol was traditional, part of an older pattern of shipowning. The division of ships into parts had

---

[1] SP16/16 and 17; Appendix B below. The calculations in the text are not derived from the tables, but directly from the certificates. These figures refer to certificates in which an individual is stated to be sole owner. There may have been sole ownership in the few other cases where only one owner is mentioned. On the general characteristics of shipowning in early-modern England see Scammell, 'Shipowning' and Davis, *Shipping Industry*, pp. 81–109.

[2] North Kent: SP16/132, fols. 31–8. Dorset: SP16/138, fols. 31–46. Bristol: SP16/138, fols. 4–14.

THE SHIPOWNERS

but slowly advanced: none of the Bristolmen reported in 1629 had more than 6 owners and 30 of them had fewer than 4. The detailed and apparently thorough account of the ownership of the 48 listed vessels mentions only 51 owners in all, among whom a dozen men clearly dominated the shipping of the port, owning parts in several ships and sometimes whole ships as well. McGrath's picture of 'a little shipowning aristocracy in early seventeenth-century Bristol', drawn from the ranks of the city's Society of Merchant Venturers, is amply confirmed.[3] Most of the major owners, like Giles Elbridge (2 large ships and parts of 5 others), John Gonning (parts in 15) and Thomas Colston (parts in 9) were merchants. One or two, like Charles Driver and Thomas Wright, were master mariners, but by and large the 15 or 20 masters who figure here as owners had only a minor interest, holding simply a share in the ship they commanded. Small groups of merchant owners likewise tended to dominate, though less emphatically, the shipping of Plymouth, Dartmouth, Exeter, Poole, Weymouth and Lyme, and the division of ships into parts was again limited. Thus in the three main Dorset ports only 3 of the 64 ships reported in 1629 had more than 3 owners. About a dozen merchants, some of whom had been or still were masters, owned between them the greater part of Hull's shipping, and here, as at Newcastle, a master was part-owner of his ship more often than not.[4]

On London and East Anglian shipowning the available information is scrappy: the 1629 return for London names only one (presumably the chief) owner in each case, while the Trinity House certificates usually mention two or three, but frequently add 'and others', the omission of which phrase, however, does not imply that the list is complete, for in some cases we know that it was not.[5] Nor do charter-parties identify in full the owners of the vessels concerned, unless they happened to be owned by only the one or two persons named. Even so, the occasional Admiralty Court evidence on which we must rely sufficiently indicates that the parcellation of shipowning was more advanced in this region than elsewhere. Sixteenths were common, indeed usual in larger ships, and thirty-second parts by no means rare. Ships' accounts give the 250-ton *Diamond* 14 owners, the 280-ton *Greenfield* 11, the 140-ton *Abraham* 8, the 160-ton *Bark Andever* 15 (one holding an eighth, the rest sixteenths), the *Edward and Sarah*, a collier, 21. In this last case the master held an eighth, 10 others held sixteenths and 10 held thirty-second

[3] McGrath, 'Merchant Venturers'.
[4] SP16/16/30 (certificate for Hull ships); Brooks, *Early Judgements*; Brooks, *First Order Book*; Willan, *Coasting Trade*, pp. 35–42.   [5] SP16/137; SP16/16 and 17.

parts, though at some stage one of these was subdivided into sixty-fourths.[6] There is no reason to suppose these to have been exceptional ships like the famous *Constant Warwick*, rated by her builder, Peter Pett, at 320 tons and having 9 or 10 owners.[7] Declarations concerning the ownership of vessels bought abroad show the buyers rapidly selling off parts to create partnerships of as many as 9 or 10 co-owners.[8] In certain cases sub-partnerships appear: for example the *William* of London was divided into thirds, each third being held by a partnership, the whole having 9 co-owners.[9] This suggests that depositions attributing a ship to only a few owners may in fact conceal the existence of further subdivisions. Many such statements are nevertheless clear and circumstantial enough to be taken at face value and we may safely conclude that ships of this region frequently had fewer than 8 owners. The difference between it and the southern and western ports was after all one of degree, not of stark contrast.

Centred upon the Thames, a lively market in parts of ships thus kept in constant flux a diffuse network of shipowning people, most of whom were actively interested in shipping business or closely connected with the shipping world. Even those noblemen or gentlemen who owned or shared in ships were seldom strangers to seafaring and the maritime community. Some, like Sir John Pennington, Sir John Watts and Sir Thomas Love, were commanders in the Royal Navy. Pennington as a young man captained his own vessel, the *Star*, in Ralegh's last voyage and in the wars with France and Spain combined with his brother Isaac, the wealthy City merchant and Parliamentarian, to promote privateering. Watts, son of the greatest Elizabethan merchant promoter of privateering, had commanded private men-of-war in the 1590s and set forth another in 1628. Love had been in the East India Company's service before 1620, was an Elder Brother of Trinity House and joined Captain William Stevens and certain London merchants to buy the 400-ton *George*, which the Crown then hired for the Cadiz expedition. Others were Admiralty officials, notably Sir James Bagg, vice-admiral of south Cornwall, Sir John Drake, acting vice-admiral of Devon and Sir Edward Seymour, vice-admiral of Devon until 1623. Such men interested themselves in privateering, as did Sir John

---

[6] Davis, *Shipping Industry*, p. 338; HCA 30/635, 638; HCA 13/50, fol. 253.

[7] Johns, '*Constant Warwick*', lists nine owners at her building in 1644–5, who by April 1649 had been joined by one other – the purser: HCA 13/61, fols. 392–3, 395.

[8] For example, Thomas Ascue bought the 260-ton *St Peter* at Dunkirk and within eight weeks had sold parts to eight others; Thomas Symonds, master of the *Priscilla*, which he bought at Dunkirk, acquired nine co-owners within a year of the purchase: HCA 13/50, fols. 102–3, 173.

[9] HCA 13/49, fol. 630.

Hippisley, the lieutenant of Dover Castle during the wars.[10] As for the peers, only a handful invested in shipping, again for the most part as privateering promoters, though with one exception their contribution to this type of enterprise was marginal.[11]

The exception was of course Robert Rich, second earl of Warwick. The only great shipowning aristocrat of his time, patron and chief entrepreneur of westward colonization, especially in the West Indies and the Somers Islands, promoter of privateering against Spain in the wars of the twenties and again through the Providence Company in the thirties, he finally became Parliament's Lord High Admiral in 1643. Although he may occasionally have owned a ship or two outright, Warwick generally undertook his colonial and privateering ventures with others, merchants as well as gentlemen and seamen. Like the Howards before him, he set forth his own private warship, the *Constant Warwick*, alongside the state fleet for which he was responsible, having had her built by one of the state's shipwrights, though in a private yard. She was the most effective warship in the Parliamentary service, but Warwick owned only half of her; the rest belonged to other Navy men.[12] The only other peer with a considerable interest in shipping, the earl of Carlisle, relied even more on merchants' backing – in his case the syndicate headed by Marmaduke Royden for the planting of the Caribbees.[13] In colonial enterprise as in privateering, gentlemen high or low depended on merchants for shipping as well as funds.

Equally peripheral were those people of modest affluence who, living in port towns and seeking to employ their savings, found the prospect of part-ownership attractive despite the obvious risk. Shares could be bought and sold with remarkable ease and speed by a simple bill of sale, and in practice their owners were unlikely to have to meet substantial debts should the ship be lost, since the only liability incurred once she had sailed on her voyage would be the wages of the crew, which the employers were not bound to pay in the event of loss. The shipping business was thus in large measure safeguarded against the legal and financial problem of unlimited liability which faced most partnerships in this period.[14] Nor was the minor investor expected to

---

[10] *DNB*, 'Penington'; Appleby, 'Privateering', I, 202–5; Manwaring and Perrin, *Mainwaring*, I, 102, 147; Harris, *Transactions*, no. 97, etc.; SP16/16/1.

[11] Stone, *Aristocracy*, p. 367; Appleby, 'Privateering', I, 206, II, 301.

[12] Johns, '*Constant Warwick*'. In 1649 the other owners were William Jessop, Peter Pett, Robert Moulton, Richard Swanley, Thomas Turner, William Spenser, John Gilson, William Batten and Nicholas Lucas (the purser).

[13] Harlow, *West Indies and Guiana*, p. xxii, shows that Carlisle was not merely a passive figurehead, but did set forth ships to the Caribbean.

[14] Davis, *Shipping Industry*, pp. 102–3.

play any onerous part in the management of a ship, which normally fell to the one or two leading owners. While the passivity of the shareholders doubtless varied with the circumstances, their essential function was to provide the capital cost and their corresponding proportion of the fitting out and running expenses. Otherwise their main concern was to share the proceeds, whether positive or negative, though sleeping partners might well wait in vain for such a reckoning, as did Robert Sparrow, gentleman, who claimed that the master of the collier in which he held an eighth part had rendered no accounts for several years and had paid out little or nothing for the past two and a half years.[15]

This was therefore a convenient, if sometimes disappointing investment for those without the drive, capacity, or simply the time to manage their own money. Above all it was attractive as a readily accessible speculation. The sea, as many remarked, was a lottery. It was indeed the supreme lottery in an age when all business was highly speculative and the motto 'nothing venture nothing win' expressed the common attitude to enterprise. At the same time, because seafaring was the main business of the ports—London only having other important concerns—contact between the managers of shipping and people with disposable funds was an everyday occurrence. Such more or less casual, more or less passive investors crop up irregularly in the Admiralty Court records, chiefly in the humbler, more open and expanding trades to the plantations across the Atlantic and to Newcastle for coal. But precisely because they were only occasional and inactive participants we learn little about them, nor is it possible to assess the relative importance of the capital they supplied for the industry as a whole. They were a miscellaneous assortment of people, like the apothecary and the upholsterer who owned shares in the *Susan and Mary*, along with six other petty adventurers, when she carried a cargo of servants to the West Indies.[16] Among such investors widows seem to have formed the largest single group, most of whom presumably inherited their shares from masters or other part-owners.[17]

The class of shipowners to whom shipping mattered most, whose very livelihood lay in their ships, were of course the masters: those 'masters of the Trinity House and other rough-hewn seamen', as Phineas Pett

---

[15] Harris, *Transactions*, no. 200.
[16] Shilton and Holworthy, *Examinations*, no. 391; HCA 13/54, fols. 171–2, 181–2, 305, 373, 385.
[17] In the Portsmouth and Gosport shipping return for 1629 three widows appear as owners of four and a half of the seven ships listed: SP16/132, fols. 70–3.

called them, the hard core of the shipping business.[18] Their share in shipowning was greatest in the small vessels of the minor ports and the innumerable fishing craft and coastal or short-distance carriers – hoys, ketches and barks – operating from hundreds of havens and creeks around the English coast. Here the vast majority of masters owned at least a share and very often the whole of the vessel they sailed. A study of probate inventories and other sources has revealed a shipowning pattern for the Wirral peninsula which was probably typical of many coastal districts. Most masters there were part-owners, many were sole owners, especially in the fishing boats. Even in the larger, sea-going ships of some 20, 30 or more tons the owner-master dominated the scene: of the 14 men who owned such vessels 5 seem to have been sole owners, with shares in 2, and in one case 3 ships, while the other masters were all part-owners, most frequently holding half a ship. Yet these people cannot be considered specialist shipowners because they were also farmers, combining seafaring with agriculture in a form of dual economy which could no doubt be found in sea-side villages elsewhere.[19]

Even in more substantial ships the master was normally a part-owner. In the years from 1626 to 1638 Trinity House issued certificates for 381 ships, and in 260 of these – 68 per cent – the master was named as one of the owners. Since he may have been one of the unnamed owners in other cases, 68 per cent must be read as a minimum. Nearly all these vessels were rated at 70 tons and over and the percentage of part-owning masters did not vary significantly with tonnage. The standard share of a master in this kind of ship was an eighth, quarters being not uncommon in the lower range and sixteenths in the higher.[20] But the position of the part-owning master in relation to his co-owners and to the management of the ship varied widely. Some were owner-managers, effectively the principals in a business which, for financial reasons, was capitalized by shareholders, people who knew the master and left him to run the ship as an entrepreneur. Others were merely agents of a managing owner or owners and were allotted a share in the ship to ensure their loyalty and good behaviour. The degree of a master's power or subordination depended on the particular circumstances – his personal standing and experience, the scale of his stake in the ship, the terms of his employment and the nature of the trade in which the ship was engaged. It is clear that in all the main trades

---

[18] Perrin, *Phineas Pett*, p. 165.   [19] Woodward, 'Wirral ships'.
[20] SP16/16 and 17. At Hull 'the command of a ship...in the seventeenth century, almost certainly implied being at least part-owner of the vessel': Brooks, *First Order Book*, p. xi.

the master normally received a wage and so was an employee of the partnership, whether he was in substance a managing director or, holding no share, a works foreman. Even so, such evidence as we have for this early period suggests that in most of the major sea-going trades the master's interest in the ship and her voyage and his responsibility for them tended to amount to more than they would later, in the more settled and predictable conditions of the eighteenth century.[21]

In the coal trade the typical shipmaster played an especially important part, having often a major interest in both ship and cargo. Normally owning at least a part of his collier, he would not only hire, pay and victual his crew, but would buy his coal on the Tyne and sell it to his partners' and his own best advantage. Samuel Shield, for example, a 29-year-old mariner from Rotherhithe, bought the 160-ton *Bark Andever* for £260 from a partnership headed by the earl of Berkshire in 1632 and sold shares in her to fourteen other men, reserving a sixteenth for himself. He spent £146 fitting her out in the Thames for a voyage to Newcastle, where he shipped a cargo of coal for London. Details of these transactions, of the subsequent sale of the coal, payment of the crew and distribution of the profit, together with further accounts for the Norway voyage which followed, show that Shield, who received wages throughout, was the effective head of a considerable business. The ship and her fitting-out costs were valued at over £400 and his coal cargo fetched £81. Many colliers were larger than this, but were owned and run on similar lines.[22] As for the rest of the coasting trade, much of it 'seems to have been conducted in a rather casual and haphazard manner', with masters occupying a position of great flexibility at a time when the merchant function and the shipmaster function were still in process of differentiation. Whether as factors, supercargoes, middlemen or principal merchants, coasting masters generally combined trade and shipowning.[23]

Somewhat different was the role of the master in the rich trades. In the southerly trades to the Mediterranean and the Levant, to the southern ports of Spain and Portugal, to the western shores of Africa and to the Atlantic islands, the heavy shipping costs and valuable ladings required merchants' capital on a relatively large scale, such as only merchants (or masters already self-made merchants) could afford.

---

[21] Compare Davis, *Shipping Industry*, pp. 159–62.
[22] HCA 30/635; HCA13/50, fol. 253. On the position of masters in the coal trade see Nef, *Coal Industry*, I, 441–5, and Willan, *Coasting Trade*, pp. 35–8. As Willan points out, correcting Nef in this particular, the master was usually a wage-earner as well as a part-owner.
[23] Willan, *Coasting Trade*, pp. 51–4.

Here, therefore, the typical master was essentially a servant or agent, responsible to his owners and, if the ship were chartered, to the charterers also, following their instructions and sending home reports of his activities and progress whenever possible. Yet even in this sphere he customarily held a share in the ship and played a large part in her management. In Mediterranean ventures, for example, he often had to make strategic decisions about the course and conduct of the voyage. Sir William Russell's instructions to William Goddard, master and one-third owner of the 400-ton *Aeneas*, aptly so named for her massive strength, indicate the large discretion a master might be allowed even in so important a venture. At Alicante and Messina he was expected to find freights prepared by named factors, but, if he reached Venice without freight for other ports of the Inland Sea, he was to make for Zante with the proceeds of the Venice consignments 'and there let all our money be invested in currants', the lading to be topped up if possible with other men's currants at £5 or £5 5s 0d per ton freight. If still not fully laden, he should call at Alicante and Malaga. Alternatively he might go from Venice to Smyrna where, if he arrived at the right time, he might obtain a full lading of cotton. If not, he could fill up with currants at Zante. Finally, however, all options were declared open: 'if you find employment abroad, then lade not for England from any of the aforesaid ports till want of employment abroad constrain you, for our desire is to have the ship kept out as long as she may with safety stay abroad'.[24]

What it meant in practice to take charge of such an expedition is revealed in detail by Henry Powell's accounts of the four-year cruise of the 280-ton *Greenfield*. Powell as master owned an eighth and the chief owner, William Courten, a quarter, the rest being divided between nine others. Powell handled all important business concerning the ship. He began by supervising extensive repairs and fitting her out in every respect for a Mediterranean voyage, disbursing the impressive sum of £1,120 and charging his partners proportionately. He arranged her lading with lead, pepper, tobacco and other goods for Genoa and Leghorn, recording the freight charges for the numerous consignments, among which Courten's accounted for about a quarter. Having first called at Genoa, Powell reported at Leghorn to Samuel Bonnell, Courten's factor, for money (raised by exchange) and possibly for instructions. The exact relationship between Bonnell and Powell is not stated, but the master's papers show that he managed at least the

[24] HCA 24/96, no. 357.

maintenance, provisioning and freighting of the ship, on several occasions her chartering, and of course the government and payment of her crew. Returning finally to London in December 1646, he laid out £1 7s 0d on a dinner for the owners at the Red Lion tavern in Gracious Street and 1s 4d for their meeting at the Cardinal's Cap, where doubtless the legal and financial implications of Courten's bankruptcy were considered, Powell himself being already involved in Admiralty and Chancery proceedings.[25]

In the case of the *Aeneas* Sir William Russell deposed that he, Goddard and one Brenford not only owned, furnished and victualled a third each, but also agreed to 'pay each of them a third of the merchandise sent out in her'.[26] Such a major trading investment by the master was probably exceptional in Mediterranean ventures, but it was not unusual in the transatlantic trades to the Caribbean and North America. Here the ships were generally smaller and less heavily armed and manned, while the masters often acquired a considerable interest in the cargo as well as in the ship. Thus John Fairborne, master of the *Elizabeth* in a voyage to Virginia in 1637, owned an eighth of the ship and carried with him cargo and personal property allegedly worth £4,675.[27] In the years from 1625 to 1645 certain shipmasters played an important part, in conjunction with merchant partners, in the opening up of the plantations trade in servants and tobacco: Peter Andrews, Tobias Felgate and Jeremy Blackman, part-owners of ships and substantial traders.[28] But these were only the most prominent of the many seamen who staked what they could afford – or more – in this colonial free-for-all. Mates may be found owning parts of ships and once a sole owner sailed as mate;[29] common sailors shipped out servants and brought back consignments of tobacco. In fact the customary right of seamen to take a limited amount of cargo on their own account freight-free was generally accepted, but masters were clearly the main beneficiaries, particularly in the American, Mediterranean and East India trades. Charter-parties occasionally set down the maximum tonnage or value permitted, presumably to prevent the master from

---

[25] HCA 30/638. The other owners were William Greene and Edmund Beane (eighths), Edmund Turvile, Francis Tryon, Thomas Humble, Lady Ruthven Gray and Henry March (sixteenths), Captain Jourdain and Mr Craven (thirty-seconds). The accounts give a detailed picture of the *Greenfield*'s operations. See also Chapter 5 below.

[26] HCA 13/55, fol. 339. William, who was the son of Henry Goddard the Crown shipwright, is also named as sole owner of the 140-ton *Shipwright*: SP16/17/141.

[27] HCA 24/94, no. 133; HCA 13/54, fols. 180, 229, 249, 316, 455.

[28] Hillier, 'Virginia trade'.

[29] HCA 15/4 (charter-party of the *Blessing* of Falmouth, 1638). The owner sailed as mate in the *Endeavour* of Bideford: Shilton and Holworthy, *Examinations*, no. 121.

occupying too much of the hold at the expense of his co-owners or to the detriment of the charterers.[30] Such statements of course refer only to the freight-free privilege and should not be read as an index of the extent to which masters invested in trade.

Most masters, then, owned at least a part of a ship or lesser craft; most engaged in trade on their own behalf; most earned regular wages. Nor were those wages small. In the American trades the standard rate at this time was £5 a month, rising to £6 in the larger vessels of 200 tons or so, which was the general level also in Mediterranean voyages. Still higher rates were available to commanders of powerful Levant traders, East Indiamen and the warlike merchantmen employed in the Brazil trade. Generally, masters in ships from the outports earned somewhat less than these London rates, but even so, when it is considered that masters, like all seamen, enjoyed free board and lodging for the duration of their employment, which for many masters was longer than the duration of the voyage, that they received average and portage as their personal perquisites and usually appropriated the lion's share of primage,[31] and that they could often expect to reap some benefit from their dealings in the fitting out, provisioning, manning and lading of the ship, it is evident that they must have been, in comparison with the mass of the working population, a relatively advantaged and affluent group.

Nevertheless, the lot of such men was extremely variable. They belonged to that very large and amorphous class in seventeenth-century England who made their living as wage-earning business people, dependent always upon the economic climate, unpredictable fortune and their native wit, assisted at times by those networks of mutual help, credit and charity which kept their society going. As seamen, moreover, they were particularly exposed to adversity. The Trinity House of Deptford endorsed many petitions of ruined shipmasters appealing for help to meet their debts and maintain their families, their state of poverty having been attested by their neighbours. These appeals included estimates of the personal losses incurred by the masters

---

[30] In February 1639 an experienced sailor declared that masters in the plantations trades were normally allowed two tons of goods freight-free outward and homeward: HCA 13/54, fol. 467. In HCA 15/4 several charter-parties stipulate the master's maximum freight-free allowance: two tons in two cases; eight tons in a Cadiz voyage; £10 in one case; 1,000 French crowns in another. Most charter-parties do not mention the matter, but this cannot be taken to mean that no such allowance was made, indeed the opposite is almost certainly true. On masters' use of freight-free privilege in later times see Davis, *Shipping Industry*, pp. 146–50. Brooks, *First Order Book*, p. xiv, shows that 'furthing' or 'portage' was a normal right of Hull seamen in the seventeenth century.

[31] On average, portage and primage see Davis, *Shipping Industry*, p. 146.

through shipwreck, capture by pirates or other disasters. The sums mentioned range from the £50 adventure in the *Susan* of London, lost by her master, Matthew Clarke, when captured by Barbary corsairs, to the £2,000 lost by Captain William Hockerage, also to Barbary corsairs. Clarke, unlike almost all the other petitioners, owned no part of his 80-ton ship, whereas Hockerage, a former East India Company commander, was said to be sole owner of his ship and her cargo. Both men stood in need of charitable assistance to pay their ransom. The losses in most of these cases amounted to several hundred pounds and are estimated to represent or exceed the entire estate of the victim. On this evidence masters appear to have been men of considerable property, but highly vulnerable to misfortune because they tended to put their assets at risk, though in certain cases it seems to have taken a sequence of setbacks to bring about the eventual ruin.[32] Probably most of those who had all their eggs in one basket were comparatively poor masters, whereas the more successful would invest some of their gains elsewhere, perhaps in another ship or ships.

As for the most successful, riches and sometimes power attended their progress. Sir William Batten, the most famous of these, was the son of a Bristol shipmaster. In the later 1620s he commanded the 350-ton *Salutation*, described sometimes as of London, sometimes as of Yarmouth, and in 1630 was master and part-owner of the 300-ton *Charles* of London. In 1635 he was still active as a master in the merchant service and in 1638 he commanded the merchantman *Confident* in the ship-money fleet. In the same year he became Surveyor of the Navy, allegedly for money, and in 1642 entered history as commander, under Warwick, of the Parliamentary fleet. His subsequent and distinguished career requires no re-telling here.[33] The London shipping return of 1629 identifies an aristocracy of masters commanding the more powerful traders: James Moyer the *Royal Merchant* (600 tons), William Rainborowe the *Sampson* (600 tons), George Hatch the *Exchange* (500 tons), Thomas Trenchfield the *William and Ralph* (340 tons), Bence Johnson the *Assurance* (300 tons), Richard Cranley the *Clement and Job* (300 tons), Squire Bence the *Friendship* (300 tons), Robert Moulton the *George* (300 tons), Roger Twiddy, as owner and master, the *Lesser George* (240 tons), John Morris, as owner and master, the *Blessing* (200 tons), Robert Salmon the *Pleasure* (250 tons), Tobias Felgate the *William and John* (240 tons), Nathaniel Goodlad the *Peter and Andrew* (300 tons). All these men,

[32] Harris, *Transactions*, nos. 166, 266, *et passim*.
[33] *DNB*; SP16/17/25; *Cal. Muncaster MSS*, p. 289.

already well placed in the shipping world, were to prosper in the coming years, and some of them rose high in a wider world as well.[34]

James Moyer, of Tower Wharf, born in Leigh, Essex, about 1585, died in 1638. The seventeen parts of ships and the 'stocks belonging to them' inherited by his widow were valued in a schedule attached to his will at £2,880, and his 'adventure' in the *Royal Merchant* at £1,100. He left lands and £500 to his eldest son, £500 each to three other sons and various other legacies, including rings for Nathaniel Goodlad and others of the Goodlad and Salmon families, who also came from Leigh. An Elder Brother of Trinity House, Moyer left £100 to be distributed by the House to poor seamen.[35] Samuel, a younger son and also an Elder Brother, was a leading merchant shipowner in the 1640s, interested in American and Mediterranean trade and closely associated with Maurice Thompson, particularly in the interloping East India trade. He collaborated with Thompson and other radicals as a commissioner for the removal of malignants from the Customs and the Navy as well as Trinity House in 1649.[36] The Goodlads were a numerous tribe of shipmasters and shipwrights based in Leigh and linked by marriage to other leading Trinity House families. William Goodlad (c. 1590–1640) was Master of that corporation in 1638–9, apparently succeeding Robert Salmon (c. 1567–1641). The latter, who is described as owner (presumably meaning chief owner) of three 200-ton ships in the London 1629 return, had been Master at least twice before and in 1638 declared himself gent. of Stepney, where he had lived eighteen years, having been a subsidy man for forty. His estate appears to have consisted mainly of lands in Essex at the time of his death.[37] Nathaniel Goodlad became a commander in the Parliamentary Navy.[38]

Another who served Parliament at sea was Thomas Trenchfield (c. 1579–1646), whom Warwick sent with a squadron of the fleet to Hull in 1642 and whom the Commissioners of the Navy commended the following year for his 'extraordinary care'. Rear-admiral Trenchfield, gent., of St Mary Gray, Kent, declared in his will that he had been born in Ipswich 'not of eminent, yet of honest and religious parents', his

---

[34] SP16/137. The *Sampson*'s tonnage appears to be overstated here. She was usually rated at 500 tons. On tonnage estimates generally see Appendix A below.
[35] Prob. 11/176, proved 2 March 1637/8.
[36] Dewar, 'Naval administration', pp. 419, 425; Farnell, 'Navigation act', p. 446; Harris, *Trinity House*, p. 38; Pearl, *London*, p. 331.
[37] Harris, *Trinity House*, pp. 274, 278–9; Harris, *Transactions*, nos. 238, 307, 334, etc.; Prob. 11/186, fols. 354–5; HCA 13/54, fol. 319.
[38] Powell and Timings, *Documents*, pp. 70, 276.

grandmother have suffered death for Christ 'in the time of the persecution in Queen Mary's reign'. Having gone to sea from the age of about twenty, he was a master at twenty-seven and 'never went to sea in any ship but I came home again in the same, nor did never make voyage but with good benefit to the interested – blessed be thy great name for all thy goodness towards me'. An Elder Brother of Trinity House, he left the House money for the building of four almshouses, and to his heirs two houses on Tower Wharf, a great house with stables, orchards, outhouses and lands in the parish of St Mary Gray and Orpington, another house in that neighbourhood, and an unspecified quantity of 'shipping'. He called upon his son-in-law, Gregory Clement, leading shipowner and insurance merchant, to oversee the execution of this remarkable will.[39]

John Morris, Richard Cranley and Roger Twiddy all began as mere shipmasters, rising to become Commissioners of the Navy in 1642, along with William Batten and the two Bence brothers, Squire the master and Alexander the merchant, both of whom, like Rainborowe, their close associate, represented Aldeburgh in Parliament. Politically City men and Presbyterians all, they lost their places and their control of the fleet in the 1649 purge, but seem to have done quite well for themselves meanwhile.[40] Morris, a mariner of Wapping, had been part-owner and captain of the *Blessing* in the later 1620s, when she sailed with letters of marque, backed by Sidrach Williams, who at this time promoted three other such ventures, including that of the *Clement and Job*, commanded by Richard Cranley.[41] The *Blessing*, said to be of 230 tons, for which Morris and others obtained a Trinity House certificate in 1636, may have been the vessel he had commanded before and the same as the *Blessing* employed by the Parliamentary Navy in 1643.[42] Cranley in October 1639 declared himself *nauta*, aged about forty-two, of the parish of All Saints, Barking. A part-owning master in the 1620s, he became an Elder Brother of Trinity House and Master thereof in 1648–9, when he was purged as a malignant. By then he was a well-known trader. In 1642–3, for example, he partnered the prominent merchant Richard Hill in promoting the Mediterranean trading voyage

---

[39] Prob. 11/197, fol. 255, dated 22 August 1636, proved 26 September 1646. The text relates three seafaring incidents in which he was delivered from danger by 'miraculous mercies received from the hand of Almighty God'. On his service in the civil war see Powell and Timings, *Documents*, pp. 4–8, 32–3, 244; BL, Additional MSS, 22546, fol. 1. A deposition by him concerning the privateering expedition of the *Discovery*, promoted by Gregory Clement and others, is in HCA 13/54, fol. 22.   [40] See Chapter 8 below.
[41] Appleby, 'Privateering', II, 9, 14, 16, 37.
[42] SP16/17/118; Tanner, *Holland's Discourses*, pp. lxii–lxv; Powell and Timings, *Documents*, p. 71.

of the *Richard Bonaventure* and in his will he described himself no longer as a sailor but as a merchant.[43]

Perhaps the most impressive example of upward mobility among these London masters was Roger Twiddy, or Tweedy, of Rotherhithe, who originally hailed from Berwick. In his will he bequeathed £10 to the eldest son of the merchant George Dunscombe, deceased, 'who first employed me and made me master of the ship *George*', and £10 each to Sir George Strode and Alderman Abraham Reynardson, 'in remembrance of the love they always bore unto me and in whose service I got part of my estate'. Twiddy was apparently a master before 1625 and during the following years of war commanded the *George Bonaventure*, a merchantman of some 230 to 250 tons, equipped with letters of marque and backed by Strode, Reynardson and others. In 1629 Twiddy was chief owner of the *Lesser George* (presumably the same ship renamed).[44] At this time he was still only, though aged forty, a Younger Brother of Trinity House, but by 1636, as master of the 500-ton *Rainbow*, one of the greatest of the Levant traders, he had clearly arrived as a leader in his profession. Two years later he was consulted by the Admiralty Court as a shipping expert and in 1642 his appointment as a Navy Commissioner doubtless opened further doors. Purged along with Morris, Cranley and the Bences in 1649, he was evidently a rich and busy merchant still when he made his will in 1652, the greater part of his estate, consisting of merchandise, shipping, 'adventures', plate and jewels, being then 'out of my hands at present' in home and foreign ports. He died in 1655, having arranged for 'some godly Presbyterian minister' to preach a sermon at his funeral.[45]

There were of course other eminent masters: Peter Andrews, Thomas Best, the Bushells, the Jordans, the Swanleys, John Totten and Anthony Tutchin, for example, the last of whom, at the age of fifty-six in 1638, having lived twenty years in Limehouse, boasted that his ship-money rate was among the highest in that district.[46] Such men often came from well-established and well-connected shipping families and had a parent, relative or patron who gave them the head start which was perhaps their most valuable advantage, placing them in

---

[43] HCA 13/55, fol. 304; Harris, *Trinity House*, pp. 34, 39, 42, 274; BL, Additional MSS, 5489, fols. 49–50; Prob. 11/252, fol. 227, proved 23 February 1655/6. On Hill see Farnell, 'Navigation act', p. 448.

[44] The *George*, the *George Bonaventure* and the *Lesser George* were probably names for the same ship: looseness in this respect was not unusual at this time.

[45] Prob. 11/250, fol. 57, proved 12 October 1655; Appleby, 'Privateering', II, 24; SP 16/16/36; Harris, *Trinity House*, pp. 39, 284; Harris, *Transactions*, no. 228; Dewar, 'Naval administration', pp. 420, 423, 426; Tanner, *Hollond's Discourses*, pp. lxii–lxv; Shilton and Holworthy, *Examinations*, no. 611; HCA 13/55, fols. 536–8.   [46] HCA 13/54, fol. 319.

charge of a ship when they were still comparatively young. A seaman who had to work his own way up would usually have to wait until middle age for the command of a substantial ship.[47] Shipmasters like the Moyers and Salmons, Elder Brethren of Trinity House in many cases, mutually supportive as such and interrelated by marriage and business associations, formed the cream of their profession, as far above the ordinary run of masters in status, wealth and living standards as the ordinary master was above the common sailor.

The preponderance of merchants' capital in English shipping above the burden of some thirty tons in the early seventeenth century is hardly to be doubted, even though the paucity of data makes it impossible to quantify the sources of investment. We have seen how merchant owners dominated the shipping of Bristol, the southwest ports and Hull, and to judge by Elizabethan evidence a similar pattern probably prevailed in Southampton and Chester.[48] Even in the east-coast coal trade, where masters and miscellaneous part-owners occupied a more significant place than elsewhere, 'almost all the capital which financed the collier fleet came from influential and wealthy merchant townsmen' of Ipswich, King's Lynn, Yarmouth and Newcastle.[49] As for London, all the available evidence points to the dominance of merchant owners.[50] It remains to be considered what kind or kinds of merchant took an interest in shipping, to what extent, and why.

The day of the specialist shipping firm lay far ahead in the nineteenth century. In Caroline, as in later Stuart and eighteenth-century England, shipowning was 'no man's whole business and few men's main business',[51] and those few tended to move their capital from shipping into trade. Almost specialist owners were the masters like Twiddy and the Moyers who built up their interest in shipping until retiring ashore and retained or increased it thereafter, though such men would invariably put some of their gains into trade and land as they grew rich. Since this was a particularly favourable time for 'adventures' in ships of size and power, the incentive to persist was perhaps stronger than at other times in early-modern England, but social custom and

---

[47] The 1629 shipping return for Dorset lists twenty-five masters, giving the ages of sixteen, all of whom were 40 and over: SP16/138, fols. 31–46.
[48] Wiggs, 'Southampton'; Woodward, *Chester*, p. 115.
[49] Nef, *Coal Industry*, II, 23–7. Davis's statement that in this trade 'ownership went outside the normal ring of merchants' rightly moderates Nef's emphasis without actually contradicting it.
[50] The great majority of chief owners mentioned in the Trinity House certificates in the years 1626–38 were merchants. Merchants also formed the great majority of London owners named in Admiralty Court cases and in letters of marque. [51] Davis, *Shipping Industry*, p. 159.

commonsense caution told against it. Conversely, few merchants became interested mainly in shipping. The brothers Alexander and Squire Bence, born in the 1590s, provide a rare, yet significantly qualified example. They were members of the leading merchant family in Aldeburgh, which was probably the fastest-growing shipping centre in the country in the first half of the century, serving with substantial vessels both the booming coal trade and London's overseas trades. In the previous generation, Alexander, William and Robert Bence were shipowners, as was also John, merchant and elder brother of Alexander and Squire. While John founded the county family of Bence of Thorington Hall, another elder brother, Robert, was a citizen and salter of London. Alexander as a merchant and Squire as a master seem to have concentrated on shipping business, but they too had important other interests. Both represented their town in the Short and again in the Long Parliament, where Squire replaced William Rainborowe, another outstanding figure in shipping, in 1642. In the same year both became Navy Commissioners and so, combining political influence with nautical connections and expertise, assumed a vital role in the conduct of the civil war at sea. Alexander, as a member of the London Grocers' Company, moved in City circles and is said to have married the sister of Samuel Vassall the radical City MP and Navy Commissioner, himself much interested in shipping. As a Presbyterian and City man, Alexander was secluded from the House in 1648 and about the end of that year Squire died, leaving lands in Aldeburgh and elsewhere as well as tenements and grounds in Ratcliffe. As a dutiful Presbyterian he endowed a lectureship in Aldeburgh. Alexander became politically active again under Cromwell and in 1655 was described as a rich man, having an income of £1,200 a year, lands with an annual value of £300 and a large estate in Ireland. He became Master of Trinity House in 1659. At some point the Bences intermarried with the Aldeburgh Johnsons, shipwrights, shipmasters and shipowners, one product of which alliance, presumably, was Bence Johnson, master of the *Mary and John* in 1626 and of the 300-ton *Assurance* in 1629 and part-owner (with Alexander and Squire) of the *Elizabeth* of Aldeburgh (100 tons) in 1636. In the next generation Henry Johnson of the same family took over the East India Company's Blackwall yard and became perhaps the largest shipowner of his day.[52]

[52] Keeler, *Long Parliament*, pp. 106–7; Brunton and Pennington, *Long Parliament*, p. 77; Harris, *Trinity House*, pp. 34, 39, 65, 271; Harris, *Transactions*, nos. 45, 228, 253; Davis, *Shipping Industry*, pp. 55, 83; MacCormack, 'Irish adventurers', p. 45; Appleby, 'Privateering', II, 23, 40; 'Dietz bounty list' (see Chapter 1, n. 27); SP12/262, no. 126; SP16/16/102; SP16/17/85, 110, 135; Prob. 11/207, fol. 164, proved 23 February 1648/9.

Even the Bences, however, had nothing like the eminence, as shipping magnates, of the Tudor Hawkinses. In the provincial ports of Caroline England leading merchants frequently invested in parts of ships, as we have seen, and for some of them shipping was evidently a major concern: John Delbridge of Barnstaple, for example, the so-called 'free trader', who engaged himself deeply in supplying the young plantations, especially the Bermudas, with servants and stores – a type of trade in which shipping was important. Giles Elbridge of Bristol, who inherited the business of Robert Aldworth, one of the Elizabethan pioneers of new trades, likewise combined a strong shipping interest with colonial enterprise. Arnold Brames of Dover, brother of the Customer of Dover, acquired an increasingly impressive stake in shipping as that port developed its remarkable entrepôt trade in the 1620s and 1630s.[53] But these and some other outport men of like stature and interests were merchants rather than shipping men, and the same must be said of those few City magnates who had some considerable commitments as shipowners. Leading members of the Levant Company are known to have been part-owners of the great ships in that trade – Sir Morris Abbot, Sir Anthony Abdy, William Abell and Henry Andrews, for example – and detailed research would doubtless reveal many more, but very few had major holdings on the shipping side. Sir John Cordell and William Garway, heirs to the outstanding shipowners of the early Levant trade, were exceptions in this respect.[54]

Some of the largest shipowners of the day were to be found among those great Londoners who participated widely in the overseas trades and other spheres of commerce, including finance. Such were the brothers Ralph and William Freeman, leading exporters of cloth to

---

[53] Delbridge's many-sided trading and political activities are described in a valuable essay by Alison Grant, 'John Delbridge of Barnstaple, merchant, 1564–1639', in Fisher, *Innovation*, pp. 91–109. C. M. Andrews judged him 'probably the most influential and important of all the west country merchants': Andrews, *Colonial Period*, I, 236. On Elbridge see McGrath, 'Merchant Venturers', p. 77; Powell, *Bristol Privateers*, p. 73; SP16/138, fols. 4–14. On Brames: Kepler, *Exchange of Christendom*, p. 110; Appleby, 'Privateering', II, 69–70; SP16/17/53 (*Tristram and Jane*), 47 (*Samuel*), 100 (*John*), 125 (*Blessing*), 154 (*Dover Merchant*).

[54] Thomas Cordell and Sir William Garway were the biggest shipowners in the Turkey trade in the 1580s and 1590s. Sir John Cordell appears as chief owner of the *Sampson* (500 tons), the *Royal Merchant* (600 tons) and the *Mary* (340 tons): BL, Additional MSS, 37816, fol. 55; SP16/137; SP16/16/120; SP16/17/43. William Garway appears as chief owner of the *Barbara Constance* (c. 300 tons), the *Levant Merchant* (400 tons), the *William and Thomas* (300 tons), the *London Merchant* (380 tons), the *Angel* (350 tons) and the *Mercury* (300 tons): SP16/16/123; SP16/17/37, 81, 139, 162. Both merchants probably owned parts of other vessels. John Mun, who (with his brother Thomas, the famous author) was connected with the Cordells, had also a significant stake in shipping, owning parts of the *Angel* (350 tons), the *Love* (300 tons) and the *Golden Fleece* (400 tons): SP16/17/139, 147, 151; Appleby, 'Privateering', II, 12.

Europe, who undertook a rich slice of the Levant trade and a lion's share of that with Russia, holding also for a time a monopoly of 'Greenland' whaling, in addition to important interests in the East India Company, Newfoundland fishing and tin exports.[55] Whaling in particular was very much a shipowners' trade and Muscovy traders also sometimes put capital into their shipping. John and Humphrey Slany likewise diversified their overseas business, moving out of the limited range of the Merchants Adventurers into the markets of the Levant, Spain, the Atlantic islands, Barbary and West Africa, adventuring also in the East India, Virginia and Somers Islands companies. In partnership together or with other merchants, the Slany brothers combined importing and shipowning on a large scale, most notably as pioneers of the Guinea trade, in which Humphrey collaborated with his son-in-law William Cloberry and with Sir Nicholas Crispe. In the powerful ships employed in the Barbary, Guinea and African islands trades these great merchants invested heavily, for shipping here still constituted a major – and in the Guinea trade probably the main – element in the trading account. In time of war their ships sailed with letters of marque and occasionally took prizes which handsomely supplemented their owners' profits.[56] In the strength of their shipping interests, however, the Freemans and the Slanys were by no means typical of the great overseas traders of their time. A few others such as Sir William Russell and Sir Marmaduke Royden invested considerable capital, but for men of their wealth these were modest outlays, while for the majority of City merchants the money they put into shipping was more or less marginal.

Of all the shipowning traders of London the wealthiest and the most ambitious in maritime enterprise were the Courtens. Sir William (1572–1636) and his younger brother Sir Peter were the sons of William, a Dutch Protestant who took refuge in London in 1568 and prospered mightily in the new draperies. By judicious marriages and

---

[55] Friis, *Cockayne Project*, p. 56; Cell, *Newfoundland*, pp. 54–5; Lang, 'Greater merchants'; Brown, *Genesis*, p. 893; Ashton, *City and Court*, p. 17. Among the ships in which the Freemans held shares were the *Trial* (200 tons), the *Blessing* (280 tons), the *Freeman* (450 tons), the *William and Ralph* (400 tons), the *Talbot* (200 tons), the *Hector* (400 tons), the *Assurance* (250 tons), the *Delight* (350 tons), the *Eagle* (340 tons) and the *Merchant Bonaventure* (230 tons): SP16/16/148; SP16/17/7, 39; Appleby, 'Privateering', II, 12, 17, 18, 27, 41; SP16/137. Sir Ralph became Lord Mayor in 1633.

[56] Friis, *Cockayne Project*, p. 100; Cell, *Newfoundland*, pp. 54–5; Newton, *Colonizing Activities*, p. 124; Brown, *Genesis*, p. 1004; Marsden, *Law and Custom*, I, 385, 413–16, 442–3; Shilton and Holworthy, *Examinations*, nos. 41, 66, 73, 118, 445; Lang, 'Greater merchants'; Appleby, 'Privateering', I, 195–6, 200–1; SP16/137; SP16/16/143; SP16/17/28, 50. The Slanys were chief or part-owners of at least eighteen vessels between 1625 and 1637, when Humphrey died, John having died in 1631. On the importance of shipping in the Guinea trade see Andrews, *Trade, Plunder and Settlement*, pp. 105–6.

business acumen the sons further developed the family firm, ploughing their capital (reported to amount to £150,000 in 1631) into a variety of speculations, including large loans to the Crown and extensive overseas ventures. The most impressive of these – the initial colonization of Barbados and the sustained challenge to the East India Company's monopoly of England's oriental trade – failed, and in the end these and other misfortunes reduced Sir William's son William to bankruptcy. Meanwhile, in pursuit of their overseas undertakings, the Courtens invested many thousands in shipping. The assertion that Sir William built more than twenty ships and employed between 4,000 and 5,000 seamen over a period of years is probably, to judge from the random evidence available, little if at all exaggerated. In his will he left gold rings to Captain John Weddell, Captain Robert Moulton and 'every captain and master of all and every my ships and pinnaces', including, presumably, the faithful Henry Powell and his nephew John. As a merchant prince, Sir William gathered about him a galaxy of merchants like Samuel Bonnell and Thomas Kynaston, who were considerable shipowners in their own right.[57] Sir Peter Richaut, another very rich immigrant from the Low Countries, was essentially a financial magnate, but engaged also in foreign trade and owned shipping on a scale lesser men could not have contemplated, though for him this was no more than a side-line.[58]

Poorer men altogether, the Thierry brothers, John and James, had, in proportion to their wealth, much greater commitments to shipping. Their father John, a French-speaking Walloon and Huguenot who came to London around 1599, died in 1627, after which James and a third son, Stephen, moved abroad to Amsterdam and Naples respectively, while John remained in London. The brothers then exploited their positioning to promote an international enterprise centred upon London and operating to places ranging from Naples to

---

[57] *DNB*; Kippis, *Biographia*, IV, 322–52; Foster, *Court Minutes, 1635–9*; Foster, *Court Minutes, 1640–3*; Ashton, *Crown and Money Market*, pp. 21–2, 169–70, 195–6; Harlow, *Barbados*, pp. 4–12; Harlow, *West Indies and Guiana*, pp. xxix–xxx, 25–40; Marsden, *Law and Custom*, I, 492–5; Shilton and Holworthy, *Examinations*, nos. 356, 358, 502, 529, 540, 605; BL, Sloane MSS, 3515, fol. 32; HCA 15/4 (charter-parties for the *Samaritan* and the *Roebuck*); HCA 13/54, fols. 139–40, 249, 308–9, 378; HCA 13/55, fols. 59, 230; HCA 13/60, 27 June 1645; HCA 24/94, no. 226; HCA 24/96, no. 435; HCA 30/636 (Anthony's accounts); HCA 30/638 (*Greenfield* accounts); SP16/17/56, 67, 86, 94, 97, 160; SP16/137. The Courtens were particularly interested in Moroccan trade: Castries, *Angleterre*, III, 307, 323, 345, 399, 519–45, etc.; SP71/13, fol. 19.

[58] *DNB*; Ashton, *Crown and Money Market*, pp. 183–4; Kepler, 'Fiscal aspects', p. 267; Taylor, 'Trade, neutrality', p. 241; Shilton and Holworthy, *Examinations*, nos. 253, 261, 289, 325, 331; HCA 13/49, fol. 575; HCA 30/636 (Anthony's accounts); SP16/16/69; SP16/35/101; SP16/43/79.

Newfoundland – most notably to the Cape Verde coast and islands, Mina, Principe, São Tomé and Annóbon – a remarkable feature of which business was the volume of shipping directly owned and employed by the partnership. They seem to have bought ships in the early 1630s with a view to servicing the Iberian trades, but to have fallen foul of Dutch marauders.[59] Yet another member of the French Church, John Delabarr (c. 1599–1664), son of a Huguenot refugee, launched ventures in a variety of trades and was a principal owner of several ships, in partnership more than once with his younger brother Vincent and his sister's husband John Kipp, also a London Huguenot.[60]

Tradesmen who built or supplied ships were often apt to acquire parts of them, whether by way of payment in kind for their contribution or as a result of some personal connection with an owner-master or merchant owner. Some may have offered to take a share in order to attract business. The master shipwright John Dearsley, who had docks at Wapping and Horseydown, owned parts in several ships, as did Robert Clement, shipwright of Stepney and mast-maker of Wapping, Peter Pett of Deptford and Phineas, his famous kinsman.[61] Among the variety of dockside dealers who ventured into part-owning – many no doubt but once – a few developed large stakes in shipping, most impressively William Greene of St Dunstan's-in-the-East, fishmonger by trade but ropeseller by profession. Supplying ships with cordage, pitch, tar and so forth, he is known to have held parts in twenty-three substantial ships, some of them colliers, some powerful Levant traders and the like, in the years 1626 to 1640, and probably in fact held many more.[62] His name is often found side by side with that

---

[59] Shilton and Holworthy, *Examinations*, pp. xxvii–xxviii and nos. 1, 5, 10, 18, 77, 103, 104, 107, 122, 158, 187, 219, 239, 241, 267, 284, 364, 448, 466, 483; HCA 13/50, fols. 19–20, 25, 205, 230, 254; HCA 13/54, fol. 70; HCA 13/55, fols. 135–6; HCA 24/96, no. 285. Before going bankrupt John made over to James no less than 1,200 tons of shipping, including seven ships owned outright and five eighths of another, of which James already owned another quarter: HCA 15/4 (assignment dated 16 February 1634/5).

[60] Moens, *French Church Registers*, pp. 14, 47; Prob. 11/315, fol. 284, proved 2 December 1664; Shilton and Holworthy, *Examinations*, nos. 28, etc; Cell, *Newfoundland*, p. 19; HCA 15/4 (charter-parties for the *Matthew*, the *George* and the *Tristram and Jane*); HCA 24/94, no. 90; HCA 30/635 (an account book of receipts for sums paid by John, Vincent and Robert Delabarr, 1620–35); SP16/16/186; SP16/17/59; CSPD 1629–31, p. 38; HCA 13/54, fol. 164 (referring to John Delabarr's house in Crutched Friars).

[61] Dearsley: SP16/137 (twice); SP16/16/23, 37; Harris, *Transactions*, no. 426. Clement: Shilton and Holworthy, *Examinations*, no. 483; SP16/17/84, 163; HCA 15/4 (charter-party for the *Thomas*); HCA 13/49, fols. 418–19. Peter Pett of Deptford owned part of the *Constant Warwick*; Phineas owned part of the *Resistance*: McGowan, *Jacobean Commissions*, p. xv.

[62] In a personal deposition dated 8 October 1639 Greene gave his age as about 52: HCA 13/55, fol. 271. He owned parts in the *Greenfield*, the *Jeremy*, the *Affection*, the *Tristram and Jane*, the *Samaritan*, the *Lydia*, the *Mary Constance*, the *James*, the *Josias*, the *Susan*, the *Protection*, the *Joseph*, the *William and Ralph*, the *Four Sisters*, the *Increase*, the *Centurion*, the *Pelican*, the

of Edmund Turvile, who supplied ironware on one occasion, guns, gunpowder and munition on another.[63] William Pulman, ropemaker of Limehouse, owned parts in at least eleven ships and is named as chief owner of several colliers.[64] In a complex of suits relating to the 400-ton *Aeneas*, several claimants alleged that William Goddard, the master, had sold them shares in return for materials used in her building. If all these claims were justified, the improvident Goddard must have disposed of more than the third which properly belonged to him, but even if they were not they imply the normality of such dealings.[65] With luck such investments might yield a painless profit, but they might sometimes become an embarrassment. Phineas Pett, for example, pleaded that he became indebted for ironwork done by a certain blacksmith on Sir Walter Ralegh's *Destiny* because Ralegh, for whom he had built this ship, could not or would not pay, obliging Pett to venture that sum in the ship, which was seized by the Crown after the voyage. He was consequently unable to honour his bond to the smith — such at least was his story.[66]

In most cases, unfortunately, the source and motivation of a part-owner's interest remain obscure for want of evidence. Thus we may surmise, but cannot be sure, that Gregory Clement, merchant, of St George's, Buttolph Lane, MP for Fowey from 1646 to 1652, rumper and regicide, came by his parts in various vessels, numbering at least ten, in the course of the assurance business he undertook from 1632 onwards. Shipping evidently occupied an important place in his business activities in the 1630s, as his marriage with Captain Trenchfield's daughter suggests, though later he speculated heavily in Irish and royalist lands.[67] The path of James Duppa into shipowning is

---

Providence, the *William and John*, the *Desire*, the *Anne*, the *Elizabeth and Susan* and the *Diamond*: SP16/137; SP16/16/9, 75, 173; SP16/17/9, 22, 32, 35, 44, 53, 54, 57, 62, 66, 71, 73, 88, 102; Harris, *Transactions*, nos. 306, 307; HCA 13/49, fols. 418–19; HCA 15/4 (charter-parties for the *Jeremy*, *Affection*, *Tristram and Jane*, *Samaritan*, *Lydia* and *Mary Constance*).

[63] SP16/16/181; SP16/17/10, 32, 44, 56, 57, 58, 66; HCA 30/638 (Greenfield); HCA 13/49, fols. 418–19; HCA 13/55, fols. 230, 271.

[64] Shilton and Holworthy, *Examinations*, nos. 6, 8, 421, 432; Harris, *Transactions*, nos. 306, 307; SP16/137 (six ships); SP16/16/24, 157, 149; SP16/17/33, 70, 127, 166; HCA 13/54, fol. 230; HCA 15/4 (charter-party for the *Speedwell*).

[65] SP16/17/149; HCA 15/4 (bill of sale for one eighth of the *Aeneas*); HCA 13/55, fols. 204–6, 306–39; HCA 24/96, nos. 45, 62, 99, 103, 349, 357–66. [66] Perrin, *Phineas Pett*, p. 211.

[67] Brunton and Pennington, *Long Parliament*, pp. 59–60, 65, 135–6; MacCormack, 'Irish adventurers', p. 46; Bottigheimer, *English Money*, pp. 71, 156; *CSPD 1636–7*, p. 350; Marsden, *Law and Custom*, I, 499; Steckley, *Paige Letters*, pp. 62–3; Shilton and Holworthy, *Examinations*, nos. 31, 196, 202, 224–5, 248, 256–9, 270–6, 287, 356, 358, 435, 453, 515, 522, 524, 531, 557, 573, 589, 595, 598, 601, 611–12; HCA 15/4 (charter-parties for the *Centurion* and the *Anne and Elizabeth*; policy of assurance for the *Mary*); HCA 13/54, fols. 17, 19, 21–2, 309 (deposition), 377; HCA 13/55, fol. 156; HCA 13/60, 4 June 1645; Clement had some interest in the *Aeneas*

equally conjectural. His father was a brewer of East Smithfield supplying the king's Navy with beer, but James, though still working in the family firm in 1608 at the age of twenty-six, became by the later 1620s a gentleman commander and promoter of powerful privateersmen, enjoying the special confidence and favour of the Admiralty. Was it the family's official connection which opened his way to advancement, or did he buy his parts of ships with beer? Influence and beer no doubt worked wonders together, but we do not know precisely how.[68]

From Limehouse ropeseller to empire-building plutocrat, from Barnstaple free trader to millionaire monopolist, a variety of merchants took shares in shipping for a variety of reasons, and the active participation of such diverse and generally successful business men argues the attractiveness of shipowning at this time. Though few made it their chief concern, many obviously thought it a good investment, fitting well their other interests. Men like William Greene and Humphrey Slany were not in shipping by chance or for fun. Either, like the former, they were close enough to perceive and to exploit its opportunities, or, like the latter, they thought it advantageous as overseas traders to have ships or parts thereof at their disposal. It has been persuasively maintained that in the eighteenth century the merchant owner was not as a rule primarily interested in carrying his own cargoes, but preferred to lade his ship with other men's goods.[69] Even then, however, as the argument admits, many exceptions occurred, and in the early seventeenth century the exceptions were probably more important still. Where ownership groups were small, as in Bristol and the minor ports generally, merchants frequently laded their own cargo in their own ships, as John Smythe of Bristol had done in Henrician days and many Elizabethan Bristolians in the Peninsula trade. Such was common practice also in the triangular trade of the southwest ports with Newfoundland and Iberia. Privateering then assumed a much larger place in the employment of shipping than it did later, and encouraged merchants to invest in ships, particularly in the hope of supplementing their trading profit with the proceeds of prize. Above all, this was a time of new trades, when merchants, anxious

---

(see n. 65 above); in 1652 he lost his seat for 'lying with his maid' and was eventually executed – for regicide.

[68] McGowan, *Jacobean Commissions*, p. 125; Appleby, 'Privateering', I, 204, II, 16, 21, 31; BL, Additional MSS, 37816, fols. 58–9, 61, 86, 102, 104, 110; Marsden, *Law and Custom*, I, 438; Nef, *Coal Industry*, II, 263–6; *CSPD 1629–31*, p. 133; SP16/16/133. Duppa participated in an attempted plantation on the Amazon in 1629: HCA 13/49, fols. 404–20, 547.

[69] Davis, *Shipping Industry*, pp. 90–9.

about the conduct of unfamiliar voyages, tended to seek direct control by venturing in both ship and goods, though normally in partnership with others in order to spread the risk of losing the whole.

The extreme case of the absorption of the shipping function by the trader was the East India Company, which at this stage built and owned all the ships it employed. The big Guinea traders – Crispe, the Slanys, Cloberry and Wood – also relied on their own ships in this highly expensive, dangerous and lucrative commerce. Whereas in the settled trade with the Canary Islands chartering and freighting predominated (though traders were not always averse to employing ships they partly owned),[70] the unstable conditions of the Barbary trade (since the death of the great sherif in 1603) and of Portugal's Atlantic trades (since the Dutch invasion of Brazil) seem to have favoured the use of powerful ships wholly or partly owned by those who laded or partly laded them. The Caribbean and North American trades, on the other hand, present an interestingly varied pattern, in which the shipping and trading functions are sometimes divorced, sometimes merged, often overlapping.

This was the sphere, *par excellence*, of the so-called 'new merchants'. These men, who developed the colonial trades in the 1620s, 1630s and 1640s, were new, it has elsewhere been argued, in the sense that, with only a few exceptions, they did not belong to the established aristocracy of trade which then dominated the great chartered companies and controlled the government of the City. They came generally from more modest, often provincial, backgrounds, from families of, in the current phrase, 'the middling sort', landed, commercial or, more usually, both. Lacking the means or patrimony to enter the exclusive Levant and East India Companies or the more venerable establishment of the Merchants Adventurers, they became interested in American trade perhaps as planters, perhaps as provisioning merchants or shopkeepers, perhaps as seafaring people.[71] These young trades across the Atlantic offered opportunities to adventurers without the substantial resources of capital and specialized knowledge which the older trades required, even when nominally open. They were in practice free for all after the demise of the Virginia Company in 1624. Numerous small business men were tempted to take a hand, some of whom evidently made money, a few their fortunes, and, among these last, shipowners were prominent.

[70] Steckley, *Paige Letters*, p. xxix.
[71] Brenner, 'Social basis' and Brenner, 'Civil war politics', which derive from Brenner, 'Commercial change and political conflict'.

THE SHIPOWNERS

The most famous and successful of the new merchants, a moving spirit in much of their enterprise, was Maurice Thompson. Born in 1604, a younger son in a gentry family, he was already at an early age the owner-master of a ship engaged in the Virginia trade, where he and his brothers also acquired land.[72] In 1627 he joined Thomas Combe of Southampton to send three ships with slaves from Africa to St Kitts.[73] From then on he participated in the Virginia and West Indies trades as a merchant, a promoter of plantation and a shipowner, collaborating in a kaleidoscope of partnerships with merchants and masters interested in shipping, planting and provisioning. He and Simon Turgis, tobacco trader and part-owner of ships, took a third share, for example, in the abortive project to colonize Kent Island, off the Virginia coast, in a joint stock with William Cloberry, William Cleborne and John Delabarr, for which purpose they dispatched William Tucker, Thompson's brother-in-law and a leading merchant planter himself, in the *Africa*, of which Tucker was master and chief owner. In the years down to 1640 Thompson was responsible for sending some twenty-five ships to Virginia.[74] Again in partnership with John Delabarr, he promoted fur-trading in the St Lawrence in defiance of the monopoly claimed by Gervase Kirke's Canada Company.[75] When he and his partners lost their ship the *Robert Bonaventure* and her lading of tobacco to Dunkirkers, Thompson joined with Gregory Clement, Robert South and other injured parties to set forth the *Discovery* on reprisal, beginning thus in 1637 a series of successful privateering ventures.[76] In 1642 he helped to finance the well-known buccaneering expedition of Captain William Jackson to the West Indies.[77] In 1638 he began interloping in the West African trade, challenging the monopoly of Sir Nicholas Crispe's company, and by 1649, in partnership with John Wood and others favoured by Parliament, had usurped control of that branch of English commerce.[78] He traded with the Bermudas also and in 1655 played a great part in promoting Cromwell's Caribbean expedition.[79] In the 1630s he supported Sir William Courten's efforts to

---

[72] Brenner, 'Commercial change and political conflict', ch. 3.
[73] Harlow, *West Indies and Guiana*, pp. 26–7; Appleby, 'Privateering', II, 47, 49; *APC Col. 1613–80*, p. 122.
[74] HCA 13/55, fols. 527–9, 569–70; HCA 13/60, 6 September 1645, etc.; HCA 24/96, nos. 278, 318; Hillier, 'Virginia trade', p. 24. In 1633 Thompson was accused of attempting to establish, with the help of others, a monopoly of the Virginia tobacco trade: *APC Col. 1613–80*, pp. 187–8.   [75] Kirke, *Canada*; *APC Col. 1613–80*, pp. 169–79; HCA 13/49, fols. 565–6.
[76] Brenner, 'Commercial change and political conflict', pp. 125–6; Shilton and Holworthy, *Examinations*, nos. 515, 522, 524, 531, 573, 612; HCA 13/54, fols. 17–22; *CSPD 1636–7*, p. 554. On the later activities of this ship see Chapter 8 below.
[77] Harlow, *Voyages of Jackson*, pp. vi, xi.   [78] Porter, 'Crispe family', pp. 66–8.
[79] Harlow, *West Indies and Guiana*, p. 26.

57

break into eastern trade and after Courten's death in 1635 continued interloping, though eventually he joined the East India Company and dominated it increasingly in the 1650s, to become its governor in 1658.[80]

Though principally a merchant, Thompson had from the start a strong interest in shipping. He is known to have owned chiefly or partly ten ships and undoubtedly held shares in others. Moreover, all the trades in which he engaged were shipping-intensive: the Guinea trade, the slave trade, eastern trade, colonial trade and privateering. In 1645 he declared himself one of the 'adventurers for prizes', setting forth armed ships to pursue the civil war at sea by seizing, as a business, the vessels and goods of merchants unfortunate enough to reside in royalist-held ports.[81] A radical in politics, Maurice Thompson of St Dunstan's-in-the-East came effectively to power in January 1649, at the culmination of the English revolution, when he was appointed to the new 'committee of merchants for regulating the navy and customs', along with his business associates and fellow-radicals, Thomas Andrewes, regicide and Lord Mayor in 1650, William and Samuel Pennoyer, Stephen Estwick, Samuel Moyer, Richard Hill, Richard Shute, James Russell and Major Robert Thompson, his own brother, while George, another brother, soon became a member of the Council of State.[82] The new committee carried out the purge of the Navy and the Customs, leaving them completely in the hands of Thompson and his friends, who at the same time took over the government of Trinity House.[83] They then proceeded to manage these affairs according to their own devices and ambitions. Thompson and William Pennoyer together drove a lucrative trade in saltpetre acquired in India for sale to Cromwell's army and awarded themselves contracts for provisioning both the Commonwealth Navy and the army in Ireland. Above all, Thompson became the architect of commercial and maritime policy, the prime mover behind the Navigation Act of 1651.[84]

Not all Thompson's numerous commercial partners were new men in the sense noted above. Courten, though indeed an outsider, was no small business man, nor radically inclined in politics. Matthew Cradock came from the merchant aristocracy, having graduated from the firm of Alderman Cockayne, a City magnate of the first rank, to leading positions in the Levant and East India Companies. It was probably his Puritan conviction which brought him into American trade and led

[80] Farnell, 'Navigation act', pp. 443–4.   [81] *Ibid.*, p. 445; HCA 13/60, 6 July 1645.
[82] Dewar, 'Naval administration', pp. 419, 425.   [83] Brenner, 'Civil war politics', p. 96.
[84] Farnell, 'Navigation act', pp. 445–6.

him to 'root and branch' politics alongside his fellow-aldermen Thomas Andrewes (whose son married Cradock's daughter) and John Fowke. Cradock, however, was an important shipowner. Fowke, also a shipowning merchant, is not easy to classify as a new man: certainly he was a most cantankerous radical and came from a minor armigerous family, but he speedily rose into the aristocracy of trade, becoming a prominent figure in the Levant and East India Companies.[85] Nor does Randall Mainwaring fit neatly into that category: he shared his cousin Cradock's religious and political views and his interest in colonial trade and shipowning, having married Elizabeth, sister of Joseph and Nathaniel Hawes, leading tobacco traders and major shipowners; but, as a gentleman of ancient lineage, a freeman of the Mercers and a prominent Common Councilman, he was a highly respected figure in the City long before the civil war.[86] As for Nathan and Nathaniel Wright (apparently father and son respectively), they were already well-established merchants in the 1620s. The father, aged about 50 in 1631, claimed then that he had lived fourteen years in Biscay, had hired the Biscayners who taught the English whaling, and had been the chief director of the Muscovy Company's 'Greenland voyage' (viz. their Spitzbergen whaling operations). The Wrights' wide-ranging commercial activities included Moroccan and Levant trade and involved them to a relatively large extent in shipowning.[87]

As for that restless opponent of the Caroline régime, Samuel Vassall, MP, he seems to have been, like many of those above-mentioned, more distinctively a shipping merchant than a particularly 'new' one. He was the son, by Anna Russell of Ratcliffe, of John Vassall, a London merchant of Huguenot origin who equipped and commanded his own ship, the 140-ton *Samuel*, against the Spanish armada in 1588. John lived in Ratcliffe and later married the daughter of Stephen Borough the great

[85] Pearl, *London*, pp. 316–20. Fowke was part-owner of the *Levant Merchant*: SP16/16/123. He and Cradock promoted the voyage of the *Golden Cock* with letters of marque in 1627: Appleby, 'Privateering', II, 26. For detail on Cradock's shipping interests see Chapter 4 below.
[86] Pearl, *London*, p. 323; Shilton and Holworthy, *Examinations*, p. xxviii, etc.; HCA 15/4 (bill of sale for the *Safety*). Joseph Hawes owned half the *John and Dorothy* and some at least of her cargo: Shilton and Holworthy, *Examinations*, nos. 108, 136, 164, 414; HCA 13/54, fols. 166–7; Joseph Hawes and Company appear to have owned entirely the *Elizabeth* of London and her cargo: HCA 13/54, fol. 141; HCA 13/60, 6 May 1645.
[87] Pearl, *London*, p. 331; Nathan (of St Olave's, Hart Street) and his son Nathaniel (of St Sepulchre's, West Smithfield) are frequently found in partnership and easily confused. Nathan's will (Prob. 11/274, fol. 337) was proved on 5 February 1657/8; Nathaniel's (Prob. 11/297, fol. 143) on 16 March 1659/60. One or both were part-owners of the *Lion's Whelp*, the *Nathaniel*, the *James*, the *Concord*, the *Reformation* and the *Whale* (SP16/16/142; SP16/17/12, 29, 80; CSPD 1629–31, p. 133; HCA 13/49, fol. 565). They were among the promoters of Digby's voyage (APC 1627, p. 222).

navigator, who had with his brother William pioneered the northern sea-route to Archangel and beyond. Samuel, baptised in Stepney in 1586, was thus born and bred at the heart of the shipping world. According to his own declaration, he became a merchant in his middle twenties and lived for a time in Italy, presumably as factor for Abraham Cartwright, Draper and member of the Levant, East India and Virginia companies, whose daughter he married. As a wholesale clothier, Vassall traded in cloth, principally to the Mediterranean and the American plantations, importing currants and silks from the Levant, tobacco, hemp and flax from the East Indies and Virginia. Along with Matthew Cradock, he was a founder of the Massachusetts Bay Company and a defendant in the proceedings of the Crown against the company in 1635, he and his brother William having a large interest in the colony. In 1626 he set forth the *Thomas* of London with letters of marque and about the same time bought up Moorish prisoners for shipment as slaves to Leghorn. He dispatched his own 400-ton *Mayflower* more than once to Virginia under the command of Peter Andrews, his brother-in-law, with whom and others he undertook planting in Virginia and Carolina. He was imprisoned for opposition to Charles's forced loan in 1627, resisted the Crown's imposition on currants the following year and the illegal levy of tonnage and poundage in 1630, and in 1635 was again imprisoned for refusing ship money. Elected by the City to the Short and Long Parliaments, he was appointed a Navy Commissioner in 1642 and a Commissioner for the Plantations in 1643. In the 1640s he developed an interloping trade to Guinea, with a particular interest in the slave trade to Barbados. Along with the Bences, the Thompsons and Gregory Clement, Vassall was a prominent adventurer in John Pym's joint-stock project for the suppression of the Irish rebellion and the annexation of Irish lands.[88]

As a Presbyterian City man Vassall was purged in 1648 and thereafter came to public notice chiefly as a beggar petitioning the government, for the most part in vain, to recompense him, with interest, for vast sums allegedly lost by him at the hands of the monarchy. Thompson meanwhile marched on in the wake of Cromwell. Nevertheless these two had much in common: in their persons they bridged mercantile

---

[88] *DNB* (John and Samuel Vassall); Pearl, *London*, pp. 188–91; Keeler, *Long Parliament*, p. 371; Bridenbaugh, *Vexed and Troubled*, pp. 425–6; Rabb, *Enterprise and Empire*, p. 261 (Cartwright); Laughton, *Defeat*, II, 328; Brown, *Genesis*, pp. 846, 1036; Rose-Troup, *Massachusetts*, p. 156; Porter, 'Crispe family', p. 69; Castries, *Angleterre*, III, 35–6; MacCormack, 'Irish adventurers', pp. 45–57; HCA 30/638 (accounts of trade in slaves, gold and ivory at Calabar); HCA 13/50, fols. 136–8 (*re* the *Mayflower*, of which Vassall is named sole owner). Peter Andrews died at sea aboard the *Expedition* in 1637: Prob. 11/176, proved 21 February 1637/8.

and maritime capital; from seafaring beginnings both grew into great merchants especially occupied with shipping-intensive trades; both laded cargo at times in ships they owned; both combined commercial, naval and political influence for their own and their associates' ends, though it is fair to suppose they identified these with the interests of the nation and, no doubt, the protestant religion. For after all they did represent, however obliquely, a growing segment of the national interest: seafaring trade, colonial development, naval power.

CHAPTER 3

SEAMEN AND MUTINY

IN THE common opinion of contemporaries, Caroline seamen were generally discontented, disorderly and mutinous. Captain Nathaniel Butler, in his *Dialogicall Discourse Concerninge Marine Affairs* (1634), observed that 'the insolencies of these men are so overgrown of late as upon every slight occasion they have nothing more ready in their mouths than that mutinous sea cry "One and all"; and on the shore you have seen some of them affronting justice in the very high streets of the City'. In the wars of the twenties Butler had commanded a royal ship as well as a merchantman hired by the Crown. He considered that the repeated mutinies and tumults of sailors in the king's service during those years had been 'rather fuelled than quenched by an over-indulgency'. Without terror and the use of martial law neither sailors nor soldiers were to be 'orderly governed'. In particular he deplored 'that loathness, or rather loathing, which of the late days hath so possessed this kind of people against all service in his Majesty's ships and fleets', attributing it to the counter-attraction of privateering, which promised pillage and liberty, and of trading voyages, which offered profits to the mariner over and above his wages.[1]

Another experienced gentleman, Nathaniel Knott, also writing in 1634, warned of the difficulties to be expected in manning an expedition against the Barbary corsairs: 'how lewd, loose and debauched the common sort of sailors are I blush to think ... Our English nation of late years were esteemed the choice men of the sea for patience and endurance, but now are grown so feeble that they cannot, or so mutinous that they will not endure the least inconvenience of war.' He was especially worried about friction between common sailors and

---

[1] Butler, *Dialogues*, pp. 35, 44. Butler was a follower of Robert Rich, second earl of Warwick, became an early governor of the Somers Islands, served in the expeditions to Cadiz (1625), the Ile de Rhé (1627) and La Rochelle (1628), and was governor of Providence Island from 1638 to 1640.

gentlemen: 'beware how thou nourish dissension between thy gentlemen servants or favourites and them, lest the company be rent in twain'.[2] Such anxieties and strictures, easy to find in the writings of pundits like Sir William Monson, Sir Henry Mainwaring, Sir Richard Hawkins and Sir Kenelm Digby, are familiar enough. They were all referring to the behaviour of sailors in men-of-war: privateersmen as well as royal warships. Privateering crews were notoriously unruly and inclined to take matters – particularly matters of prize – into their own hands, and when 'each man went upon his own venture', sailing not for wages but for shares, this was hardly surprising.[3] There had been mutinies aboard the queen's ships in Elizabeth's time – notably the case of the *Golden Lion*, whose crew revolted, took over the ship and deserted their commander, Sir Francis Drake, in 1587, for which they went unpunished. In King Charles's wars the scale and frequency of mass protests, refusals of duty, desertions and marches ashore were worse than anything seen before. It may well be that commanders like Butler and Monson were expressing an authoritarian attitude which chimed well with a certain political tendency in Court circles, but the state papers amply demonstrate that their censures were founded on fact. Butler's call for captains to use more corporal punishment for 'the reduction of these libertines of our age, to their old (Queen Elizabeth) [*sic*] obedience and discipline'[4] distorted both the history and the meaning of the unrest, but mutinous outbreaks had actually developed to a new level.

What is less familiar and puts the matter in a different light is evidence that the authorities were also concerned at this time about the incidence of mutiny in merchantmen on trading voyages. On 10 May 1631 Sir Henry Marten, Judge of the High Court of Admiralty, issued the following decree:

> Whereas great complaints is daily made to the judge of his Majesty's High Court of the Admiralty by the masters and commanders of ships employed from this kingdom into foreign parts that their mariners serving under them in those voyages are grown very mutinous, insolent and disobedient, in so much that the master cannot bear command amongst them, but also many times they so unite and themselves join together in such their rebellions, that if the master do not conform himself to their pleasure they will dismiss him and set up another master of their own choosing, and by such their ill carriage their voyages are

[2] BL, Harleian MSS, 6893, fols. 41, 63.   [3] Donno, *Madox*, p. 285.
[4] Butler, *Dialogues*, p. 46.

not only much hindered, but many times utterly overthrown, to the great loss of their employers and discouragement of their commanders. And forasmuch as it is found by experience that these insolencies and factions commonly spring from one evil spirit that secretly seduceth the rest, and when he hath drawn them to a head sheltereth himself under their common answer of One and All, or else by writing their names in a round circle under their mutinous resolution, so that it cannot be known who first set his hand to the same or is ringleader therein, whereby he escapeth such punishment as his desert requireth; the said judge for the removing and avoiding of such evils for the time to come did this day order and decree: that in what ship soever any mariner shall use that pernicious phrase One and All, or shall make any order among themselves and subscribe it about a circle as aforesaid, the mariners so answering and subscribing shall not only lose their wages for the voyage, but shall be noted for principal mutineers and otherwise severely punished as the quality of their offences shall deserve; which order the judge decreed to be published upon the Exchange.[5]

A copy of this order occurs in the records of the Trinity House of Deptford under the date 28 August 1635, which suggests that the House had occasion to refer to it at that time, and in the following year the Trinity House of Hull noted, in dealing with an allegedly mutinous letter, that a copy of the decree was kept hanging 'above the table' and ordered that the seamen responsible for the letter should suffer the punishments mentioned in the decree, unless they could come to an agreement with the master concerned.[6] The original decree did not specify punishments other than loss of wages, but the Hull Brethren had probably added the penalties they thought fitting. Indeed, the presence of the decree in both sets of records suggests that both Houses took it seriously enough to think of enforcing it four or five years later. As corporations of masters, they may well have prompted the judge in the first place and no doubt collaborated with the Admiralty Court in implementing the policy.

In examining these phenomena of a particular period, a particular generation of seamen, the longer term must not be forgotten. Such behaviour was not peculiar to the second quarter of the seventeenth century. The customary law of the sea embodied in the *Black Book of Admiralty*, which drew upon the Laws of Oleron and other medieval

---

[5] The decree is inscribed in the Admiralty Court Act Book covering that date: HCA 3/33, fols. 514–15.

[6] Harris, *Transactions*, no. 490; Brooks, *First Order Book*, p. 21; another copy occurs in BL, Additional MSS, 5500, fol. 17.

sources, clearly implies that mutinous conduct was part of the traditional pattern of sea life. The right of a master to discipline members of his company was recognized. The twelfth law of Oleron states that a master hires his mariners and ought to keep them peaceably and offer to be their judge. He can fine them for giving the lie to each other or to him. If he smites a mariner, the latter must abide the first buffet, but can defend himself if smitten again. If he smites the master he should pay five shillings or lose his fist. The 'Inquisition taken at Quinborough' in 1375 ordered inquiry to be made about mariners who laid violent hands on their masters or rebelled against their honest commands, and about masters who failed to keep their mariners quiet at table and elsewhere.[7] Of the Elizabethan period Oppenheim remarked that 'the sailor expected to have a voice in the conduct of a voyage and, if he was not listened to, became, to say the least, very unaccommodating'. He cited a number of examples to show 'how readily the English sailor flew to mutiny when discontented'.[8]

After the Restoration and through the eighteenth century, sailors and masters in merchantmen and Jack Tars and captains in the Royal Navy were no strangers to mutiny. In 1674 Samuel Pepys, recently appointed Secretary of the Admiralty, wrote in reply to one Captain Rooth: 'It is with great affliction that I read what you observe concerning the universal loss of discipline amongst the seamen of England, to the degree of their making no difference between his Majesty's service, where the want of payment of their wages may in some measure give excuse for it, and that of the merchants, where they not only have their pay certain, but their wages excessive, a vice which I pray God grant I may see rectified before it prove too fatal, not only to his Majesty's service, but to the whole navigation of the country.'[9] As Pepys acknowledged, the main cause of discontent in the king's service was 'the length and badness of the payment of the seaman's wages'.[10] Mutinies aboard and demonstrations in London in the miseries of the second Dutch war recalled the appalling scenes of the later 1620s.[11] In his study of the merchant service in the first half of the eighteenth century Rediker found evidence of sixty mutinies and is no doubt justified in claiming that many more actually occurred.[12] Davis, referring to the whole period from the Restoration to the American Revolution, writes of 'endless cases of crews, either as a whole or in groups, refusing duty, sometimes for good but often for bad reasons'.[13]

[7] Twiss, *Black Book*, I, 105, 161.   [8] *Monson's Tracts*, II, 247–8.
[9] Tanner, *Catalogue*, I, 198–9.   [10] *Ibid.*, I, 127.   [11] *Ibid.*, I, 117–20.
[12] Rediker, *Between*, pp. 308–11.   [13] Davis, *Shipping Industry*, p. 155.

Rodger describes mutiny in the Royal Navy in the middle decades of the eighteenth century as 'a formal system of public protest to bring grievances to the notice of authority'. Mutinies were generally non-violent and 'happened quite frequently'.[14] Hannay took much the same view, classifying mutinies of this type as 'simply strikes'.[15]

Yet in this long record of maritime disorder a change, both in the incidence and in the character of mutiny, is evident, and it is the reign of Charles I which marks the turning point. The collective type of mutiny indicated by Davis, Rodger and Hannay, as distinct from individual indiscipline or mutinous behaviour of the kind condemned in the medieval laws, appears seldom in our sources before 1625. The actual rarity of mutiny in merchantmen in Tudor and Jacobean times is reflected in Oppenheim's assertion – albeit a mistaken one – that no instances of it occurred before 1625.[16] The Elizabethan events he cited were outbreaks of disorder aboard royal men-of-war or privateers. Then, as ever, privateering crews were quick to riot or revolt, but mutiny in the queen's ships was by no means such a common occurrence as it became in the wars of the later 1620s and in the Navy from Pepys's day to Nelson's. Was it a coincidence that in both royal and merchant services the frequency of mutiny rose to a new level in the second quarter of the seventeenth century? Conditions in respect of recruitment, pay and discipline in the Navy differed markedly from those which prevailed in commercial shipping. On the other hand both services drew upon the same pool of seamen and were, particularly in war-time, closely connected and interdependent. Some further and more detailed examination of the causes, character and treatment of mutiny in the Royal Navy and in private shipping may serve to shed light on this question.

In the early seventeenth century mutiny was as ill-defined in law as it was in ordinary parlance, and was treated for the most part by procedures which have left little on record and remain obscure. Even then, however, the difference between the king's service and the merchant service was fundamental. In the former mutiny was a serious crime, punishable by courts martial with powers of life and death, whereas in the latter it was treated as a misdemeanour, with light penalties.[17] Even so, commanders in the Navy did not normally have

---

[14] Rodger, *Wooden World*, pp. 237–44. [15] Hannay, *Naval Courts Martial*, pp. 115–18.
[16] *Monson's Tracts*, I, 244.
[17] Course, *Nautical Terms*, said that mutiny was subject in the Royal Navy to court martial under law deriving from the Naval Discipline Act of 1661 and was punishable by extreme penalties,

authority to hold a court martial or to inflict capital punishment. If in independent command, they would be instructed by the Admiralty to treat all offences 'according to the known orders and customs of the sea', without further elaboration as to the nature of the offences, the procedure or the punishments. Surviving accounts of the penalties a captain might inflict serve only to illustrate the discretion exercised in practice in the absence of precise regulations.[18] When a set of 'Instructions for the Admiralty' was at length issued in 1647, based explicitly on 'the known orders and customs of the sea', it denied captains authority to try murder or manslaughter, but empowered them to punish with due severity other offences, including raising faction, tumult or conspiracy and 'any other insolency and disorder'.[19] The earl of Lindsey's commission as admiral of the first ship-money fleet authorized him to hold a court martial which could inflict the death penalty, but his instructions to his captains permitted them to deal only with relatively venial offences.[20]

Mutiny itself was not a felony and so could not be tried by jury. Sir Henry Marten, Judge of the Admiralty Court, made this clear in 1627 when his Majesty in Privy Council ordered the Lord High Admiral to subject certain mariners to exemplary punishment. They were duly presented by a grand jury to the High Court of Admiralty on a charge of mutiny. But the deputy registrar of the court had to report to Edward Nicholas, Buckingham's secretary, that the judge could not lawfully satisfy 'the lords' desire to have them capitally punished'. That, he declared, must be done by martial law. The case had political implications, for the mutinies had occurred on two merchantmen

---

whereas in the merchant service it was dealt with under the Merchant Shipping Act of 1906 and subject to a maximum penalty of twelve weeks imprisonment.

[18] SP16/157, *passim*. For accounts of punishments see Butler, *Dialogues*, pp. 16–19 and *Monson's Tracts*, III, 436, and IV, 200–1. [19] Tanner, *Catalogue*, I, 183.

[20] SP16/288/84; *Monson's Tracts*, IV, 3. Sir Sackville Trevor, admiral of a fleet led by HMS *Assurance* in 1627, gave the following account of a court martial. On receiving information of a mutiny in a merchantman under his command, 'I called all the captains and masters of the fleet to have this business heard before them. I found all these offences proved by those that have subscribed to them. The boatswain of this ship, being the master's brother, came aboard the *Assurance*, which I command, with 30 men in the long-boat, having put both them and the rest aboard in a mutiny. His offence being so apparent, I with the consent of most of the captains ducked him thrice at the yard arm and then turned him ashore for a mutineer. I hold the master aboard me a prisoner, with the opinion of all the captains, till your Grace's further pleasure be known.' He enclosed a list of 'articles proved against William Rudes, master of the *Esperance* of Ipswich, and Thomas Rudes, boatswain of the same', each signed by several witnesses. The captain of the mutineers' ship wrote to Nicholas, Buckingham's secretary, on the same day about the master, emphasizing the gravity of his offence, but adding: 'his life I hope my lord duke will spare out of his clemency, which (if his trial be by a council of war) will be deeply in question': SP16/62, fols. 120–4.

pressed with their crews for the king's service, the accused having allegedly questioned the Lord Admiral's warrant, refusing to put to sea.[21] No prosecutions for mutiny are to be found among the indictments recorded for the Admiralty Court, most of which refer to piracy, and some to murder and other felonies. Even the men who cast Henry Hudson adrift were not indicted for mutiny.[22] The Council of course could and did issue special commissions for the execution of martial law upon sailors rioting in port or marching to threaten the Navy Commissioners in London, but it ran the risk of demeaning its authority and arousing opposition by over-zealous interventions. In that same difficult year of 1627, being informed that certain mariners aboard his Majesty's ships did 'in a mutinous and seditious manner cause a horn to be blown for the calling together of their fellows to the end to invite and encourage them to depart from the said ships without leave, and to come to London on pretence of demanding their pay', their lordships, thinking it not fit to suffer an insolence and misdemeanour of so high a nature to pass unpunished, ordered the Navy Commissioners 'to cause strict inquiry to discover, as well the person who blew the horn, as such others who were his principal abettors and adherents, and to cause them to be apprehended and brought before the board'.[23]

Such disorders in King Charles's service have often been described. They took the form of refusal of duty by large numbers of men reacting to sheer deprivation – of food, of health and of pay. Fleets returned from disastrous expeditions such as those to Cadiz or La Rochelle with thousands sick or starving and little or no money to discharge them. Some might be discharged with tickets, in which case they might flock in hundreds to besiege the Navy Commissioners, rioting in the City, mobbing the duke of Buckingham or threatening to march on Whitehall. Some deserted in desperation, forgoing their pay, others mutinied, refusing to move their ships until paid off. The same pattern is to be observed year after year throughout the wars with France and Spain. Mutiny of this type was a recurrent symptom of naval, administrative, financial and ultimately political failure. The disaffection of the sailors was obvious. 'The common men voice the king's service worse than galley slavery', protested Sir Henry Mervyn. He blamed 'the ill-management of maritime affairs' and warned

---

[21] *APC 1627*, pp. 37, 139–40; *CSPD 1627–8*, pp. 85, 141, 156; SP16/60, fol. 128. Examinations of four of the accused are recorded in HCA 1/49, fols. 52–3.
[22] HCA 1/6 and 1/7, *passim*. Indictment of Robert Bileth, HCA 1/6, no. 133.
[23] *APC 1627*, p. 163.

prophetically that without better order the king would lose 'the love and loyalty of his sailors'.[24]

In these circumstances the authorities found it very difficult to deal with mutiny. We hear of captains dealing out punishments – the bilboes, prison, ducking, even putting down an uprising sword in hand. But we also hear Mervyn describing the miseries of his men and asking 'with what confidence can punishment be inflicted on men that mutiny in these wants?'[25] Other captains expressed sympathy in this vein and some were clearly helpless, baffled by passive resistance. Mervyn on another occasion said that in preparing certain merchantmen for service he found the masters so mutinous that he was obliged to replace them, which hardly sounds draconian.[26] The courts martial, which have left no records, were presumably more ruthless, but not always effective. At Plymouth in 1628 pressed men broke out of the town house, where they were locked up pending embarkation, for which a ringleader was condemned to death, whereupon the mutineers attacked the prison to rescue him. The outcome is not known, but it evidently disappointed the Privy Council, which reprimanded the Devon commissioners for remissness in prosecuting the offenders.[27] One suspects that many of those in authority lacked both the power and the will to punish mutiny with the severity demanded by the king and Council, who continually barked about 'exemplary punishment', 'pain of death' and so forth.[28] Modern writers who cite draconian codes of punishment should explain how they could be enforced upon mutineers in the absence of marines, who had not yet been invented.

In private ventures the master, as we have seen, had a right and a duty in customary law to keep order aboard. Disputes were of course common and depositions in the civil suits arising frequently allege ill-treatment on the one hand or mutinous conduct on the other. The normal recourse in such matters was to the High Court of Admiralty for legal settlement or to the Trinity House of Deptford (or of Hull) for arbitration. Cases might be referred from the Admiralty Court to Trinity House or vice versa. Both bodies had parallel powers to deal summarily with seamen's misdemeanours, including mutiny. Referring to this, one deponent in a civil cause described a master warning his men in 1632 'that he would acquaint the Judge of Admiralty in

---

[24] *CSPD 1629–31*, pp. 64–5.   [25] *Ibid*.   [26] *CSPD 1627–8*, p. 536.
[27] *APC 1627–8*, pp. 360, 363, 375; Oppenheim, *Administration*, p. 233; SP/16/98/26. About the same time the Privy Council complained of the slackness of JPs and constables in dealing with a similar incident in Southwark: *APC 1627–8*, p. 354.
[28] *APC 1625–6*, pp. 72–3; *APC 1626–7*, pp. 34–40, 101, 221, 306, 371, 386; *APC 1627*, pp. 37, 99.

England of such their abuses and misdemeanours, or the Master of Trinity House, to receive such punishments as their deserts required'.[29]

The Trinity House of Deptford, incorporated by charter in 1514, was essentially a gild of shipmasters. Its by-laws included a number concerning the conduct of seamen, whom it had power to punish, power explicitly recognized in its extended charter of 1604.[30] In making an award concerning wages in 1611 the Master and Elder Brothers declared that certain mariners who had behaved in a factious and mutinous manner should receive no wages, adding, however, that this was the heaviest penalty they could impose.[31] The Deptford corporation, unlike that of Hull, had no gaol of its own. Nevertheless, in 1622 it was stated in the Admiralty Court that the Brethren had imprisoned a master's mate for refusing to obey his master, and in 1628 they committed the seaman John Goodlad to the Marshalsea for five or six days for having urged four or five hundred sailors on Tower Hill to demolish Trinity House if the Brethren failed to secure their wages from the Crown. In 1632 they punished a body of men who had signed a round robin, ordering them to pay out of their wages the costs of sending their ringleader to the Marshalsea. Although we know little about this aspect over the corporation's activities, these cases show its disciplinary powers to have been limited, and in 1647 it complained about its lack of power over seamen. In practice its punishments were light, nor did it always take the master's side.[32] The Hull House in 1645 punished a mutiny by confining two men to its prison for twenty-four hours, fining them 10 shillings each, and penalizing another four with fines of 5 shillings. Negligence, insolence and refusal to sail were not uncommon charges, but the Hull Brethren rarely used their prison, preferring fines, and generally treating the ordinary seamen fairly in their disputes with masters.[33]

Unfortunately we know even less about the treatment of mutiny in the Admiralty Court, though the decree of 1631 and other references indicate that the judge did try sailors for misdemeanours, presumably by a summary procedure like that of a magistrate. An entry in the Trinity House transactions bears this out in reproducing an Admiralty Court order that mariners proved guilty before the judge of hiring

---

[29] HCA 13/54, fol. 175. In May 1625 the Privy Council ordered that seamen who absented themselves from work in the preparation of HM ships should be committed to prison 'to answer their abuses and contempts in the Admiralty Court or otherwise': *APC 1625–6*, pp. 72–3.
[30] Harris, *Trinity House*, pp. 256–7.   [31] Harris, *Transactions*, no. 16.
[32] *Ibid.*, nos. 316, 317, 406, 418; Harris, *Trinity House*, pp. 256–7.
[33] Brooks, *First Order Book*, pp. xvi–xviii, 71–2.

themselves to several masters at the same time should be imprisoned for one month.[34] The statutes of 1536 and 1537 concerning the criminal jurisdiction of the court do not, however, refer to such summary powers, being devoted only to felonies, in particular piracy, robbery, murder and theft, which were to be tried by jury according to common law. Neither mutiny nor any of its specific forms was mentioned, nor do such offences figure in the recorded indictments.[35] Mutinous conduct is sometimes mentioned incidentally in examinations relating to felonies and of course more often in the much more voluminous depositions in civil causes.[36] These, in fact, provide the bulk of the historical evidence about mutiny in merchantmen on private enterprise as distinct from the king's service, but it is oblique because mutiny was not the issue, and liable to heavy bias because masters and men often bandied charges and counter-charges of misconduct to promote their claims. All the same the evidence is usable with due care.

It shows that mutiny in the merchant service nearly always expressed disharmony between the master and some or all of his company. The master and crew had much in common and what bound them together prevailed most of the time over what divided them. The concept of the merchantman of that era as a cockpit of class struggle, even if plausible for the early eighteenth century, does not fit the early seventeenth.[37] Yet conflicts of interest did often occur to test the master's authority. He was usually a part-owner of the ship he sailed, typically having a one-eighth share, or perhaps a quarter or sixteenth.[38] He was responsible to the other owners for the profitable management of the voyage, for the ship's safety, and at least partly for the shipment of the cargo according to the charter-party or bills of lading. His own wage would amount to four or five times that of a common sailor, twice that of a mate and about three times that of his other chief officers. He would often invest in a freight-free portion of the cargo. In some ships he was essentially a superior employee, but in others a petty employer and in most a sort of hybrid employer–employee. His personal background seldom differed significantly from that of his companions, and his control over them depended primarily on his personality, age and skill. His authority was sanctioned rather by custom and nautical necessity than by any physical or legal power, of which he had none to hand: only

---

[34] Harris, *Transactions*, no. 489.
[35] *Statutes of the Realm*, 27 Henry VIII, c. 4; 28 Henry VIII, c. 15. HCA 1/6, 1/7.
[36] HCA 1/48–50; HCA 13 series.   [37] Rediker, *Between*.
[38] In 260 out of the 381 ships issued with Trinity House certificates (see Appendix B) the master was named as one of the owners; in the remainder he may well have been one of the unnamed owners in some cases.

his dim and distant Brethren of Trinity House and the less predictable if more august Judges of the Admiralty.

A master's command might become insecure for a variety of reasons, including his own incompetence. This was presumably at the bottom of some of the many quarrels between master and mate, which could cause serious trouble because the mate was a potential master and might have experience as such. In one case a mate claimed to be master on the grounds that the commander was appointed as captain and that a captain normally had a master under him. He was accused of attempting to win a following and take over the ship.[39] A mate who took command on the master's death might well feel exposed, particularly when he owed his position to the approval of the crew. On the death of the master in one Virginia voyage the company chose first one mate and then the other to succeed him, with resulting confusion about who should be responsible for the disposal of the late master's possessions.[40] The not infrequent violence directly involving the master in fighting, vindictive punishments or murder reflected not only the tension and hardship of life at sea, but also a degree of familiarity and disrespect which put discipline at risk in some voyages.[41]

Usually, however, disputes between masters and men concerned economic matters – sometimes victuals, more often wages. As a small business man, most of whose assets were tied up in the ship, many a master ran the risk of ruin on every voyage, as numerous Trinity House petitions for assistance pathetically show.[42] Sometimes he would have to raise a loan to finance the venture, pledging the ship by bottomry and paying an exorbitant rate of interest.[43] Always under pressure, masters had many opportunities to reduce their wages and victuals bills.

---

[39] HCA 13/49, fols. 387, 396–401, 406. In the *Mary Anne* of Newcastle, Browne Bushell was reputed to be captain and master, being called sometimes the one and sometimes the other: HCA 13/54, fol. 351; HCA 13/55, fol. 57.   [40] HCA 13/54, fols. 180, 455.

[41] References to brutal treatment of crew by masters, though not uncommon, indicate that seamen had some notion of an acceptable level of violence. In the case of a master who ducked the carpenter three times at the mainyard, thrashed him with a rope's end and finally dragged him ashore at the stern of a ship's boat to leave him there, a witness declared that the ducking and dragging ashore were 'allowed by the custom of the sea...but not to drub him': HCA 13/55, fol. 179. The Admiralty Court records give the impression that masters had more trouble with their crews in transatlantic than in other voyages at this stage: see, for example, Shilton and Holworthy, *Examinations*, nos. 49 and 51, concerning the *Amity*'s Barbados voyage, which was marked by violent and drunken disputes among the crew, particularly about the choice of master.   [42] Harris, *Transactions*, passim.

[43] Two bills of bottomry occur in HCA 15/4: in February 1635 Richard Girling of Ipswich, master of the *Hope* of that port, raised £300 to be repaid with £366 (22 per cent); Thomas Emery in February 1638, master of the *Greyhound* of London, raised £20 to be repaid with £25 (25 per cent). John Fairborne, master of the *Elizabeth*, in 1637 raised £50 to be repaid with £60 (20 per cent): HCA 13/54, fols. 229, 249, 316.

It was convenient, for example, to leave men behind in a foreign port on the grounds, justified or not, that they had been idle, drunk or disorderly, failed to return aboard when summoned, or otherwise behaved mutinously. When seamen sued for wages the defence often alleged misconduct, which plaintiffs would counter with charges of harshness or cheating.[44] The rights and wrongs of particular disputes are difficult to assess, but some cases smell strongly of fraud.[45]

The Admiralty Court decree on mutiny in 1631 indicates that disputes between masters and men were becoming rife at that time. A few years later, in 1635, a petition of common sailors underlined their economic content. 'The daily controversies that arise among us', they maintained, 'are principally occasioned by reason that the owners, masters and pursers of ships always hire their common sailors by verbal contracts, which they generally do in secret, and of purpose without any witnesses, because one shall not know what they promise to another, whereby it many times comes to pass when the poor sailor hath performed the voyage and comes to demand his due, he is so neglected and delayed from the purser to the master and from the master to the owner, and so round as it were in a circle without end, that he doth not only lose his best opportunities of present voyages, but

---

[44] The case of Neale *et al. contra* Maddock illustrates these disputes well enough. Maddock, master and part-owner of the *William and John* of London, was sued for wages allegedly withheld by him from members of the crew left behind at Kinsale. They claimed that he signed on a number of men for a voyage to Lisbon and back, but then at Lisbon extended the voyage to Setúbal for no further pay. Those who refused to go were told to leave the ship and two men and a boy were deliberately left behind at Setúbal. When the ship put into Kinsale owing to bad weather, Neale and others spent two or three nights ashore and on attempting to re-embark were physically assaulted by Maddock, who refused to have them aboard. They complained that Maddock used his men harshly throughout the voyage. Maddock's defence was that all the plaintiffs (except Neale himself) had behaved mutinously, refusing to go to Setúbal, saying they would rather leave the ship and serve the king of Spain and swearing that they would not defend the ship in case of attack. They would not permit him to punish any younker for misdemeanour, so that he and his mates were 'deprived of the command in the said ship'. They spent night after night drinking ashore at Kinsale and refused to come aboard, so that Maddock had to get a warrant from the recorder of the town to round them up, with the assistance of two constables. The master had been 'a very mild man among his company': HCA 13/50, fols. 32–59.

[45] In Hurdidge *et al. contra* Wilde, master and part-owner of the *Dragon* of London, the latter was sued for wages by his crew, who alleged that at Leghorn he refused them wages then due and persuaded them to invest that money in corn, to be brought by the ship from the 'Arches of Pelago', promising them 30 per cent interest. On returning to Leghorn with the corn, the crew refused to unlade until they were paid by the owners' factors there, but in the end they were still owed three and a half months' wages. The defence was that the ship had been arrested at Constantinople in reprisal for the actions of another English ship, and that wages were not due and had not been paid for that period, since the ship was then idle and made no profit. As for the investment of their wages in the venture, the crew had insisted upon it and the master had agreed only under duress. Whereas the plaintiffs argued that the master connived at their refusal to unlade the corn, he denied it: HCA 13/50, fols. 183, 209–17.

is many times enforced to wage law for his due. And when he comes to a trial, having no speciality to produce, but alleging a bare verbal contract which without witness is not forcible in law, he is left to the misericord of his adversary and is constrained to take what he is pleased to give...Much more miserable is the case of his wife, children and friends if he die in the voyage, or do not return to demand his own, whereby great numbers of poor wives and children are left to the parishes.' The petitioners asked that written contracts be obligatory thereafter and suggested a procedure for recording and enforcing them. Since this request was not granted and written contracts did not become statutory until 1729, it may be assumed that the practices mentioned continued.[46]

The significance of the petition, however, lies not only in its reference to sailors' problems in obtaining their wages and to the frequency of wage disputes at this time. It is also remarkable evidence of sailors' power to resist and organize. Law suits for the recovery of wages were now, as the petition remarks, common in the Admiralty Court. At times, moreover, the sailors may be found taking the offensive, using their power of combination not merely to defend their interest but to increase their earnings by what amounted to strike tactics. Thus in 1630, 'by the general voice of one and all', the company of the *William* of London at Leghorn refused to proceed to Acre to lade corn unless paid double wages, which they extracted from the factor by renewed pressure on their return to Leghorn.[47] In 1637 the men of the privateer *Discovery*, having brought in several prizes, refused to resume the voyage unless they were paid £1,000 over and above their agreed wages, alleging a promise of one sixth of prize. They rejected compromise offers by the promoters and the voyage was consequently abandoned.[48] Sailors certainly understood and frequently used the strike weapon, which came easily to men living together, working as a team and bound by a common material interest. Seamen were also taking the initiative individually by hiring themselves to several masters at the same time, a practice which became common enough to evoke an Admiralty Court order in 1635 threatening severe penalties for the offence.[49]

These tensions, increasingly evident in the merchant service in the 1630s, were symptoms of the unprecedented growth of demand for

---

[46] SP16/306/87; BL, Additional MSS, 9301, fols. 156–7; Oppenheim, *Administration*, p. 243. Written contracts are found in the early years of the eighteenth century: Rediker, *Between*, pp. 116–17. See also Davis, *Shipping Industry*, p. 142.   [47] HCA 13/49, fols. 391–2.
[48] Shilton and Holworthy, *Examinations*, nos, 515, 522, 524, 531, 573, 612; HCA 13/54, fols. 17–22.   [49] Harris, *Transactions*, no. 489.

seamen during Charles's reign. We have seen that the nation's shipping more than doubled its tonnage between 1582 and 1640, but the returns of seafaring men (see Appendix D) argue a rather less steep rise in their numbers. The steady expansion of the Royal Navy after 1618 imposed extra pressure on the stock of seamen and, with the advent of war in 1625, the Navy was quite unable to meet the heavy manpower requirements of the great expeditions and at the same time protect an enlarged and in part more vulnerable merchant marine. Consequently the Crown conscripted private shipping for patrolling, fighting and transport on a scale previously unknown. All of these, like the royal fleet, were manned with pressed seamen, since the permanent staff of the state Navy consisted only of skeleton crews. The cessation of the wars in 1629–30 eased the pressure for a time, but it was renewed with the powerful surge of trade which followed. Now the heavily manned ships of the southerly trades, the substantial vessels of the Atlantic trades, and the prospering fortunes of the coal trade and Newfoundland fishery, the latter especially demanding of manpower, together brought English seamen nearer to full employment than they had ever been in peace-time. The merchant marine owed this prosperity to England's neutrality in Europe's great war, as we have observed, but those wars even increased the pressure upon supply by attracting Englishmen into foreign service, a drift repeatedly but vainly condemned by government.[50] And finally those same wars led the government to institute the regular and full-scale fleets financed by ship money from 1635 onwards until this, the first operational navy in peace-time became, in 1642, the Parliamentary Navy. The commanders in these ship-money fleets continually complained of their manning difficulties: widespread evasion of the press, a high rate of desertion and the chronic undermanning of his Majesty's ships, problems created not simply by naval mismanagement, which was of course perennial, but also by the intensity of the current demand for seamen.[51]

These cumulative developments combined to strengthen the seaman's bargaining power. Although the meagre supply of reliable evidence makes it difficult to trace the course of wages in the early

---

[50] Proclamations forbidding this were issued in 1634, 1635, 1636 and 1639, and naval commanders were repeatedly ordered to remove English seamen from foreign vessels: Marsden, *Law and Custom*, I, 513; Harris, *Transactions*, no. 463. On Dutch–Spanish competition for men see Israel, *Dutch Republic*, pp. 194, 325.

[51] On the earl of Northumberland's complaints about his crews, see *Monson's Tracts*, III, 275. Sir William Russell, Treasurer of the Navy, wrote in 1637 that he could not find a single merchantman willing to go on the Sallee expedition. He accepted as true the owners' pleas that they were committed to trading voyages and concluded that pressing ships must cause an interruption of trade: *CSPD 1636–7*, p. 362.

seventeenth century, when in any case they probably varied more from ship to ship and man to man than in later times, the upward trend is clear enough.[52] After the Elizabethan war with Spain the pay in merchantmen slipped from its war-time heights to low levels in the depressed conditions of the 1610s, the years of the Dutch–Spanish truce. At this time the term 'common seaman' embraced the ordinary, unskilled deck-hand or 'younker' and the more experienced sailor without a special trade, later called an able seaman. The former could not expect more than 15 shillings a month in these years, and was probably no better off than similar men before the war with Spain. Fully fledged seamen would be getting a little more, up to about 18 shillings. In the next decade, under the influence first of the European war and then, more powerfully, of Charles's wars with France and Spain, wages recovered and advanced beyond any former rates to some 20 to 24 shillings. As the wars drew to a close in 1629 and 1630, privateering and naval activity fell away and common seamen were paid anything from 16 to 22 shillings down to 1633. Then in the later thirties rates from 20 to 24 shillings became normal, persisting in the 1640s.[53] The pay of men with special skills – boatswains, gunners, carpenters and the like – varied so much that no clear trend emerges, and that of mates was even more variable, depending on the type of ship and voyage as well as on the man's skill, though certainly the rates of 60, 70 and 75 shillings earned by first mates in the transatlantic and Mediterranean trades of the late 1630s and 1640s would never have been obtainable in peace-time before, unless in an East Indiaman.

These figures do not of course represent real wages. Even if we knew much more about the cost of living in general than we do, we still could not estimate how it affected seamen, who had free board and lodging for part of the year. Comparison with other occupational groups is out of the question, nor can we realistically assess the earnings of seamen from primage, average and petty trade. It cannot be argued that seamen influenced the general level of wages by collective bargaining or co-ordinated industrial action. They obviously lacked the means to do so. But the figures do acquire some significance when considered in a longer-term context. Davis found that for a century and more after

---

[52] For wage rates I have used Davis, *Shipping Industry*; Harris, *Transactions*; Croft, 'English mariners'; Hillier, 'Virginia trade'; Brooks, *First Order Book*; Shilton and Holworthy, *Examinations*; Stevens, *Dawn*; HCA 30/635, 636, 638; HCA 13 series. On the rates in HM ships see Corbett, *Spanish War*, pp. 258–62, 281–2; Laughton, *Defeat*, II, 316; Oppenheim, *Administration*, pp. 153, 225–6; Harris, *Transactions*, nos. 241, 244, 245.

[53] Brooks cites rates from 23 to 28 shillings for common seamen in Hull trades in the 1630s and 1640s: *First Order Book*, p. xiii.

the Restoration the high wage rates of war-time would quickly collapse with the advent of peace, reverting to their former peace-time level. Thus in the long run peace-time wages remained remarkably stable, showing only a very slight and gradual rise from an average 24 shillings in the 1670s to 25 shillings a century later. The period from 1580 to 1650, we now find, also witnessed fluctuation in seamen's wages from war-time to peace-time, but peace-time wages rose markedly over that period as a whole, from some 15 to 18 shillings (or perhaps less before 1585) to the 20 to 24 shillings characteristic of the years from 1635 to 1650. Thus they appear to have advanced by about one third, to reach almost the level found to prevail from the 1670s onwards.[54] The explanation of the stability of peace-time wages in the later period lies in the heavy fluctuation in the demand for seamen between war and peace. War would inflate wages, but peace would inexorably restore the all-too-familiar conditions of high unemployment and competition for work. In the early seventeenth century the same tendency is evident, but it was offset by the trade boom of the 1630s and the two more fundamental and lasting changes which accompanied it: the great expansion in the volume, range and manning of the merchant marine on the one hand, and the creation of an operational peace-time Navy on the other.

Seamen of this generation were thus favoured as well as disfavoured by the special circumstances, commercial and naval, of their day. On the one hand they suffered greater hardships than their predecessors or their successors in the relatively new and arduous ocean trades and in the king's service, the growing pains of which hurt them far more. On the other hand they were needed now more than ever and awareness of this must in due course, over a period of two decades, have encouraged insubordinate behaviour towards masters in merchantmen, passive resistance and active protest in the Navy, and generally the attitude expressed in that mutinous slogan, 'one and all'. For although mutiny in the merchant service and mutiny in the king's service differed greatly in form, in causation and in legal treatment – so much so as to constitute different phenomena – they were in fact connected. The men involved were the same and it was the difference in pay and conditions between the two services which provoked that 'notorious contempt of his Majesty's service' of which the Privy Council complained even before Charles's wars. When war came seamen looked to the promise

---

[54] See Davis, *Shipping Industry*, p. 152: 'the two middle quarters of the seventeenth century, when their wages rose substantially'.

of pillage in privateers or else to commercial wages well above peacetime rates, while the Navy conscripted them to serve at rates of pay which, even if and when received, fell far below the wages, let alone the earnings, available in trade.[55] Seamen evidently took little notice of the government's dire and repeated threats against absentees and runaways.[56] In 1637 the Principal Officers of the Navy sought the advice of the Commissioners of the Admiralty concerning the prestmasters' difficulties, posing a series of unanswerable questions, such as how to compel a seaman to take press money if he refused, and how to prevent him taking money from several prestmasters, 'it being the usual custom with divers of the ruder sort to jeer and brag that they will drink it for his Majesty's sake, though they never intend really to serve at all'.[57] By 1641 the press system had practically broken down and Sir Henry Vane had great difficulty in persuading Parliament to accept even a temporary measure of conscription for mariners.[58]

Masters and owners tended to share this dislike of the king's service. Sir John Coke, now Secretary of State though still much occupied with naval business, wrote in 1626 that 'the masters and officers of the merchants' ships which went this late voyage [to Cadiz] have generally contemned and misbehaved themselves towards their captains'.[59] Soon after the wars, in 1632, Captain Henry Stradling reported to Nicholas that 'no ships are more stubborn and unwilling to give his Majesty's ships respect than our own merchants. They hate all gentlemen, especially such as serve his Majesty at sea.'[60] Butler observed that 'our merchants like not to have any gentlemen commanders in any of their ships, but leave the command to the masters only. And this hath

---

[55] Early in the war Trinity House explained to the House of Commons that 'of late, whenever seamen have been required for any service for defence, however important, a sufficient number has been found only with difficulty, and being found, many have evaded the service of the state in favour of that of the merchants. Worse, some have fled to serve foreign princes and even enemies, and have been the instruments of great loss to our merchants. The sole cause thereof is the smallness of the pay in the king's service, which is based on an ancient rate when victuals and other provisions were much cheaper. The pay is not above 4d a day for ordinary seamen and according to the same mean proportion for officers. Since most have wives and children to support, it is far too little and not more than half the amount usually allowed (and the same well paid) by our merchants and by foreign states': Harris, *Transactions*, no. 244. A proclamation of 24 April 1626 provided higher rates of pay, the common sailor's wage being increased from 10 to 14 shillings a month: Larkin, *Stuart Proclamations*, II, 87–9.

[56] A proclamation of June 1626 threatened deserters with death: *ibid.*, II, 95–7. In April 1627 the Privy Council ordered that men be taken off ships in the Thames, the Cinque Ports and the Essex, Kent and south coasts until the fleet should be fully manned, since it was still 'unfurnished' despite an order in March staying all shipping for that purpose: BL, Additional MSS, 9295, fols. 68–9.   [57] BL, Additional MSS, 9301, fol. 7.

[58] Rowe, *Sir Henry Vane*, pp. 117–18. Vane remarked that 'without pressing and punishment no man will serve the king': Oppenheim, *Devon*, p. 63.

[59] BL, Additional MSS, 37816, fol. 77.   [60] SP16/222/13.

produced this common ill-effect, that these masters being blown up on this fashion of late, undergo the command of a captain over them with a great deal of grudging and sullenness, even in his Majesty's own ships, much more in all such merchant ships as serve in his Majesty's pay.'[61] Owners were reluctant to lend their ships to the Crown because the official rates fell well below the commercial with no guarantee of prompt payment. When in 1627 the government was reduced to offering to pay them in land, the owners understandably refused, pointing out that ships normally had several owners, sometimes including widows and orphans, and that they needed cash to pay their debts and repair their ships, having gone for two or even three years without payment. Many such debts incurred by the Crown during the wars went unpaid until ship money brought in the necessary.[62] The resistance of the City of London to providing the greater part of a fleet for the defence of the Narrow Seas in 1626–7 resulted in a badly armed and inadequately manned set of ships whose masters avoided any effective service and apparently condoned the widespread mutinies which brought this disgraceful cruise to an end.[63]

Although aversion to the king's service among owners, masters and men did not mean disloyalty, it came to be associated with political attitudes which sat uncomfortably with those of Charles I. At the beginning of the reign the seamen made their views plain in the famous affair of the 'loan ships'.[64] Charles's loan of the royal warship *Vanguard* and seven hired merchantmen to King Louis of France proved embarrassing when it became evident that Louis intended to use them against the Protestants of La Rochelle. The resistance of the English crews to being so used was therefore diplomatically convenient, but they did not mutiny on orders from above. It was their initiative in refusing service and their continuing state of mutiny, however condoned by their admiral and his political masters, which prevented the delivery of the ships for three weeks, until it appeared that French intentions had changed. Even then only one man consented to serve under French command. As Sir John Coke noted, with evident sympathy: 'it is very well known that our seamen generally are most resolute in our profession: and these men have expressed it by their common petition to their admiral and otherwise by protestation, that

---

[61] Butler, *Dialogues*, p. 31. In 1635 Kenrick Edisbury reported to Nicholas that Bence Johnson, one of the masters nominated for the ship-money fleet, was evading the service, and that, unless steps were taken to press him, other masters, likewise unwilling, would refuse to serve: *CSPD 1635*, p. 39.   [62] Oppenheim, *Administration*, pp. 273–4.
[63] Wren, 'London and the twenty ships'.
[64] Gardiner, *History of England*, v, 328–9, 378–94.

they will rather be killed or thrown overboard than be forced to shed the innocent blood of any Protestants in the quarrels of Papists'. Yet in this overtly political mutiny they expressly affirmed their loyalty: 'they are English free born and know the inveterate malice of the French, and therefore will not dishonour our nation and blemish in a sort their allegiance to his Majesty by putting themselves so far into French jurisdiction'.[65]

The wars which followed compounded this mood with an element of disaffection for the king's service and for his gentlemen commanders, as noted above. By 1637 a clear division was apparent between these last and those naval commanders who came from the merchant marine, particularly William Rainborowe and the captains who sailed with him in the Sallee expedition. He and his associates represented the Trinity House of Deptford and the shipowning, shipbuilding community of the Thames. It was this same element, closely allied with London merchants with a strong interest in shipping, which assumed control of the nation's fleet in 1642, capturing both the naval administration and the fleet itself, which it proceeded to manage and to command, under the leadership of the earl of Warwick.[66] The course of events leading to this Parliamentary coup need not be related here.[67] The accounts of Clarendon and Warwick, from opposite points of view, agree, however, as to the decisive part played by the rank and file in the winning of the fleet for Parliament. According to Clarendon, 'the devotion, generally, of the seamen [was] so tainted and corrupted to the king's service, that instead of carrying away the ships, the [royalist] captains themselves were seized, taken and carried by their own men to the earl'. Warwick said that the captains were seized by parties of unarmed men, who spontaneously boarded the ships which were preparing to resist and so won them without bloodshed. In effect, there was no resistance.[68]

As Clarendon admitted, this was a heavy blow to the king's cause, for it meant the 'loss of the whole navy'. He enlarged his explanation of the seamen's action by suggesting that 'they had been taught to believe that all the king's bounty and grace towards them had flowed from the mediation of those officers who were now engaged against the king; and that, the Parliament having seized the customs, they had no other hope of pay or subsistence but by absolutely devoting themselves

---

[65] Gardiner, *Impeachment*, p. 232.
[66] Chaplin, 'William Rainsborough'; Kennedy, 'Naval captains'; Kennedy, 'Parliament's Admiralty'. [67] See Chapter 8.
[68] Clarendon, *History*, II, 223; Powell and Timings, *Documents*, p. 18.

to their service'.[69] No doubt such economic considerations did influence the sailors: discontent over pay was already evident in 1641 with the drying up of ship money and other financial sources. But this was no ordinary mutiny. There had been reports of sedition aboard his Majesty's ships in the spring and summer of 1640 already,[70] and in January 1642 the mariners of the Thames demonstrated their support for Parliament in pledging themselves to defend it and in escorting the five members back to Westminster by river.[71] Their subsequent role in Parliament's seizure of the fleet must in reason be interpreted as a political act motivated not only by recent political and economic developments but also by attitudes longer in the making.

The political character of the fleet mutiny of 1648 was even more pronounced, however politically confused the situation and many of the participants may have been. During the first civil war the vice-admiral commanding the fleet was William Batten, long an owner-master in the merchant service and a strong Presbyterian, trusted by Parliament and the City and popular with his captains and men. With the rift between Presbyterians and Independents, the growth of radicalism in the army and the military occupation of London in 1647, the brewing of a new civil war made the allegiance of the Navy a matter of urgent concern to the royalists on the one hand and the army leaders on the other. During the summer Batten came under suspicion of plotting with royalists and had to resign his commission, to be replaced by Colonel Thomas Rainsborough, a militant radical and a leader of the more revolutionary elements in the army.[72] At the same time the influence of Warwick, a political Presbyterian and the great patron of the Parliamentary Navy, faded. The second civil war broke out towards the end of April 1648 and a month later the fleet in the Downs, consisting of Rainsborough's flagship and six others, revolted.

The mutiny may well have been prepared by Batten's agents, but to suggest that the sailors were simply manipulated is to underestimate them, for their action and their explanation of it were entirely consistent with the attitudes and loyalties they had displayed throughout the conflict and throughout the reign. This was a mutiny

---

[69] Clarendon, *History*, II, 225.
[70] HCA 1/7, no. 159: 'the information against Cooke, Toomas and others for speaking of disloyal words against his Majesty'. The boatswain and the corporal in HMS *Guardland* were accused of saying that 'King Charles was a tyrant in demanding ship moneys and that in England kings had been deposed for less matters.'
[71] Gardiner, *History of England*, X, 148–50; Clarendon, *History*, I, 507–8.
[72] He was William Rainborowe's son. On this mutiny see Clarendon, *History*, IV, 331–2; Powell and Timings, *Documents*, pp. 266–8, 287–311, 328–34; Capp, *Cromwell's Navy*, pp. 15–41.

organized by common seamen, led by a boatswain's mate. The 'declaration of the navy' stated that they had secured the ships for the service of the king and Parliament, had refused the command of Rainsborough 'as a man not well affected to the king, Parliament and the kingdom', and had unanimously joined with the Kentish gentlemen in their (royalist) demands. Appended were certain 'reasons': first, that Parliament of late had granted commissions to sea-commanders in its own name, without mention of the king; secondly, that several landsmen had been given commands; and thirdly that 'the insufferable pride, ignorance and insolency of Colonel Rainsborough' had alienated the hearts of the seamen. The simplicity of those hearts was revealed on the same day, when a captain who refused to sign the declaration asked whom they would choose for their commander and received the resounding response, 'A Warwick, a Warwick'. The Derby House Committee promptly restored Warwick as Lord High Admiral and sent him to quell the revolt. The fleet now became divided between the 'revolters', led by Batten, who went over openly with eleven ships to the royalist side, and the rest, who increasingly rallied to Warwick in the next few months. Although the men on both sides were said to be 'distempered' about pay, the royalists were much the worse afflicted by disorders and mutinies. Batten and his chief ally, Captain Jordan, fell out with Prince Rupert and returned to England. Many of their sailors deserted the royal cause and several of the revolter ships surrendered to Warwick.

Clarendon's opinion that the seamen were 'a nation by themselves, a humorous and fantastic people; fierce and rude and resolute in whatsoever they resolve or are inclined to, but unsteady and inconstant in pursuing it, and jealous of those tomorrow by whom they are governed this day', though a common enough sentiment at any time, was presumably prejudiced by disappointment with the revolters.[73] As an explanation of their conduct it will hardly suffice, nor can such dubious general notions about the character of seamen explain their mutinous inclinations throughout this ill-fated reign. Indeed no unilateral view can accommodate the complexity of the phenomena. This generation of seamen lived through a critical phase in their country's maritime history, a phase marked by rapid change accompanied by much stress and strain in shipping and naval affairs as well as in society and politics at large, conflicts leading to a civil war in which seamen were inevitably involved.

The changes in seafaring were essentially twofold. Dramatic

[73] Clarendon, *History*, IV, 332.

developments in the scale of naval warfare and naval armaments coincided with marked expansion in the range and volume of merchant shipping. These changes had begun before 1625, but now they accelerated and at the same time they converged and interacted. In conscripting the ships and manpower of the merchant marine on a much larger scale than ever before, the Crown increasingly alienated the affections of the maritime community in general. By entering into competition with shipowners and merchants for the services of seamen, it enhanced their value and so strengthened sailors in all their dealings with their employers, whether official or private. By reducing masses of seamen to sickness, penury and endemic mutiny, without having the effective disciplinary power to repress their disorders, it may well have promoted that disrespect for authority in general noted and deplored not only by naval commanders, but also by masters in merchantmen, by Trinity House and by the Judge of Admiralty. The dangers, hardships and at times sheer misery of life at sea – as depicted for example in Edward Barlow's journal[74] – worsened as voyages grew longer and crews more numerous. Yet the proportion of common seamen to officers also grew in both warships and traders, making the traditional consultation of the crew less a matter of mutual understanding and more like a mass meeting. All these conditions fostered the natural turbulence of sailors, increased their readiness to combine and assert themselves and eroded their regard for authority. The political circumstances of the time added a certain colour to seamen's attitudes. This soon faded, but the other main aspects of the maritime scene in the second quarter of the seventeenth century persisted. A pattern had become established, and part of that pattern was mutiny, a regular feature of seafaring for the next century and a half.

[74] Barlow, *Journal*.

CHAPTER 4

ANTHONY'S ACCOUNT

ONE OF the boxes of 'miscellanea' in the High Court of Admiralty records contains various papers of a certain Thomas Anthony, papers lodged as evidence in a suit brought by his heirs but presumably settled out of court.[1] These materials, jumbled together in the box with other accounts and documents concerning other cases, are themselves jumbled, incomplete and in part irrelevant, for Anthony had no time to sort his papers before he died, nor would his heirs or their lawyers have found it easy to isolate the relevant matter from the rest. The suit arose from his last voyage, of 1636–7, in which he had served as a factor, and concerned a sum of money claimed by the heirs from his employers, but alongside and partly intermingled with the accounts and letters relating to this venture there are notes of personal expenses, borrowings and investments, as well as papers relating to his two preceding voyages. Twelve main items and a number of minor pieces, some of which are mere scraps of paper, make up the whole body of Anthony material, which unfortunately is not arranged, numbered or foliated in such a way as to make precise reference possible. On the other hand the survival of this deposit from three years in the shipping business is fortunate because it gives us what is for this period a rare insight into the life and activities of an individual, albeit untypical seaman, into the conditions and circumstances of his particular job and into the workings of a particular – indeed peculiar – branch of overseas trade.

Thomas Anthony in these last three years of his life was a middle-aged man with a wife and daughter in Bridgwater and three sons, one fully grown and independent and the other two beginning to earn their living in London. In the first of the three successive voyages to which these papers relate he shipped as purser, though he complained that the master conducted the money transactions himself, treating him as a mere clerk. In the second voyage he had financial duties, but actually

[1] HCA 30/636.

signed on as one of the master's mates. In the third voyage the chief owner, who was also the chief freighter, engaged him as his factor, charging him with onerous and wide-ranging responsibilities in respect of provisions and cargo, the latter including not the least of his worries, a number of human beings. Anthony's functions thus varied from voyage to voyage and in practice he had to be ready for almost anything, adaptable as well as biddable, joining the enterprise of a man of business to the compliance of a seaman under orders. Anthony was clearly an educated man, literate and numerate far above the average. Recommended by the great mercantile adventurer Marmaduke Royden and employed in positions of trust by three such merchant magnates as Sir Peter Richaut, Sir William Courten and Matthew Cradock, he may well have had business experience ashore, as many pursers had before turning to the sea, perhaps after falling upon hard times. Like other pursers, he was poorly paid, at much the same rate as an ordinary mate, and was more or less expected to use his financial initiative for his own as well as his employers' benefit, for example by private trade. If in practice he benefited himself at his employers' expense he was a typical purser, but his accounts do not of course provide evidence of any illicit dealing. They do, however, give the impression that he lived and died a poor man, one of the many who in that age combined wage-earning with petty business.[2]

On Saturday, 9 November 1633 Anthony arrived in Bristol, having travelled overland from London with some other seamen to join the *Merchant Bonaventure*. A strong Londoner of 220 tons and 16 or 20 ordnance, her chief owner now was Sir Peter Richaut, a wealthy merchant and financier who had migrated from Brabant to England in James I's time.[3] There were probably several co-owners, but Anthony, whose papers say little about this venture, does not disclose their names.[4] John Stevens, who had commanded her with letters of marque

---

[2] On pursers see Capp, *Cromwell's Navy*, pp. 207–8; Scammell, 'Manning', pp. 152–3. Hollond remarked 'all men know that pursers are generally poor, and that some of them have no small charges to maintain, and that yet they live well'. A group of them petitioned Sir John Pennington in 1639 for 'the grant of a competent salary' on the grounds that without that or 'the continuance of what has ever been tolerated' they would be poor: Tanner, *Hollond's Discourses*, p. 163.

[3] *DNB* (Rycaut). His interest in shipping was substantial: in 1625 Sir John Coke wrote to Secretary Conway, 'the offence of Peter Rycault in selling our ships and ordnance is considerable, the Council table having already bound the delinquent in £5,000' – *Cowper MSS*, I, 191. In 1626 he owned part of the 210-ton *John and James* of London and set her forth with letters of marque: SP16/16/69; Appleby, 'Privateering', II, 33.

[4] Since the suit was against Anthony's employers in the third venture, whatever matter in these papers concerns other business is merely incidental, surviving only because it happened to be mixed with the evidence proper.

in 1628 and was now busy fitting her out, may have been one,[5] and Marmaduke Royden another.[6] Although the scrappy evidence concerning this voyage leaves much obscure, it is clear that this ship, together with Richaut's 300-ton *Peter and Andrew* of London, had been chartered by Portuguese merchants for a Brazil voyage. Of all the Iberian trades this was one of the most exposed to Dutch marauding, so that the kind of 'defensible' merchantmen the English could supply were in great demand, whereas for their part English owners were prepared, at appropriately high freight rates, to run the limited risk of capture in the expectation that the ships themselves, as neutrals, would be released sooner or later, if not immediately. The two English vessels were to sail in company with a Portuguese ship, which appears to have been a powerful trading man-of-war, all under the command of one Dom Francisco de Guevara, brother of the chief freighter.[7]

From the start, however, relations between the English and Dom Francisco were difficult. The *Merchant Bonaventure* was bound in the first place for Cork and was to join the Portuguese ship, which was already at Kinsale, for the first leg of the voyage, to the Biscayan port of Pasajes. It was not unusual for English ships thus to make one of the

---

[5] Appleby, 'Privateering', II, 41.

[6] On 13 March 1634 Anthony wrote to 'Captain Marmaduke Roddein' from Pasajes about certain iron put aboard the ship by Dom Francisco as freight, adding: 'at my being with you in London I was shipped by your good means for purser, for which your love I am bound to you. And order was that what moneys I needed I should be supplied by the master, Thomas Lee, who from his coming from London to this instant hath had the reasoning and disbursing of all payments whatsoever, and I only to copy forth what comptes he gives, and therefore I cannot give such reason of myself as otherwise I could have done.' This seems to imply that Royden was one of the owners. A very rich merchant, Royden promoted trade to Spain, France, Turkey and above all the Canary Islands, and was interested in privateering, the Northwest passage and the plantation of Barbados. He led the syndicate for which the earl of Carlisle obtained his Caribbee Islands patent and which was responsible for ousting Courten's men from Barbados. He was MP for Aldeburgh 1628–9, took the royalist side in the civil war, was knighted in 1643 and died 1646. He owned the 120-ton *Vintage* of London in 1629, was a part-owner of the *William* of London in 1632 and probably had an interest in other ships. Having been apprenticed to and factor for a Bordeaux merchant, his main interest was the wine trade. *DNB*; Harlow, *Barbados*, pp. 4–15; SP16/137; BL, Additional MSS, 37816, fol. 73; Appleby, 'Privateering' II, 23, 58; Shilton and Holworthy, *Examinations*, nos. 42, 492; HCA 13/49, fol. 630; HCA 13/54, fol. 377.

[7] On the freighting of English ships for the Brazil trade, 'sometimes with officers and crews complete, sometimes with Portuguese skippers and English crews, and at other times with mixed complements', see Boxer, 'English shipping in the Brazil trade', p. 199. In the absence of a charter-party or some report of the agreement, the terms of the transaction can only be surmised. The *Peter and Andrew* (24 ordnance) had been launched in 1626 and sailed in that year and 1628 under Captain Nathaniel Goodlad with letters of marque. Goodlad was listed as her master in 1629 and commanded her again in 1636 for Richaut, but whether he did so also in 1633–4 is not known: SP16/137; Shilton and Holworthy, *Examinations*, nos. 253, 261, 289, 325.

southern Irish ports their effective point of departure, and sailing in company was a sensible precaution in the circumstances. But the *Bonaventure* was so slow to budge from Bristol – for which Anthony blamed the 'backward and variable' local sailors – that Dom Francisco threatened to lodge a formal protest with a view to legal action. In fact the English got away from Bristol on 22 November and, having dispatched their business at Cork in a fortnight, proposed to depart before the Portuguese ship was ready, whereupon Dom Francisco secured a warrant forbidding Cork customs to clear them. In reply they 'protested by notary for all damages and interest that might ensue' and met his irate demands for a cable by offering him one of their worst, which he rejected. It was not until 16 January 1634, after nearly eight weeks in Cork, that they finally weighed for Pasajes, there to find the *Peter and Andrew* ready to sail, having arrived a month before. Here they discharged the pilchards and salted hake they had taken aboard in Ireland (though not apparently the coarse cloths and wool), laded large quantities of iron, and paid off most of the English crew, allowing them three and a quarter months' wages, including twenty days for their passage home. Spanish and Portuguese sailors signed on to take their places, and Portuguese captains were appointed to command the two English ships.[8]

Held up by storms for six weeks at Pasajes, the two ships, in company with Dom Francisco's and probably others, finally left on 15 March, only to be delayed again by foul weather, having to wait twenty-six days at Madeira before unloading their iron, cloth and wool. But now they were too late to find freight for Brazil and had to give over that voyage. Dom Francisco sent them instead to Lançarote in the Canary Islands[9] to lade wheat for Lisbon, 'much contrary to the agreement, which when it shall please God to send to Lisbon will grow in question of altering the voyage'. Unfortunately, at Lançarote wheat was very dear, so they proceeded empty to Terceira in the Azores hoping to pick up cargo for Lisbon there, but were disappointed again. As Anthony wrote thence to Richaut early in June, so few Brazilmen escaped the Dutch men-of-war that 'I stand in doubt we shall have but

---

[8] It was usual at this time to discharge most of the English crew and place the ship under a Portuguese captain when English ships reached the Peninsula to make the Brazil voyage. See, for example, the case of the *Tryall*: Shilton and Holworthy, *Examinations*, nos. 605, 607, 617; HCA 13/54, fol. 41, where deponents refer to this practice.

[9] A number of passengers came aboard at Madeira for Lançarote, 'being poor husbandmen which were to cut their corn and gather in their harvest', with two friars, three seamen and a soldier. The friars, the seamen and the soldier went free of charge and the guard and the corporal of Lançarote stood surety for some of the others. The rest paid.

little passage goods'. The *Bonaventure* anchored in the Tagus on 23 June and left for Setúbal on 10 July to fill up with salt, a routine practice of Iberian traders,[10] returning home at last to Limehouse on 18 September. What with the wars, the weather and Dom Francisco it had not been a happy cruise, nor is it likely that those ten months of frustration and wrangling left much, if any profit for the owners.[11]

As for Anthony, he came ashore by the Downs and posted to London to notify Richaut of their arrival. When the ship came into the port of London he went aboard to fetch his chest and clothes and attended to the unloading of the ship and the winding up of the venture. Meanwhile he found lodgings in Limehouse at a shilling a week, paying 6d extra for every meal and a small sum for 'bedding and washing'. From 4 October, when they joined him, his sons Raymond and George shared the room at no cost other than a trifling amount for their bedding and washing. Nevertheless by 19 November Anthony had almost run out of money, for on that day, he recorded, 'I found I had in my power £2 13s 4d'. In approximately two months he had spent over £33, of which nearly half went on clothing for the two boys, £3 to his wife in Bridgwater, together with a hat worth 12 shillings, and £3 18s 0d to one Mr Edward Payne of Bristol, probably repaying a loan. His lodgings bill, including meals, amounted to £4 7s 8d for 70 days. To meet these expenses he had £20 in wages from Richaut, received in October, £6 17s 3d representing 'rials of eight' acquired during the voyage, a few other scraps of income and presumably a few pounds cash in hand not mentioned in his accounts. In consequence of this financial crisis he moved to John Punchard's house, 'near against the Green Dragon tavern in Limehouse', a distinctly cheaper lodging, where he paid 9d a week for bed and 4d for meals from 19 November until 12 May 1635, when he joined his next ship. It must have been a thin winter until the end of April, when he received 30 shillings half-pay (an advance on wages) for himself and Raymond, who were to sail together, as well as a loan of £20 from the owner, Sir William Courten. Meanwhile he lived largely on credit,

---

[10] Trinity House in 1630 or 1635 opposed a scheme which entailed prohibiting or heavily taxing imports of salt on the grounds that English merchantmen 'employed for the Straits...are encouraged by the certainty of salt if better employment fails'. They claimed that the scheme would result in the unemployment of a third of the country's best merchant ships: Harris, *Transactions*, no. 495.

[11] The accounts are far too scrappy to warrant even a guess at the profitability of the venture. There is no evidence that the English ships derived any benefit from the prizes taken by Dom Francisco – one on the way to Pasajes and the other on the way to Madeira. On the other hand those prizes presumably helped the Portuguese to meet their obligations to the owners.

eked out with occasional windfall earnings – a pound for some writing done for Royden and a few lesser sums. In February Royden apparently gave him 6 shillings 'for my purse'. In the same month he managed to place his younger son George with a Mr Washington of Lincoln's Inn, to serve him 'five years for meat, drink, apparel and living'. For this relief, no doubt, Anthony was duly thankful.[12]

On 14 April he signed on for another Brazil venture, this time in Courten's ship the *George* (sometimes called the *St George*), a powerful Londoner of some 300 tons, armed with two whole culverins and eighteen demi-culverins and commanded by one of the most distinguished masters in the merchant service, Robert Moulton. Now aged 44 or thereabouts, he had been a master for twenty-two years already and had commanded this ship since 1629, before Courten acquired her. During the civil wars he became a leading officer in the Parliamentary Navy, a close associate of Warwick (he was a part-owner of the *Constant Warwick*), vice-admiral to Robert Blake in 1650 and a Navy Commissioner in 1651. A strong Puritan, he went out to New England in 1629 to establish Matthew Cradock's shipyard on the Mystic River. He died in 1652.[13] In this venture Anthony shipped as master's mate at 50 shillings a month and Raymond was taken on as a 'younker' at 18 shillings. A week before sailing he received from Alderman John Barker of Bristol (who had helped him to place his son at Lincoln's Inn) the sum of £25, 'which sum he doth adventure with me... and within a month of her safe return, to repay the same £25 with the half of the profit which shall accrue'.[14] With this and Courten's loan Anthony was able to invest £37 3s 5d in a trunkful of miscellaneous wares for the Brazil market, the chief items being six gross of Coventry knives (£9 10s 0d), four pieces of 'fingerweights' (£5 2s 0d) and 57 yards of dowlas (£3 9s 0d). Of this voyage he records only a bare outline of events and two or three references to personal transactions. They reached Fayal in the Azores on 7 July and on 17 September he left there to return in another of Courten's ships, the *Katherine*, while the *George* went on to Brazil under a Portuguese

---

[12] Mistress Punchard's bill for 25 weeks' bed and board for Anthony and his two sons came to £5 4s 11d. Courten's £20 was not of course a personal loan but a business arrangement – Anthony could not do his job without money. His personal borrowings were minuscule in comparison, the largest being a sum of £2. On the other hand it was normal to use business money, like public money, for private purposes.

[13] Born at Landulph, Cornwall, and probably related to the Devon family: Capp, *Cromwell's Navy*, pp. 45–55, 176; Powell and Timings, *Documents*, pp. 69, etc.; Oppenheim, *Administration*, p. 347; Powell, *Blake Letters*, p. 28, etc.; Rose-Troup, *Massachusetts*, p. 27; Johns, '*Constant Warwick*', p. 255; SP16/137; HCA 13/49, fol. 631; HCA 13/54, fol. 140; HCA 13/61, fols. 392–3.   [14] Barker had been mayor of Bristol in 1625: Powell, *Bristol Privateers*, p. 68.

captain and another master, one Thomas Spenser, to whom Anthony entrusted certain goods (other than those already mentioned) to sell on his behalf in Brazil.[15]

After his return in October he repaid Barker his £25, but mentioned no profit, nor do his accounts make any further reference to the contents of the aforesaid trunk.[16] He also paid such debts as were outstanding, sent presents and money to Bridgwater and spent some more on fitting out his boys. From December he was borrowing small sums again. Then on 17 March he agreed to sail as Matthew Cradock's factor in the *Abraham* of St Katherine's 'for Vergenye or any other where for 50 shillings the month'. Cradock would bear 'all such charges as I shall be at, by sea or land', and on the 22nd allowed him £10 'for my account, which is towards my employment in the *Abraham*, bound for Ireland and Veargenye'. This enabled Anthony to settle Mrs Punchard's bill for himself and Raymond (£6 0s 6d) on the 24th, the last day of the Old Style year. It is doubtful whether he was solvent even now, for he records that on 29 March 'I gave Mr Edward Payne of Bristol my bill for £5 0s 7d, which he disbursed to myself, my wife and my son Raymond, to pay when God shall enable me and therefore no time set down on the bill.' Alas, God did not grant him much time. He saw the last of his son on the 18th, when Raymond left Limehouse to join his ship, the *Dove*. By the end of the month Anthony was in Bristol, looking for a passage to Ireland, where there was much to do in preparation for Cradock's venture.

A great London merchant and shipowner, Matthew Cradock was a man of wide interests and strong views, a key figure in the business and politics of the City. He had been apprenticed in 1606 to William Cockayne of the Skinners' Company, Eastland trader and author of the disastrous cloth-trade project of 1614. He quickly reached a prominent position in the Eastland trade and, after his admission in 1627, in the Levant trade also, while from about the same time he had a substantial interest in the East India Company, being regularly a 'committee' thereof in the later 1630s. It was, however, as a pioneering promoter of North American trade and settlement that he made his mark and in this connection that he developed his extensive interest in shipping. As a founder and first governor of the Massachusetts Bay Company, he

---

[15] It was probably intended from the start that Anthony and others of the English crew should be replaced by Portuguese seamen at Fayal.

[16] The *George* arrived in February at Bahia, where she spent, it was said, eighteen months obtaining freight: Shilton and Holworthy, *Examinations*, nos. 605, 607. Even if goods of Anthony's were sold in Brazil, this makes it unlikely that he ever heard about it.

spent large sums upon that enterprise in its early years, being deeply engaged as head of a private partnership within the company. He was responsible particularly for that shipyard on the Mystic River which Moulton and others were sent to construct. At his house in St Swithin's Lane the directors of the infant company met, and he it was who advised the removal of its headquarters to New England under a new governor, John Winthrop, in 1629. Cradock, a Puritan in religion and a radical in politics, was connected by marriage and commercial business with the leading Puritan and radical elements in the City. His daughter Damaris married the eldest son of Thomas Andrewes, the great treasurer of the Parliamentary cause, Lord Mayor in 1650, Independent and republican, business associate of Maurice Thompson, Samuel Moyer and Nathaniel Wright. Cradock had direct business connections with Thompson and Wright, was a friend of the younger Henry Vane and a cousin of Randall Mainwaring, another radical London shipowner. He came into conflict with the government in defending the Massachusetts Bay Company against the attack upon it in Star Chamber in 1635 and from 1637 played an increasingly important part in City affairs, finally representing London in the Short and Long Parliaments until his death in May 1641. Among his fellow MPs, Samuel Owfield, Sir Robert Parkhurst and William Spurstow, all of London merchant families and all supporters of 'Root and Branch', were related to him by marriage. His fellow burgess for the City, Isaac Pennington, was a close ally, and the successor to his seat, Samuel Vassall, had interests nearly similar to his (in the Levant trade, American plantations and shipping), being an inveterate enemy of the Caroline régime and co-defendant with him in the proceedings against the Massachusetts Bay Company.[17]

Like many other traders to North America and the West Indies in this period, men engaged in the adventurous and rapidly developing fish, fur and tobacco trades, Cradock took shares in various ships employed therein, at times combining the roles of part-owner and freighter. He is known, from Trinity House certificates, Admiralty Court proceedings and charter-parties, to have owned parts of eighteen ships in the years 1627–40 and this figure certainly understates the actual extent of his shipping interests.[18] As for the *Abraham*, originally a

---

[17] DNB; Pearl, *London*, pp. 169, 176–91, 282–3, 309–11, 316–20, 323, 331; Keeler, *Long Parliament*, pp. 144–5, 291–2, 296–7, 302, 346–7, 371; Rose-Troup, *Massachusetts*, pp. 16–31, 139; Friis, *Cockayne Project*, p. 283; Farnell, 'Navigation Act', pp. 443–6.

[18] SP16/16, nos. 139 (*Employment*, 1629), 142 (*Lion's Whelp*, 1629), 152 (*William*, 1629); SP16/17, nos. 39 (*Freeman*, 1631), 59 (*Mary*, 1632), 65 (*Society*, 1632), 112 (*Beaver*, 1635), 143 (*Ambrose*, 1637); HCA 15/4 (*Ambrose*, 1637; *Anthony*, 1637; *Exchange*, 1638; *Mary Constance*, 1640;

French bottom, she was estimated at 140 tons in a Trinity House certificate dated 6 April 1636, where Cradock, Grace Hardwyn and the master, Abraham Hugesson, were named as owners. Hugesson, a Dover privateering captain in the late wars, had probably captured her then. But by 7 June, as Anthony's letters show, he had departed this life, to be replaced as master by Andrew Hardy, who at the same time acquired a sixteenth share. Cradock, with a quarter share, was the chief owner, while Thomas Stigg, a Virginia merchant, William Penneye, Edward Meredith, Thomas Colthurst and one Cockayne held eighths and Grace Hardwyn the other sixteenth.[19]

Cradock was not only the chief owner but also the chief freighter of the *Abraham* on this occasion. The partnership referred to in Anthony's accounts as 'Cradock and co.' comprised at least himself, Penneye, Cockayne and Stigg, and probably the other owners also. Anthony therefore, as Cradock's agent, was concerned with both ship and cargo, acting in certain respects as purser and in others as supercargo. In practice, however, he shared such duties with others. The master undertook most of the business 'for the use of the ship', including advances of pay to the crew, though he also had an interest in the lading and took part (as we shall see) in the procurement of human cargo. Another factor, James Hooke, kept the account of cargo laded in London and worked together with Anthony to manage the transactions at Barbados, where he remained to complete the outstanding business while Anthony returned with the ship. Finally, at Middleburg he had to work in concert with another of Cradock's factors, who eventually took charge of the operation there. Since the surviving evidence contains no explanation of Anthony's duties, it is not possible to be precise about the distribution of responsibility among Cradock's various agents, but the division of labour appears to have been somewhat informal and blurred. In fact Anthony's position was

Rebecca, 1639); Appleby, 'Privateering', II, 26 (*Golden Cock*, 1627); Andrews, *Colonial Period*, I, 393–5 (*Ambrose, Arbella, Jewel*, 1630); HCA 13/49, fols. 428–9 (*Golden Cock*, 1631), fols. 565–6, 572, 600, 604–5 (*Whale*, 1631–2); CSPD 1636–7, pp. 376–7 (*Unicorn*, 1637). Shipowning merchants with shares in these were, notably, Maurice Thompson, Nathaniel Wright, Ralph Freeman, John Delabarr and John Fowke. Although Cradock promoted the Massachusetts shipyard, he is not otherwise known to have undertaken or invested directly in shipbuilding. Shipwrights, like ship masters, might become merchants, but merchants rarely became shipbuilders.

[19] SP16/17/121. Hugesson commanded the *Black Dog*, the *Hunter*, the *Hopewell* and the *Spy*, all of Dover, during the wars (Appleby, 'Privateering', II, 66–9) and in 1629 owned a Flemish prize, the *Costly* (SP16/137). Anthony's spelling of personal names is such that his 'Penneye' or 'Pennrye' may well have been William Pennoyer, another radical, shipowning merchant, who was Cradock's partner in various other business and political affairs and was mentioned in his will (Prob. 11/186, proved 4 June 1641).

no easy one, particularly because, though only a subordinate employee receiving a stream of instructions from Cradock, he had to use his own discretion in many matters affecting the success or failure of the enterprise.

On 1 April 1636 he was at Minehead, seeking a passage to Ireland, but it was not until the 20th that he finally reached Kinsale, via Youghal, and set about ordering stores and cargo for the ship, which still lay in the Thames, lading. Kinsale in the early seventeenth century was a small but busy port in the economically advancing province of Munster, the rapid development of which was associated especially with overseas trade and the increasing 'new English' element brought in by the plantation. Kinsale itself, with a population of some 1,500 in 1641, contained a remarkable proportion of new English, most of them engaged in seafaring business as mariners, rope-makers, chandlers and so forth. Not far behind its neighbours, Youghal, Cork, Waterford and Limerick, the port gave access to a region whose flourishing corn, cattle and cloth trades and relatively cheap products attracted many America-bound ships seeking provisions both for the voyage and for the plantations. Here, too, the necessary commercial facilities were available by courtesy of local merchants, including some of the new English, notably Tristram Whetcombe. The latter was probably related to Simon Whetcombe the Dorset wool merchant who, as a leading figure in the Dorchester, New England and Massachusetts Bay companies, was well known to Cradock. On arrival at Kinsale Anthony delivered a letter from Cradock to Whetcombe, and on 29 April reported to his principal: 'as occasion doth present I do take moneys from Mr Tristram to earnest and buy such commodities as I shall see fitting'.[20] In his accounts he noted 'Mr Whetcombe's charges for exchange on money I received: £5 14s 0d' and sums so received totalling £315 15s 0d. This made up almost all the money Anthony spent on ship and cargo in Kinsale, for Cradock had provided only £5 in cash, and receipts for outward freight amounted to a mere £9 10s 0d for one and a half tons at £3 a ton and one passage (for a merchant) at £5, these being standard charges. As Anthony duly recorded in one of his letters (faithfully rehearsing the terms of his employer's last, as was his wont), Cradock and Co. were determined to make full use of their own ship: 'and for passengers or lading from or for other men, you desire neither,

[20] MacCarthy-Morrogh, *Munster*, pp. 223–43, 258–9. This makes specific reference to the supplying of the *Abraham* on pp. 235, 237, 239–40. On Whetcombe see *ibid.*, pp. 258–9, and Rose-Troup, *Massachusetts*, p. 159. A letter written by him to his brother in England, apparently alleging royalist inspiration of the Irish rebellion, was cited in the 'declaration of the two Houses' in 1642: Clarendon, *History*, p. 189.

but rather that the ship be laden with those things advised and as may be likely to find good market in Virginia for your own accounts'.

When the *Abraham* reached Kinsale towards the end of August she was already laden with a miscellaneous stock of goods required in the plantations: boots, shoes, blankets, hose, shirts, petticoats, doublets, waistcoats, hats, linens, silk, mohair, thread, garters, laces, ribbons, points, coarse cloth, buttons, combs, spoons, stewpans, basins, cups, hatchets, nails, lead, pewter, needles, chamber pots, knives, shot, pistols, fowling-pieces, soap, candles, resin, vinegar, sweet oil, malt, butter, meal, flour, sack, claret, white wine, strong waters, prunes, sugar, currants, pepper, nutmegs and green ginger. Anthony added 64 dozen Irish stockings, large numbers of shirts, petticoats, blankets, breeches, jackets and smocks made up by a local tailor whom he supplied with Irish wool and linen; rugs, cadows,[21] sack-cloth and friezes, the staple products of the local cloth industry; and substantial quantities of butter, flour, oatmeal, malt, candles, barrelled beef and cheese, as well as 268 bundles of Irish linen and a half-barrel of soap. Of Whetcombe's money he delivered about a third – a little over £100 – to Hardy 'for the ship's use'.[22] Most of the remainder went upon charges incurred in the recruitment and equipment of 'servants'.

By 1636 the traffic in servants was already well established as a regular and major feature of England's colonial trade. Having been adopted in the first place by the Virginia Company, it quickly became the chief means of supplying the plantations of the Caribbean and North America with the labour they so eagerly sought.[23] Normally by this system a merchant, skipper or specializing agent would engage servants by indenture, a legal contract binding one party to serve for a term of years and the other to pay his or her passage and keep for the period specified, and perhaps some reward on completion of the term. The length of service varied, but was usually four years, and occasionally there was mention of an annual wage. Indentures were brief and vague documents, which in fact left many questions unanswered, referring cryptically to 'the custom of the country', though at this stage that too was somewhat indefinite. Since, however, the servant bound himself to serve the other party or his assigns, it was

---

[21] Or caddow, a rough woollen covering.
[22] The ship must have been partially provisioned already, and Hardy received other moneys from the owners.
[23] On the servants trade in general see Smith, *Colonists in Bondage*, which cites the *Abraham* evidence on pp. 62–6. The episode is also mentioned in Bridenbaugh, *Vexed and Troubled*, pp. 417–18; Bridenbaugh, *No Peace*, p. 14; and Dunn, *Sugar and Slaves*, p. 57. All of these contain minor errors.

in most cases understood that he would be 'set over' – or in effect sold – to some planter on arrival in the colony. The standard charge for a passage throughout the colonial era was £5 or £6 and merchants asked the same for transporting a servant, though they would normally charge extra for the servant's equipment and clothing and for expenses incurred while awaiting departure. Although the actual cost of a passage to the merchant might well be less than £5 or £6, since he no doubt expected to cover the expense and make some profit, the amount he might spend on the servant's clothing and equipment and on his keep in port varied considerably according to the circumstances, so that the total cost of procuring, fitting out and carrying a servant to the plantations is reckoned to have ranged from £4 to £10 and might sometimes amount to more. The merchant would no doubt attempt to pass on such costs to the buyer in the colony, but the mass of evidence concerning sales suggests that the merchant's profit on such transactions was, though comfortable, not generally exorbitant. As Smith observes, 'the real point was that servants provided a convenient cargo for ships going to the plantations to fetch tobacco, sugar, and other raw products available'.[24] The sale of servants and other supplies needed by the planters was important to the merchant because it gave him in exchange a cargo which would return a high profit in the European market. These considerations are closely relevant to the case of the *Abraham*.

Anthony's very first letter from Kinsale towards the end of April implies that Cradock intended to ship servants and that Kinsale was a recognized centre for their recruitment. He reported the presence there of a ship of Amsterdam 'which hath gone from here at other times, who doth use to carry 120 or 140 passengers for St Christophers, and likewise a ship of this town which will carry about 100 and will be ready within three weeks or a month'. Servants there were, he observed, 'to be had, but as I am informed, such as go herehence, those which entertain them do give some more some less in money by the year for as long time as they can agree'. This remark suggests that Anthony as yet knew little about the servants trade, for all the other evidence indicates that wages were paid only in special cases. He had apparently formed a false impression on the basis of a local rumour that servants in St Kitts received wages. In any case he did nothing to obtain servants for the time being. As he explained in a letter of 8 June: 'until the ship be here there will be no providing of servants, the reason, for that as soon as we have agreed with such as will go, they will be

[24] Smith, *Colonists in Bondage*, pp. 35–9. 345.

forthwith on our charge, and doubtful that after some time at such expense they will run away...for since my being here I have seen sufficient proof thereof, which causeth me to be the more doubtful of the sequel'. This was wise, but the sequel was to show that wisdom was not enough without good fortune.

Preparations for the voyage went forward at a snail's pace. In June Anthony still did not know its destination, referring to 'our voyage for Virginia or New England according to direction', but on 13 July he acknowledged new instructions which clarified a number of matters. The *Abraham* would soon be on her way, 'and by your letters sent in the said ship I shall perceive your resolve to sail from here to Virginia, where God willing I shall find Mr Thomas Stigg, a merchant who is enterprised with you and your partners in the ship and her lading, and by whose means you doubt not the ship will find speedy dispatch home from thence. And now the ship is to proceed directly to Virginia, there will be no cause to send any cattle...and you desire I should provide as many servants as I can and upon as good conditions and for term of years the best I may, their time being to be set over to Englishmen in Virginia, which you are rather desirous to have done than to take in passengers. You wish me to take in 100 servants at least, and if not able to provide so many, then to take in some passengers to improve the freight.' In effect, what might be lost on the trading account should be made up on the shipping account: that was one advantage for merchant partners using their own ship. 'And for such servants as I do agree withal', he continued, 'you hold it fit that they covenant to serve Mr Thomas Stigg in Virginia, or myself or either of our assigns. If Mr Stigg should not be there, then myself, with the help and advice of the master, Andrew Hould [*sic*], are to set over their time to other men as is the usual custom in Virginia.' Finally in this letter Anthony dealt with the crucial question of the terms of the indentures. Cradock had evidently reacted firmly if not sharply to his agent's talk of wages: 'for hiring of servants you wish to observe there is no wages to be given, but their masters whom they serve are to give them meat, drink and apparel, and land when their time is expired, according to the custom of the country, which is understood. And what I wrote in my former touching wages was for such as went for St Christophers, which for not expressing you took it that I meant for Virginia: which I fear will be our hindrance, for that their use here is all for St Christophers.'

Was it the Hollander or some English trader bound for St Kitts who spread this illusion? We do not know, but the lie was apparently effective. Anthony himself seemed convinced. On 1 August he wrote, 'here all are inclined rather for St Christophers, where they are entertained for early wages' and, on 1 October, 'every man's mind in this place is bent that way, and had your order been that way we should have had so much freight and passengers [*sic*: he clearly meant servants] as we could have carried'. The suggestion is that he had failed to obtain the desired amount of cargo, animate or inanimate, and that the fault lay in the choice of Virginia as market, which he had questioned all along. By this time, too, he had other worries, as will appear. Meanwhile, at long last the *Abraham* reached Kinsale on 27 August and he was able to go ahead with the recruiting of the servants. In a letter accompanying the ship Cradock reiterated that he wanted all the servants on his own account rather than passengers and told Anthony to confer with Hardy, who could advise him better about such matters. The master presumably had experience of this business and seems to have undertaken some at least of the work required to procure men. 'Charges by the master in riding into the country to get servants' amounted to £9 13s 6d. The drum was beaten in Cork, Youghal and Bandon as well as in Kinsale.

It proved a troublesome business to find, to keep and to equip these people. Anthony was looking for men aged from sixteen to thirty years and during September he noted outlays on the 'entertainment' of a dozen or so servants. On the 15th, for example, 'at the making of Thomas Green's bond in beer and for his purse and his company – 6d'. At the end of the month, 'spent in beer on Henry Quarrel, John Rider, Agnes White and Dorothy Gering – 1s 0d'. The signing of the indenture was evidently eased by a glass or two. Similar small gratuities went to individuals assisting the work: 'given to Thomas Belchard of Bandon, spirit of wine and sugar to procure servants – 4d' and 'bestowed on beer on Martin Johns and three others and on the two men that were employed for procuring servants – 8d'. During September the majority of the recruits were men, but in October Anthony must have been anxious at the slow rate of progress, for now the entries relate mainly to women. By 22 October he had 'entertained and forthcoming', he reported, '61 persons, whereof 41 are men servants, the rest women kind, from 17 to 35 years', but lack of money had been a great hindrance and 'the procuring of men servants hath been very chargeable'. In fact the women now were 'readier to go than the men'. At the beginning of the month Whetcombe had refused to advance further money on the grounds that he had none of Cradock's in hand. As Anthony later explained, 'sickness in London' had stopped credit on the exchange, and the resulting shortage of cash caused delay in the preparations, which in turn cost money: 'and being thus hindered and whiles we stay, there runneth one or other of the men servants daily'.

In one instance at least runaways were brought back, presumably under duress, for Hardy recorded in his account the expenditure of 6 shillings 'for bringing two of our passengers that run away'. Finally, towards the end of October, the servant problem landed Anthony in trouble with the civil authority. On the 26th he reported: 'we entertain all such as come. And we are abused by these false Irish, for when they will and are disposed to have anyone from us, they feign thievery on them, and then being for the king there is no resisting. And now but yesterday I was committed and imprisoned by the sovren[25] or mayor's command, whose name is John Galloway, and there remained until the parties which he demanded were delivered him, which was by constraint performed, and then I released, with the cost and expense of 4s 6d. And thus they have served us at other times, and we no redress or ganseth,[26] though men wrongfully abused as thus we are.' It is of course impossible to get to the bottom of this contretemps, but Anthony may well have been more the abuser than the abused. On 22 October, three days before his arrest, he noted the expense of 6d 'for carrying aboard of 2 servants', which may indicate that these men were kidnapped or 'spirited' aboard, perhaps under the influence of drink. It may be significant, moreover, that the two servants concerned were, as Anthony's accounts reveal, Irish, at whose binding one William Smith, employed by Anthony as a procurer, spent a generous 8d on beer. William and Samuel Smith, Anthony's main agents in this business, received from him money, shoes, shirts, stockings and linen, as well as their rent and diet, all amounting to the considerable sum of £6 4s 0½d.

The identification of the two surrendered servants as Irish has, however, another significance. Among some thirty such bindings recorded in the accounts, these two alone specify the subjects as Irish and, whereas nearly all the others are named, these are, in the several references to them, invariably described as the anonymous two Irish. It may well be, as MacCarthy-Morrogh has cogently argued, that they were so distinguished because the rest, or most of them, were not Irish but New English, as indeed their names seem to indicate. Kinsale and other parts of Munster had a substantial New English element, among whom many, having parted from their roots in the English West Country, remained unsettled, mobile, exposed both to adversity and to promises of betterment elsewhere. The propensity of emigrants to re-

---

[25] The 'sovereign', or mayor, elected by the burgesses.   [26] Or 'gainsaw' = gainsaying.

emigrate and of colonists to move on to new colonies has frequently been observed. On the other hand, the evidence relating to this single, comparatively small shipment cannot be regarded as conclusive with respect to the nature of emigration from Munster at this time, when large numbers of Irish people were in fact appearing in the plantations.[27]

It is not possible to make any realistic estimate of the amount of money spent on the servants' food, clothing and other requirements. Apart from sums employed in their procurement, the chief items noted in the accounts are diet (£25 11s 8d), cadows, bed-sacks, rugs and cushions, clothing (shirts, coats, waistcoats, smocks and stockings), tobacco (3 lbs at 2s 8d a lb) and unspecified charges, totalling about £70. Even if complete in this respect for the period up to the departure from Kinsale on 7 November, the accounts do not cover the cost of maintaining the servants at sea, though there is an entry of £7 7s 1d for money spent on them at Cowes. Here they were obliged to interrupt the voyage for almost five weeks to repair the ship and supply their needs after running into bad weather out of Kinsale. Anthony now wrote asking Cradock to send linen and smocks for the women servants, whom he had not been able, for lack of money, to fit out adequately at Kinsale. A month later, on Christmas Eve, as they finally set sail for the New World, he reported that he had discharged three women found to be infected with 'the nasty pox'. These were given passes for their safe travelling, while another, who had 'the French disease' (syphilis), was left on the Isle of Wight where she had been recruited.

In the same letter he acknowledged a message, brought by Mr Meredith from the promoters, that the *Abraham*, if unable to 'clear' Virginia, should make for St Kitts or Barbados, for both of which letters of assistance were provided. One of these was addressed by William Penneye to a certain Captain Bowyer, one of the leading planters in Barbados, promising payment for help in disposing of goods and servants, referring him for further advice to 'John Haies who is acoming'. The other, also from Penneye, was addressed to Thomas Ball, also of Barbados. Cradock and Co. appreciated the advantage of having an agent acquainted with the country and this was the reason why they had arranged for Stigg, who apparently made his own way to Virginia in the course of this year, to manage the transactions there. Indeed, they might have done better in Kinsale had they engaged the services of a local merchant to advise and supervise Anthony and Hardy. Whetcombe had provided only cash – and that inadequately. As things

[27] MacCarthy-Morrogh, *Munster*, pp. 210–12.

stood, the *Abraham* put out from Cowes with only fifty-six servants, seventeen of them women, whereas Cradock had called for at least a hundred men.

By that time, moreover, eight months had elapsed since Anthony's arrival in Kinsale and the wearisome length of the preparations had caused problems with the crew. The master, wrote Anthony in October, 'hath been very much troubled with some part of his unruly company', who demanded he should pay their outlays 'in this expensive place'. Hardy had shipped seventeen men at London in June, two of whom deserted, two others being dismissed for 'mutiny'. Three signed on at Plymouth, but left when the ship reached Cowes, where seven more were taken on. Hardy had to advance his men considerable sums and at the end of the voyage the wages bill was reckoned by Cradock's Flushing factor at no less than £405 18s 9d. This may not represent the entire outlay on wages, for Cradock meanwhile had paid the wives some money. At least eight of the men received wages for fourteen months' service. In sum, the crew cost far more than they would have done in an American voyage of normal duration. Perhaps the worst effect of the loss of time, however, was the decision to make for Barbados instead of Virginia. As Anthony explained in his first letter from that island, which they reached on 25 January 1637, 'we were desirous to have gone for Virginia, but that we much doubted in making our voyage, by reason that there have been so many ships laden from thence, and doubtful that we should not procure our lading but in long time, and therefore thought better to take a certain port for an uncertain'. This was doubtless reasonable, but had the *Abraham* set out several months earlier, this regrettable decision would not have been necessary.

It was regrettable, of course, because Barbados tobacco was notoriously inferior to Virginian. Indeed Peter Hay, one of the biggest planters there, was told in 1637, 'your tobacco of Barbados of all the tobacco that cometh to England is the worst'. It fetched a poor price in the home country, where it could not compete with the Virginia product, and when in the later thirties they tried peddling it on the Continent, at Amsterdam, Middleburg and Hamburg, they always found bad markets. Since its foundation as an English colony in 1627, Barbados had experienced a rapid growth in population, so that in 1637 there were nearly 4,000 payers of poll tax. In 1635 the island took about 20 per cent of the emigrants from London to the West Indies and North America, and in 1638 had 764 planters owning 10 or more acres. Most of these, however, were poor planters struggling to make a living from a crop which in the later thirties was glutting the European market. Already they had turned to cotton in part, but it was not until the next decade that the island economy was rescued by the beginning of sugar production. Meanwhile they depended for their supplies and for the disposal of their produce more upon Dutch than upon English traders, in spite of the efforts of the home authorities to exclude foreign shipping and monopolize the colony's trade for the mother country.[28]

Upon arrival, Anthony had to report another misfortune: the bad weather experienced between Kinsale and Cowes had spoiled some of the meal, and much of the wine and strong waters had been lost by leaking. However, with the help of Captain George Bowyer, he and James Hooke, the other supercargo, quickly disposed of the servants, of whom 56 were sold – 39 men and 17 women.[29] Of these Henry Hawley, the governor, took 10 men at 450 lbs of tobacco per head, while Richard Pierce, his brother-in-law and president of the island, took 10 men and 2 women, at 500 lbs each. Captain Bowyer also took 12 at the same rate, including one woman. Edward Cranfield took 5 men and a woman at 500 lbs each and the remaining 16 were sold among 10 other planters for 500 lbs a head, except for 3 women, who fetched 550 lbs each. In all, therefore, the servants yielded 27,650 lbs. The governor, a notorious tyrant, obviously had preferential treatment, but otherwise the customers paid a fair, standard rate such as was paid there and elsewhere in the plantations, though when the market price of Barbados tobacco is taken into account they would appear to have obtained their servants relatively cheaply.[30] It is noteworthy that the women fetched the full price, and in three cases more than that. There is nothing in the record to indicate the period for which the servants were bound, nor their reaction to being sold in Barbados after agreeing to go to Virginia. Perhaps they did not care: apparently no one else did.

The servants were disposed of immediately after arrival, on 28 January, but the rest of the cargo sold slowly over the next four months. The goods, human and other, of Cradock and Co. yielded returns worth 71,056 lbs of tobacco, of which 24,347 lbs remained unpaid at the ship's departure. The actual amount of tobacco discharged

---

[28] Dunn, *Sugar and Slaves*, pp. 49–56; Bridenbaugh, *No Peace*, pp. 53–5.
[29] Smith, *Colonists in Bondage*, p. 66, mistakenly suggests that only 53 were sold, 3 having died. The remarkable fact is that none died on the voyage, which took only a month. On a voyage the following year 80 out of 350 were lost in the Atlantic passage: Dunn, *Sugar and Slaves*, p. 57.
[30] The servants aboard the *Tristram and Jane* in 1636 were sold in Virginia at an average price of 527 lbs of tobacco, which was worth considerably more than that of Barbados: Smith, *Colonists in Bondage*, p. 38. 49 servants in the *Susan and Mary* were said to have fetched 4 cwt (400 lbs) of tobacco apiece at St Kitts and Barbados in 1636: HCA 13/54, fol. 172.

for them at Middleburg amounted to 38,492 lbs, the difference being made up of other goods, including a small but interesting quantity of sugar.[31] The *Abraham* also freighted 63,436 lbs of tobacco for other parties, the largest consignment being Peter Hay's 24,872 lbs, and the next largest 8,499 lbs for Messrs Holland and Fletcher, closely followed by John Bruckhaven, who laded 7,808 lbs. Lesser amounts on behalf of eleven others, including James Hooke the supercargo, account for the rest. Thus a total 101,928 lbs of tobacco paid freight at $2\frac{1}{2}$d per lb.[32] Anthony mentioned in his private notes, however, 443 lbs of tobacco laden in the *Abraham* and 'marked with my mark', which presumably went freight-free, as also probably did 5 lbs for his friend Edward Payne and 190 lbs 'received of Richard Bishop for the use of my son John'. Hardy too did some business for himself, and doubtless other members of the crew brought back their rolls, bags and boxes without charge.[33] Anthony also left 76 lbs of tobacco in debts to be collected by a friend of his. Six of the planters who laded tobacco took passage in the ship, paying £4 a head, except for one Jehu Bolton, mariner as well as planter, who travelled for £2 only, while another of the six brought his wife and two small children, paying £10 for himself and family.

On 1 June the lading was completed, and there is no further news of the *Abraham* until 31 July, when Anthony reported to Cradock her arrival at Middleburg. She had evidently put in first to Cowes, probably in order to receive, according to some pre-arranged plan, Cradock's instructions concerning the last stage of the voyage. They were, of course, to make for Middleburg, where duties were lower and where Barbados tobacco might realize some profit, and to avoid London, where its prospects were poor. Not only smokers, but also the government preferred Virginian, which since 1632 paid 4d a lb in duties, whereas Caribbean had to pay 6d.[34] This discrimination, which was part of a policy of discouraging tobacco cultivation in the islands, was accompanied by strenuous efforts to force English traders to bring their cargoes from the plantations to England. Thus already in 1632 the Privy Council, being informed that divers ships from St Kitts, Barbados and other plantations went into foreign countries with their

---

[31] 376 lbs valued at $1\frac{1}{2}$ lbs of tobacco per lb.
[32] Few shipments amounted to as much as 100,000 lbs of tobacco in this period: Hillier, 'Virginia trade'. The freight actually paid was a little over 2d a lb, though the nominal charge was $2\frac{1}{2}$d.
[33] Giles Milford, trumpeter of the *Truelove* in a Virginia voyage of 1638, laded a barrel, a hogshead and three bags, and in his own and a shipmate's cabins stowed 200 lbs in loose leaf, two great rolls and a little white box, as well as some in his chest, together with 'good store of apparel and two bottles of strong waters': HCA 13/55, fol. 63.
[34] Dietz, *Public Finance*, p. 355.

goods and merchandise, to his Majesty's great loss and prejudice to his customs, required the lords of the Admiralty to compel ships to come to London or some other port of this kingdom. Accordingly captains of English merchantmen in the tobacco trade were obliged to give bonds to return to an English port, and those suspected of intending to evade this obligation were boarded on occasion by naval commanders and ordered up the Thames.[35] Nevertheless, the financial incentive to head for Holland often proved stronger than the capacity of the Navy to enforce the policy and men like Cradock no doubt found some political satisfaction in thwarting that fiscal drive which was so important to the Caroline régime.

Jeromie Williams Ashman, who acted as Cradock's factor at Middleburg, advised Anthony to forbear selling the partnership's tobacco because the market was then 'plentiful' and the price 12 or 13 stuivers a lb – 14d or 15d sterling.[36] By 9 August, however, the presence of the *Abraham*'s cargo had reduced the price to 10 stuivers (a shilling sterling), and two days later Anthony reported that 'the planters and likewise the factors that received goods forth of our ship go selling and making away at 8 and 9 stuivers the pound...and the buyers proffer but 6 and 7 stuivers the pound, such is the misery of the time and place'. Cradock consequently decided to have his consignment warehoused at Amsterdam until the market should improve. He also wrote to Ashman that the ship should now go under the name of the *William* of London and that he and Hardy should appoint a new master, 'which we pray you to do for some particular respect'. The bills of lading for goods taken aboard in Middleburg were to be signed by the new master giving the ship's new name. Cradock was not prepared to explain any further, but it is difficult to escape the conclusion that his object was to conceal the evasion of his Majesty's customs. Hardy, who was expected to perpetrate the fraud, was understandably unhappy: 'the master', observed Anthony, 'will assent, but strains thereat and what your intent should be, and that his name cannot be altered; who feareth how you will deal about his bond, and offereth to sue you till the said be cleared and taken up'. It was a well-justified objection, for the penalty specified in the bond might well have been enough to ruin the master, but he was presumably reassured

---

[35] Harlow, *Barbados*, p. 22–4; Shilton and Holworthy, *Examinations*, no. 593; HCA 13/54, fol. 558 (resort to Dunkirk by the *Edward and George* from the Caribbean, the crew being 'shipped for no such port' and demanding security for their wages before proceeding there from Falmouth); HCA 13/54, fol. 322 (engagement of a Dutch pilot to bring the *Dolphin* of London from Barbados to Elsinore in 1638).

[36] Roberts, *Merchants Mappe*, p. 103, gives 10 stuivers to one shilling sterling.

to his satisfaction, since his account contains a copy of a covenant between himself and one Andrew Rainie of Dunfermline, witnessed by notary public at Middleburg on 10 September 1637, by which Rainie agreed to go as master of the *William* of London to deliver her to her owners in London, for which service he should receive £6.[37]

By Christmas the *William* was being readied once more in the Thames, bound for Virginia, but in the meantime Ashman returned an account for approximately £1,300 received for freight and passage money, out of which he had paid customs duties on Cradock's consignment and various other charges, remitting to Cradock a sum of £200 and holding in hand a small quantity of tobacco worth £30 18s 1d. The amount finally due to the owners was a mere £43 19s 0d and, since the *Abraham/William* would require refitting for her next voyage and at least one other debt had yet to be settled in connection with her last, it may safely be said that the ship had made a losing venture. On the other hand the returns on the partnership's tobacco may well have realized a profit for the owners as traders, though even there the net gain cannot have done much more than balance the loss on the shipping account. For in 1638 the price of tobacco plunged still lower – so precipitously that English ships stopped coming to Barbados. It had been a chargeable and unfortunate venture from start to finish, exemplifying the hazards of the early plantations trade, a rough and risky free-for-all, with few winners and many losers.

Anthony was one of the losers. Late in August he reported sickness among the sailors at Middleburg: 'the most part of our men are fallen sick with the ague, and therewith so weak, that by means thereof, and others that quitted the ship, he [the master] was constrained to get other men in their places'. On 9 September he wrote from Flushing: 'I learn that you desire Mr Ashman to haste away the ship, who is ready at the Ramikins to take the first opportunity of wind and weather that shall please God to send, if not crossed by reason of sick men, which have been very much visited here with fever, hardly five sound men, by means whereof and for that some fell sick here, the master was forced to get others, and as it was not manned as she should be to carry her home, for that men do sicken daily... the master is looking and seeking to get men... It hath pleased God to take Philip Hacker to his mercy, and another of our company deceased in Middleburg two days past. I pray

---

[37] In 1637 and 1638 many merchants chose to warehouse their tobacco because the return would not cover customs and freight charges: Hillier, 'Virginia trade', p. 280. The master's bond was normally for £1,000 and replacement of the master to evade the penalty became a common practice in the later 1630s: *ibid.*, pp. 247, 250.

God send health amongst us and well to see you.' This was apparently his last letter, and he was probably ill when he wrote it. In March 1638, when his heirs filed his papers in the Admiralty Court, they claimed wages for him up to 20 September 1637, which must have been the day he died. Allowing for sums offset, their claim amounted to £27 0s 7d, and the fact that this was levied proportionably upon the owners indicates that they did not contest the matter. Andrew Hardy, the master, appears to have died during that autumn or winter.

It would be a mistake to pretend that these meagre memoranda enable us to know Anthony as a person. He seems to have been an ordinary, decent man, who eked out a mean existence, toiling for little reward at a thankless job and struggling to make ends meet in the idle winters. He left only one scrap to provide a dubious clue to his character, a ragged sheet of paper covered with scribbled notes from various dates, in the midst of which appear these garbled and much-corrected fragments of religious verse: 'the lord is only my support and he that doth me feed / how can I then lack anything whereof I stand in need / how he doth me fold in God's most might the tender grace past by / and a star drives me to the streams that run most fervently / he doth me fold in God's most might his tender grace past by / and afterwards doth drive me to the streams that run most pleasantly'. Did he, like Digby's men, die in the grip of fever, babbling of green fields?[38]

---

[38] See p. 116 below. Does this help the critics so long baffled by Shakespeare's famous line describing Falstaff's death?

CHAPTER 5

DIGBY AT SCANDEROON

ACCORDING TO Aubrey, 'Sir Kenelm Digby was held to be the most accomplished cavalier of his time', whose Oxford tutor, himself an eminent man of learning, called him the 'Mirandola of his age', referring to Pico della Mirandola, the great humanist. Ben Jonson, his friend, sang his praise: 'he doth excel / In honour, courtesy, and all the parts / Court can call hers, or man could call his arts. / He's prudent, valiant, just and temperate: / In him all virtue is beheld in state; / And he is built like some imperial room / For that to dwell in, and be still at home.' Such hyperbole of course breeds doubt, and we are fortunate in having the considered opinion of another who knew him well – Clarendon, a shrewd judge of men: 'a man of very extraordinary person and presence, which drew the eyes of all men upon him, which were more fixed by a wonderful graceful behaviour, a flowing courtesy and civility, and such a volubility of language as surprised and delighted; and though in another man it might have appeared to have something of affectation, it was marvellous graceful in him, and seemed natural to his size, and the mould of his person, to the gravity of his motion and tune of his voice and delivery... He had all the advantages that nature and art and an excellent education could give him, which, with a great confidence and presentness of mind, buoyed him up against those prejudices and disadvantages... which would have suppressed and sunk another man... but never clouded or eclipsed him from appearing in the best places, and the best company, and with the best estimation and satisfaction.' He was, Clarendon concluded, 'very eminent and notorious throughout the whole course of his life, from his cradle to his grave'.[1]

Something perhaps lay concealed by Digby's legendary charm, and, for all that critics and admirers have written since, it remains difficult

---

[1] Aubrey, *Brief Lives*, II, 323; Jonson, *Works*, VIII, 262–3; Clarendon, *Life*, I, 33.

106

to grasp so extraordinary a personality. Our concern is only with a particular episode in his life, the famous exploit at Scanderoon, since that incident is of considerable interest both as a naval action and as an event in domestic and international politics, but the entire adventure – like all his deeds – bore so strongly Digby's personal stamp as to make some account of the man indispensable. In treating the Scanderoon affair simply as a manifestation of the Digby phenomenon, his biographers have missed much of its significance, but conversely Scanderoon cannot be explained without some sketch of its hero – or anti-hero. One cannot have *Hamlet* without the Prince.[2]

Those 'prejudices and disadvantages' of which Clarendon spoke were real enough. Kenelm was born in 1603, the son of Sir Everard Digby, who was executed two years later as one of the conspirators in the Gunpowder Plot. Moreover Kenelm was brought up in the Roman Catholic faith. These handicaps did not prevent his rise at Court: he was allowed to inherit an estate of some £3,000, became a gentleman of the Privy Chamber to Prince Charles in 1623 and was then knighted. Later he naturally assumed a place in the queen's Catholic coterie, along with Endymion Porter and others. Even so, the current distrust of Papists kept him out of any important office until he opted for Anglicanism in 1630 and after he reverted to Catholicism in 1635. During that interval, which followed his return from the Scanderoon voyage, he served for a short time as a supernumerary Principal Officer of the Royal Navy,[3] and evidently sought a career in public affairs. Digby's private letters and published works show a serious interest in religious questions, with no trace of scepticism, but rather a restless inclination to indulge a taste for philosophical speculation. His shallow and derivative ideas about the immortality of the soul, infallibility, the nature of matter and so forth were those of a dilettante eager to display his limited intellect to the world. Finally, after a phase of acute emotional distress on his wife's death, he acknowledged the strength of his attachment to the Roman church by returning to the fold, but it is not difficult to imagine that ambition was the spur to his initial apostasy.

Not for nothing was Sir Kenelm called the Mirandola of his age. He not only counted Hobbes and Descartes among his friends and metaphysics among his pursuits, but dabbled in the magic arts of

[2] The chief secondary authorities on Digby are: *DNB*; Bligh, *Digby*; Petersson, *Digby*; Gabrieli, *Digby*.
[3] In October 1632 he was given a special appointment as an additional Principal Officer of the Royal Navy, to act as Assistant Comptroller, and retired from this office in May 1633: Johns, 'Principal Officers', p. 48.

astrology and alchemy, conducted amateur scientific experiments and claimed the invention of that entirely unscientific piece of quackery, his notorious 'powder of sympathy', which was supposed to cure wounds without coming into contact with the patient's body. A connoisseur of painting, a friend of Van Dyck, a collector of books and antiquities, a student of Spenser and a companion of Ben Jonson, Digby himself wrote indifferent poetry, elegant letters and fluent prose, all in a very fine hand. Yet the greater part of his abundant energy seems to have been devoted to practical affairs, particularly affairs of Court. From the late 1630s he was active in the royalist cause, for which he suffered imprisonment in 1642–3, and he became Henrietta Maria's Chancellor in 1645. In 1653, however, Cromwell allowed him to return to England. The matter of toleration for Catholics was then canvassed, and Digby acknowledged the Protector as a rightful ruler, serving him subsequently as an agent abroad. Not surprisingly, royalists – among them Clarendon – denounced him, perhaps unfairly, as an unprincipled turncoat, but when he returned after the Restoration he was well received. He died in 1665, deeply in debt as a result of extravagance in expense which matched his extravagance in everything else.

'Very eminent and notorious' throughout his life Digby certainly was, by dint of a natural talent for self-display which at times deteriorated into posturing and downright braggadocio. Thus in 1641, while in France, taking offence at some insulting remarks about King Charles uttered by a French nobleman, he challenged and killed the man. Not content with that nor with the French king's pardon, he felt impelled to publish the whole story as a pamphlet applauding 'brave Digby's worthy deed'.[4] Alas for Digby, his worthier claims to fame are mostly forgotten and he is remembered chiefly for the preposterous love affair he conducted as a very young man with Venetia Stanley, a lady admired more for her beauty than her reputation and three years his senior. After their marriage in 1625 Venetia appears to have reformed, but three years later, on his way home from Scanderoon, Sir Kenelm chose to concoct, under the title 'loose fantasies', an allegorical romance which has been generally received as an account of their courtship, even though a sympathetic biographer describes it as 'the strangest mixture of Arcadian love, heroic exploits, shallow philosophy, baroque fantasy, and special pleading for a lady's reputation, ever to be written down'.[5] Although ostensibly not intended for publication, this

[4] *Sir Kenelm Digby's Honour Maintained*, London, 1641.
[5] Petersson, *Digby*, p. 42. Venetia was the daughter of Sir Edward Stanley of Tonge Castle in Shropshire, and granddaughter of Thomas Percy, 7th earl of Northumberland.

farrago was composed and revised with scrupulous care, and in his closing pages Digby took the trouble to excuse the work to a hypothetical reader. In the event it was not published until 1827, but it may well have circulated in manuscript while Digby lived, for somehow the whole affair then became public property.[6]

Such was the individual who decided in 1627 to undertake a private naval expedition against the king's enemies. Honour and plunder were traditionally legitimate objects of noblemen in war, and from Elizabeth's time in sea war especially. Moreover this particular young gentleman's hunger for fame and money had been sharpened by his invidious position at Court. For Sir Kenelm was a kinsman of Sir John Digby, earl of Bristol, who was James's ambassador to Madrid in 1623, when Charles, accompanied by Buckingham, came there to woo the infanta, and a principal reason why this courtship came to grief was that Bristol and Buckingham could neither agree as to policy nor tolerate each other's influence. Thenceforth the two grandees were deadly enemies, and Sir Kenelm, whom Bristol had recommended to Charles at precisely that unfortunate time and place, found his preferment at Court blocked by the all-powerful favourite.

Urged by Bristol to 'employ himself on some generous action', his choice of privateering suited the moment as much as his self-image, for privateering flourished in Charles's wars no less than it had in Elizabeth's, reaching its peak in the year 1627. Exhaustive analysis has established that during those five years of warfare at least 737 prizes were adjudged lawful by the Admiralty Court and that, allowing for the incompleteness of the evidence, the actual total cannot have fallen far short of a thousand, while the value of the 737 alone amounted to some £800,000 or £900,000. It is true that the country lost many ships and much merchandise to her enemies, but those losses did not approach in number or value the prizes and prize goods returned to English ports. Merchants and shipowners setting forth trading ventures found it attractive to take out letters of marque in the hope of extra profit, while many were encouraged to fit out vessels as men-of-war simply for plunder. At the outset of hostilities the notion of a sea war conducted by private enterprise in the Elizabethan tradition was popular in Parliament and the ports. Indeed the earl of Warwick and his political friends, inspired partly by false memories of Elizabethan glory and partly by the current success of the Dutch West India Company, saw

---

[6] Digby, *Private Memoirs*. A strong reason for supposing that the text was intended to be read is the fact that it is largely devoted to justifying the author's conduct and defending his wife's reputation.

the war as a great opportunity for aggressive maritime expansion at Spain's expense. Charles and Buckingham, of course, did not share that view. Their wars were European wars, in which private shipping would perform necessary services at the king's command, whether in great expeditions or in more routine duties. Privateering thus became a secondary and separate dimension of the sea war, valued by Buckingham only because, as Lord High Admiral, he was entitled to – and took considerable pains to harvest – a tenth of all legitimate prize.[7]

Privateering had aroused increasing disapproval in official naval circles in Elizabeth's last years, when its popularity with seamen already caused severe manpower problems for royal commanders. With the renewal of sea warfare in 1625 competition for seafaring men between the royal and private services became intense, men being pressed wholesale from privateers and merchantmen by royal officers on the one hand, and hiding as best they could – or deserting – on the other. Buckingham, as chief of the Royal Navy, had ample cause to look askance at privateersmen. It was his responsibility to impose discipline on the nation's sea forces, and the propensity of voluntaries to attack neutral shipping, to smuggle prize goods into the realm, and in general to defy law and order was notorious. Furthermore, tighter control over privateering would bring no mean financial return to the Lord Admiral and his staff. For these reasons the Admiralty under Buckingham regulated privateering much more carefully, effectively and lucratively than it had done under Nottingham. It enforced more strictly the licensing of privateersmen and the system of bonds for good behaviour, and it strongly opposed direct grants of special commissions by the Crown.

Elizabeth had on occasion authorized commissions in the form of letters patent, issued under the Great Seal, to favoured privateering promoters like the earl of Cumberland. Such commissions conferred special privileges, summoning the queen's officers to assist the grantee and empowering him, for example, to press mariners, to exercise martial law, to take prizes from subjects of princes not in league and amity with her, and to return prizes without paying customs duties or the Lord Admiral's tenths.[8] Thus might the complaisant Nottingham be circumvented by an influential courtier. Buckingham, however, was altogether more powerful and more jealous of his power. When in 1627 the king proposed to grant such a patent to the earl of Warwick,

---

[7] Appleby, 'Privateering', I, 260, 270; Appleby, 'West Indies'; Kepler, 'Ships gained and lost'.
[8] Marsden, *Law and Custom*, I, 278–80. Cumberland obtained six such patents at different times.

Edward Nicholas, Buckingham's secretary, protested that it was derogatory to his master's office and did all he could to hinder the grant and the expedition itself. Buckingham's interest in this dispute was personal in respect both of the tenth he stood to lose and of the political enmity between himself and Warwick, who had backed the Parliamentary onslaught upon him the previous year. Resisting the infringement of the Admiralty's authority by special favours of this kind could plausibly be presented as sound policy in the Crown's best interest, but Buckingham and his secretary were in fact defending a private empire within the state, an anomaly symptomatic of the régime's structural weakness. In the event Warwick secured his commission unaltered, but his success did nothing to diminish the duke's resentment and determination to stop any more such grants.[9]

Consequently, when later in that same year Nicholas learned that young Digby had persuaded the king, in Buckingham's absence at the Ile de Rhé, to let him have a special patent to go to sea, he vehemently objected. As he wrote to Sir Henry Marten, 'I conceive it is a commission derogatory to the honour of my lord's place, and to the jurisdiction of the court of admiralty.' Sir Kenelm, he argued, was 'a private gent., whereas such commissions have not been used to be granted to any other under the degree of a baron, unless it were for the king's service'. He attacked in particular the grant of power to execute martial law, and in general the latitude of Digby's licence to take ships and goods of any not in amity with his Majesty.[10] 'I am resolved to use all the power I can of my lord's friends at court totally to dash that commission and all others of that kind', he wrote later, adding, 'I honour Sir Kenelm Digby and think him worthy of encouragement, so as it be not at my lord's cost and to the dishonour and diminution of his grace's place.'[11] Digby defended himself with some spirit, but in the end the commission was reduced to little more than a licence 'to enter and take in hand a voyage to sea', and he was obliged to take out letters of marque from the Lord Admiral and to give bonds for good behaviour stipulating that he must bring back all prizes intact for adjudication in the Admiralty Court. In addition he was required to sign a declaration, the terms of which are not known, before he finally left London to join his ship on 21 December 1627.[12]

---

[9] Warwick's patent was similar to that which he acquired in 1629: Marsden, *Law and Custom*, I, 457–60. On this dispute see also Appleby, 'West Indies', pp. 229–30, and Craven, 'Earl of Warwick', pp. 467–8.   [10] SP14/215, fols. 50–1: 9 October 1627.
[11] SP14/215, fols. 64–5: 28 October 1627.
[12] SP16/84, fols. 56–9, 112; SP16/87, fols. 33–4.

This was all rather humiliating, but Digby seems to have borne it with good grace. Meanwhile he had prepared two ships, the *Eagle* of 350 or 400 tons and 26 cast-iron pieces, in which Peter Milbourne was to sail as master under his command, and the *George and Elizabeth* of 250 tons and 20 iron pieces under Sir Edward Stradling.[13] With some 250 or 300 men between them, these were formidable men-of-war. Details of the costs are entirely lacking, but such a heavily armed and manned expedition must have been far more expensive than an ordinary privateering venture. Digby, like other gentlemen commanders, of course found merchant partners, the most important of whom were George Strode, Nathaniel Wright and Abraham Reynardson, all Londoners,[14] but in this case the commander himself probably bore the main risk, selling part of his property to finance a gambler's throw in the best tradition of aristocratic promoters.[15]

Although his original intention allegedly was to make for Guinea, there to capture some island,[16] Digby for reasons unknown changed his plans and decided to make his main objective the Turkish port of Scanderoon (modern Iskenderun or Alexandretta) in the far north-eastern corner of the Mediterranean, where he expected to find French merchantmen from Marseille, richly laden and lawful prize. Well travelled and well informed, this Italianate Englishman must have known also that a Mediterranean cruise offered many other attractive opportunities to an English man-of-war. The great inland sea teemed with a bewildering variety of craft of many nations and innumerable ports: argosies, galleons, saettias, caramusals and tartans; galleys, galleasses, galeots, brigantines, feluccas and frigates; merchantmen, warships or both at once, like the most useful and formidable of all, the so-called *bertoni*. These were the tall and broad ships, three-masted and square-rigged with lateen mizzens, strong carriers and strong fighters, in which the northerners – and above all the English – specialized,

[13] SP16/137; Appleby, 'Privateering', II, 18, 25; Bruce, *Journal*, p. 1; *CSPV 1628–9*, p. 392. In 1630 Digby sold the *Eagle* to Matthew Cradock and others, who set her forth (again under Peter Milbourne as master) in the first Massachusetts Bay Company voyage that year: Andrews, *Colonial Period*, I, 393–5. Stradling, eldest son of a Glamorgan gentleman, seems to have shared Sir Kenelm's interest in literature, since the two of them spent some of their idle hours on this voyage discussing Spenser's *Faerie Queen*, Digby's obscure thoughts upon which he embodied in a letter to his friend, duly published as a pamphlet in 1644. Stradling fought on the royalist side in the civil war and died in 1644.

[14] Abraham Reynardson was elected an assistant of the Levant Company in 1634 and treasurer from 1639 to 1641. Prominent also in the East India Company, he was sheriff of London in 1639–40 and an alderman from 1640. In 1649 he was deposed from the mayoralty for refusing to make public the act abolishing the monarchy. His wife was a daughter of Sir Nicholas Crispe the customs farmer: Pearl, *London*, p. 305. Nathaniel Wright was an important shipowning merchant: see above, p. 59. [15] *CSPV 1628–9*, p. 211. [16] *Ibid*.

though others owned or employed them too. For half a century before Digby passed the Straits of Gibraltar the English *bertoni* had been developing a major role in Mediterranean commerce as well as a reputation for piratical behaviour.[17]

In the last quarter of the sixteenth century the long struggle between the two great powers of the region – Spain in the west and Turkey in the east – receded as both turned their attention elsewhere. At the same time Venetian trade and maritime power entered a decline, which became steep and irreversible in the early 1600s. With the land-routes from the Netherlands to northern Italy disrupted by warfare, the sea-route from northwest Europe to Italy and beyond revived, and from the 1570s the roomy and powerful traders of the north came back, bringing fish and cloth to Leghorn, which became their principal centre, as well as to the Spanish ports, to Genoa, to Civitavecchia in the Papal States, to the ports of Barbary and Sicily, and beyond to Venice and its colonies – Crete and the Ionian Islands of Zante and Cephalonia especially – and further into the Levant. The advance was swift, taking a fresh leap with the admission of English merchants to the Ottoman Empire and the founding of the Levant Company in 1581. In a short time the Levant trade became the most profitable branch of England's overseas commerce and Turkey merchants among the wealthiest in the land. The English were able to compete successfully with the Venetians and the French partly because they exported their own commodities – cloth, tin and lead – cheaper than others could, saving themselves thereby the necessity of acquiring silver; partly because they were able eventually to supplement these exports with the precious returns of the East India Company – pepper, spices and so forth – which had formerly reached the Levant from further east; partly because they combined their Levant trade with the currants trade of Patras and the Ionian Islands; and not least because their ships could defend themselves against all comers in their long voyage through seas infested with corsairs and pirates.[18]

Those substantial ships, ranging for the most part between 200 and 500 tons, could be used (and in war-time often were) as men-of-war, but in the Mediterranean they rarely interfered with other shipping. The merchants condemned prize-hunting, not only because it put their own precious cargo at risk, but more still for fear of commercial reprisal, especially in Turkey, where their funds and property were always liable to arrest and those arbitrary exactions known as *avanias*.

[17] Tenenti, *Venice*, pp. 152–5.
[18] Pullan, *Venetian Economy*; Davis, 'England and the Mediterranean'; Wood, *Levant Company*.

The Levant Company could not afford to tolerate misbehaviour by its own ships, but theirs were not the only English ships in the Mediterranean – indeed they were outnumbered by the rest. Most of these were irregular traders, sometimes making a simple return voyage to some Spanish or Italian port, sometimes disposing first of their own cargo and then freighting goods from port to port for months or even years on end. Such a ship was the 280-ton *Greenfield* of London, owned by William, son of Sir William Courten, William Greene the ropemaker and others, including her master, Henry Powell, whose surviving accounts relate the complex transactions of a Mediterranean venture lasting from September 1642, when he left the Thames, to December 1646, when he returned. In those four years he worked most of the Mediterranean apart from the French coast and the Levant ports north of Alexandria, returning repeatedly to Leghorn and to Courten's factor there, Samuel Bonnell.[19] In this era of unremitting warfare and maritime disorder there was plenty of work for ships like this beyond the Straits.[20]

Trading *bertoni* like the *Greenfield*, well armed and well manned, were more likely than the Levant Company's ships to use their power against other shipping, particularly in time of war, when they usually sailed with letters of marque. But, leaving aside a few outright pirates, the *bertoni* which caused the most trouble were privateersmen more concerned with plunder than with trade, though they often took out cargo from England and sometimes carried freight within the Mediterranean. These were not inclined to lose the chance of rich pickings by over-scrupulous discrimination between enemy and neutral ships or goods, particularly since they were always welcome to sell their booty in the Barbary ports, evading thus the awkward questions they might otherwise face at home, not to mention the customs and admiralty tenths due on legitimate prize. In the last years of Elizabeth, private men-of-war wrought such spoil as to cause her government serious embarrassment. The Venetians, who suffered most, protested angrily and Anglo-Venetian relations deteriorated, for this and other reasons, almost to the point of trade war in 1602, while the Levant Company, finding itself held responsible for attacks on the Grand

---

[19] HCA 30/638. The *Greenfield* was arrested at the suit of Courten's creditors when Powell returned to London, his accounts being filed in evidence. Henry Powell had played an important part in Sir William Courten's colonization of Barbados: Harlow, *Barbados*, pp. 4–12; Harlow, *West Indies and Guiana*, pp. xxix–xxx, 25–40. See also Chapter 2 above.

[20] Compare the journal of Ralph Gosnold, captain of the *Richard Bonaventure*, promoted by Richard Cranley and Richard Hill, merchants of London, October 1642 to August 1643: BL, Additional MSS, 5489, fols. 49–50.

Turk's subjects, demanded the suppression of this 'corsair insolency'. From 1598 to 1603 the government responded by issuing proclamation after proclamation forbidding privateers to enter the Straits, but to little effect, partly because some of the most powerful men in the realm, including Sir Robert Cecil, the queen's Principal Secretary, and the earl of Nottingham, her Lord High Admiral, were interested parties. True, Cecil and Nottingham themselves promoted two expeditions into the Mediterranean to apprehend the culprits, but their gamekeepers turned poachers, achieving nothing for law and order and returning with prize goods which embarrassed as much as enriched the ministers.[21]

Relevant though this murky history certainly was to Sir Kenelm's own plans (as indeed to their outcome), there is no reason to suppose that he was aware of it. After the end of Anglo-Spanish hostilities in 1603 most of the English privateers withdrew, but some chose to continue overtly as pirates, joining the Barbary corsairs and greatly enhancing their aggressive power. The Mediterranean became no safer, but in certain respects the political complexion of the matter changed: the Levant Company, relieved, had less cause to complain to the government, which was itself less embarrassed by protests and threats from foreign powers, and as the uproar died down the whole episode faded into the past. Consequently, when war broke out again in 1625, the authorities took no step to enforce or renew the ban on privateering within the Straits. In fact it was left to Digby to teach them the lesson all over again. When news of his deeds reached London the Privy Council had to ask Sir Henry Marten to look into the precedents with a view to revising the terms of letters of marque and at last in June 1629, when the wars were almost over, the stable door was belatedly re-locked.[22]

Having departed from the Downs on 6 January 1628, Digby's two ships passed the Rock of Gibraltar on the 19th. Thus far the cruise was enlivened by nothing more than occasional fruitless chases (the English men-of-war being without a pinnace and far too slow themselves to catch anything) and officious boardings of innocent neutrals, and so it continued while they plied the most westerly waters of the Mediterranean in search of prize. By the end of the month the men began to sicken, as Digby related in his journal, 'of an infectious disease that took them with great pain in the head, stomach and reins, and putrified the whole mass of blood and caused much vomiting, yet they died not suddenly of it, but lingered on with pain and extreme

[21] Andrews, 'Cecil and Mediterranean',
[22] *APC Charles I*, IV, 222; Marsden, *Law and Custom*, I, 456–7.

weakness'.[23] In his 'loose fantasies' he evoked the ghastly scene in more vivid language: 'from those who were infected with it, it took hold of others that were in perfect health, like fire when it is joined to combustible matter, and if they did but come within distance of each other's breath, or touch any part of their garments, it came to pass that in a very short time almost all were possessed with it, by reason of the great number of men enclosed in a small room; and although every one strived to avoid those that were sick, whereby they died in much desolation without any help, yet the infection was so rooted in the ship that they could not fly from it: and if the natural affection of his friend or charity moved any one to be so tender as to do another the offices belonging to a sick man, many times with a sudden death he prevented the other's languishing one: and by this means it happened often that dead bodies lay many days in their cabins and hamacas, nobody daring to go overlook them, and much less to throw the noisome carcasses overboard, until their intolerable stink discovered them; but sometimes there were of mean fellows that would come to steal what they found about the bodies of those that were of better quality, and then by their own sudden death in the same place, they would bewray their theft. But that which of all others seemed to cause most compassion, was the furious madness of most of those who were near their end, the sickness then taking their brain; and those were in so great abundance that there were scarce men enough to keep them from running overboard, or from creeping out of the ports, the extreme heat of their disease being such that they desired all refreshings, and their depraved fantasy made them believe the sea to be a spacious and pleasant green meadow.'[24]

On 15 February, with more than eighty of his company disabled, Digby put into Algiers, and here he stayed, while his men recovered their health, until nearly the end of March. Relations between England and the corsairs were as usual unsettled and equivocal, blowing hot and cold at the same time. Sir Thomas Roe, having contrived capitulations at Constantinople in 1623 for the release of captives and mutual toleration at sea, had been trying without much success to have them enforced since then.[25] England wanted peace, trade and freedom to frequent Algiers, but in practice these were difficult to achieve because the Algerines, who lived by plunder, were ever ready to resume the

---

[23] Bruce, *Journal*, p. 12. This was published from the original MS in 1868. Another copy, with slight variations, is in the library of Worcester College, Oxford: Gabrieli, *Digby*, p. 45.
[24] Digby, *Private Memoirs*, pp. 311–12. This doubtless exaggerates for the sake of effect. It is not known how many men were lost. Digby presumably replenished his company from other English ships – he had 270 English crew on his five ships at the end of May.
[25] Wood, *Levant Company*, p. 62; Richardson, *Roe's Negotiations*, pp. 572–4.

offensive upon any plausible grounds. Nor were such grounds lacking at this juncture. Not long since, Squire Bence, master of the 300-ton *Assurance* of London, had removed Christian slaves and renegades from a ship of Algiers, in reprisal for which the Algerines had seized three prizes belonging to the earl of Warwick. The English consul, James Frizell, had been imprisoned and he and other English residents relieved of much of their property.[26]

There is no evidence, nor did Digby himself claim, that he had any authority to act or speak for the Crown on these matters, but in the journal he pictures himself playing the part of a royal emissary. According to his own account he was courteously received by the 'king' (presumably the Pasha, nominal ruler of Algiers), who promised redress of 'all former errors', and by the Divan (the effective ruling body), who 'swore solemnly that they would religiously observe the capitulations, and that private wrongs done to any of their men at sea should not be righted by them upon our consul or merchants here...but complaint should be made to the king of England'. He had hopes, he wrote, of securing the release of forty or fifty English captives there, and of reaching an agreement that would frustrate the French, who were then negotiating for an alliance 'to overthrow English trade in the Straits'. When, however, he presented certain formal proposals, he obtained in exchange only oral assurances: the wrongs would be redressed, the capitulations observed, safe conducts granted to any English ships, and the captives released upon payment of ransom. Digby claimed that he thus obtained 'full satisfaction', but in fact all those 'many meetings in the Divan and private negotiations' were no more than a charade: the disputes remained unsettled, the captives remained captive and reprisals continued. At best Digby's vanity was satisfied.[27]

After leaving Algiers on 27 March Digby took several prizes in the western Mediterranean, including a 250-ton French flyboat, which he made his rear-admiral, under the command of Henry Stradling,[28] and a saettia, a light, fast, lateen-rigged craft which proved a valuable

[26] Marsden, *Law and Custom*, I, 454–5; Bruce, *Journal*, p. 18.
[27] Bruce, *Journal*, pp. 15–19. In December 1628 the *Adventure* of London, set forth by George Rookes and others, was seized in Algiers in reprisal for losses sustained at the hands of Squire Bence, Charles Driver and other English captains, and a swingeing fine exacted before her release: HCA 13/49, fols. 417–18; HCA 13/50, fols. 3, 7; Marsden, *Law and Custom*, I, 454–5. In September 1628 the Privy Council ordered that letters of marque must in future contain a clause prohibiting acts of hostility against subjects of the Barbary States, and in October a proclamation forbade such acts: Larkin, *Stuart Proclamations*, II, 209–11.
[28] Younger brother of Sir Edward, he afterwards served as a commander in the Royal Navy until 1642, when he refused to obey Parliamentary orders: Kennedy, 'Naval captains'.

addition to the fleet. Scattered then by storm, the ships reached Zante and Cephalonia around the middle of April, there to refit and find new boats, several having been lost, and to dispose of such prize goods and vessels as were not required for the fleet. The currants trade here was a source of rich profit to the Venetians who controlled it. Busy with shipping, the islands attracted especially the English, 'who forsooth', as Roe complained, 'can hardly digest bread, pastries, broth and bag-puddings without these currants'.[29] English ships were always to be found here and at the rival Greek port of Patras, with a strong presence of resident English factors. Here, therefore, Digby proceeded to make himself at home, much to the annoyance of the Venetian authorities, who disliked the domination of their ports by such a predatory force. They objected to Digby's trading away of booty taken from Frenchmen, Spaniards and others with whom they maintained friendship, they resented the disgraceful behaviour of his crew ashore and his recruitment of local seamen, and they furiously protested when, having refitted, he began to use Zante as a base of operations. In short, he did nothing to sweeten relations with Venice, which were embittered enough at this time by continual disputes about the currants trade and allied matters.[30]

On 28 May, after six weeks at the islands, he finally weighed for the Levant. Well supplied and in excellent trim, his fleet now comprised the *Eagle* with 98 English crew, the *George and Elizabeth* with 70, the flyboat prize, now re-named the *Lyon*, with 45, the *Hopewell*, another prize, with 35, and the *Swallow* (the saettia, aptly named) with 22, apart from an unspecified number of Italian and other recruits, including even some Frenchmen. By now the young amateur had amply proved his capacity for command in numerous actions and nautical as well as diplomatic difficulties, not the least of which was a threat of mutiny among his men at Cephalonia. The trouble arose, as it did very often in privateers, over shares in the proceeds of prizes. Some of the crew wanted their shares immediately and 'took occasion to sow mutinous discourses' when Digby quite rightly refused on the grounds that division of spoil before return to England would be unlawful. Anyone uttering further seditious speeches, he warned, would be sent home for punishment in the Admiralty Court. Having thus flatly denied their claims, he called a 'general assembly' and explained the matter reasonably to their apparent satisfaction. On other occasions he did not hesitate to

[29] Wood, *Levant Company*, p. 67.
[30] *Ibid.*, pp. 66–70; *CSPV 1628–9*, pp. xliii–xliv, 73–4, 81–2, 98–9, 102–3, 112, 125–6; Bruce, *Journal*, pp. 28–34.

inflict the normal penalties for misdemeanours, but now he managed to settle his men without violence. Later in the voyage, observing the disorderly conduct of the crew in another privateer, he congratulated himself on 'the good discipline in my fleet, for I think that in no private vessels, or of the king's, there was ever better correspondency in general, and better performance of every man's duty in particular, than was among my men'. It was a typically boastful overstatement, but other evidence confirms that he did command uncommon respect and obedience.[31]

On 10 June 1628 (20 June by the New Style calendar) the fleet of five stood in to anchor behind a point south of Scanderoon and prepared for action.[32] Digby expected the harbour to contain French shipping and had already learned that a powerful force of Venetian galleons and galleasses was also present, which might well resist an attempt to take prizes. That night he sent in a boat to reconnoitre, which returned in the morning with news of two galleons, two galleasses and two English ships as well as four French vessels, one of which carried 100,000 pieces of eight. Thereupon, he relates, 'I stood in with the road as fast as I could, but before, having first made a short speech to encourage my men, I sent my saettia with letters to the Venetian general and the English captains, to acquaint them who I was, contriving it so that my letters should be delivered as I came within shot'. This letter, reproduced later by the Venetian generals in their report, simply announced Digby's intention of attacking only the French, but the Venetians replied that they could not suffer the ships in their company – meaning the French – to be harmed, and warned him to desist. Digby, having already made up his mind to fight whatever opposition he might encounter, took no notice of this threat and continued on his course, deliberately holding his fire. Having issued their warning, the Venetians were thus compelled to back it up by opening fire and so enabled Digby to achieve his first object, which was to put the blame on them.[33]

The action thus begun lasted three or four hours, ending inconclusively with the disengagement of both sides after only slight

---

[31] Bruce, *Journal*, pp. 30, 31, 85; *CSPV 1628–9*, p. 392.
[32] Digby recorded the action briefly in his journal (Bruce, *Journal*, pp. 38–9) and at greater length in *A Relation of a Brave and Resolute Sea-Fight* (London, 1628, reprinted in Bligh, *Digby*, pp. 139–41). The Venetian account, written by the captain of the galleasses and the captain of the galleons, is translated in *CSPV 1628–9*, pp. 136–42.
[33] Further letters, exchanged during and after the action, were copied into the Venetian report. In the course of this correspondence Digby proposed a duel instead of a battle, which challenge was courteously refused.

damage and loss of life. The galleasses, which were large sailing galleys, were heavily armed and manned, though Digby probably exaggerated in crediting each of them with 700 men and thirty or forty brass guns 'of incredible bigness'. The galleons too were powerful ships, though encumbered by cargo on deck and without sails on this occasion. Both parties of course claimed victory. The Venetians declared eighteen of the enemy killed and wounded, while Digby alleged Venetian losses of forty-nine killed and many more hurt. Minor damage to the ships was mutually admitted. In spite of being at a disadvantage tactically, the Venetian force was able to deny the English the booty they sought, for the French had time to carry their goods ashore. Nevertheless, on points the day was Digby's. Far from being repelled, he remained in the harbour, ransacked what remained in the French ships before restoring them (at the instance of the English vice-consul, who feared reprisals ashore), and was treated with much respect and courtesy by the Venetian commanders until he departed the road (again in response to English pressure) on 16/26 June.

In naval terms the engagement at Scanderoon may therefore be considered a marginal, if insignificant victory, but in other terms it proved distinctly hollow. It yielded very little in the way of prize and caused nothing but heavy loss of money and face to the English merchants in that country. Already in their report the Venetian captains sufficiently indicated their real motive, which was not so much to do the French a favour as to ingratiate themselves with the Turkish authorities at the expense of one of their greatest rivals in that Empire – the English. 'The Aga of this port', they wrote, 'heard of the event with great satisfaction, and probably the Grand Turk will also, being greatly obliged for the favour in defence of the port, so insulted by these ships'. There followed congratulations from the Pasha of Aleppo, who committed the safety of the port to their protection and ordered the Aga to imprison the English consul. In reporting these matters the Venetian consul at Aleppo observed that 'the action has greatly increased the reputation of the Republic and of your commanders, and the Turks here will always remember it'. On the other hand he had refrained from accusing the English traders, leaving that rather to the French consul, who would thus share with the Aga of Scanderoon the odium for 'all the ruin that will fall upon those poor merchants'.[34]

[34] *CSPV 1628–9*, pp. 138, 146–8. As the editor of the Venetian papers observes, 'although the action of the Venetian commander had the full approval of his government, it is not quite clear why he thought it his duty to intervene upon this occasion. Digby was undoubtedly infringing Turkish neutrality, but it is not so obvious why the Venetians should undertake to defend it, especially when they had been so backward in enforcing it in places where their rights could

Thomas Potton, the English consul at Aleppo, in custody and desperate, thought the Venetians and the French were trying hard to overthrow the English completely. The French demanded vast sums Digby had not taken, but the Venetians were worse disposed: 'so wickedly minded against us [as] to have us staked and hanged for rebels', and offering large bribes to have their rivals expelled. Potton had saved his fellow countrymen from imprisonment, but they were not allowed to conduct any business and had been put to great expense to stop the confiscation of their property. 'For so great a contempt as this nothing can plead but money', but in any case 'there will be no longer living here so long as any man-of-war of our kingdom keep in these parts'. What he deplored above all was that certain of Digby's backers were members of the Levant Company: 'if it is tolerable that two or three members of the company can undo all the rest...then command us home to serve our own prince rather than be slaves to strangers'.[35]

Others meanwhile were doing their best to remedy the situation. Two days after the action Sir Kenelm penned for Sir Peter Wyche, the ambassador at Constantinople, what was to become the standard English version of events. Commissioned by the king for a warfare voyage (implying that with his Majesty looming in the background he could be no ordinary privateer), 'I shaped my course to come into this road to relieve myself of some necessaries after a tedious and troublesome time at sea...I wrote letters to the commanders of each vessel to acquaint them who I was, giving them assurance I would not...do any act of hostility in the road.' Whereupon the Venetians attacked him, 'which being an injury beyond my sufferance', he responded in kind. Then, finding himself attacked also by the French, he boarded them, but afterwards withdrew his men 'upon Mr Vice-consul's entreaty'.[36] This diplomatic invention was in fact accepted by the Grand Vizier in his wisdom, and Wyche obtained orders to the Pasha of Aleppo to release Potton, to allow the English to resume trade, and to remit the whole dispute to Constantinople. Unfortunately

---

not be questioned. Their action may have been inspired by resentment at Digby's behaviour in the Ionian Islands and the hope that the considerable force under Capello would teach him a severe lesson. The Republic was also, at all times, rather morbidly anxious to be on good terms with the Turks. Eager attempts were made to show the Turk what a great service had been rendered to him. These efforts made very little impression upon the Porte' (*CSPV 1628-9*, p. xlv).

[35] SP97/14, fol. 164: 15/25 June 1628. The only one of Digby's partners known to have been a member of the Levant Company was Reynardson but, since only three of them are known by name, there is no particular reason to question the truth of Potton's statement.

[36] SP97/14, fols. 154-5: 13/23 June 1628 (printed in Gabrieli, *Digby*, pp. 283-4).

Potton had already, to Wyche's disgust, 'rashly given away 50,000 dollars for an accommodation in this business, whereas he should have stood it out, making a just defence, there being nothing committed against the capitulations, which grant our men-of-war liberty to enter these ports and water freely'. There could be no hope of restitution of that money once paid, especially because it had been given freely, not forced out of him.[37] Wyche's final comment on the matter was gloomy. In the ensuing months losses at the hands of Maltese and others were laid at the door of the English, who were threatened with further *avanias*. Some merchants returned home in despair and the rest were discouraged. 'Your lordship', he concluded, 'will be hearing from the Turkey Company in London', for something must be done to keep English men-of-war out of the Levant seas.[38]

Sir Thomas Roe, at Smyrna on his way home after his long stint as ambassador, censured Digby in stronger terms, revealing some of the prejudice Clarendon alluded to: 'whatsoever Sir Kenelm Digby's commission be, Scanderoon was no fit place to execute it, to disturb the quiet trade of merchants that pay better tenths than any rover, and to give occasion to the greedy and needy Turk to prey upon us. The Company must be sensible of this at home. And for mine own part I do not like the liberty and trust given to any of that religion, for however they may be honest and brave, moral men, yet either they, or some that look further than they, may have other and vaster demands than only punishing the foolish French, or enriching the Admiralty, to cast *petram scandali*, a rock into our best trades, and if possible to work a breach with this rash state. I remember that in Queen Elizabeth's time, *beatissimae memoriae*, no papist in England could prevail for a letter of mart: not that some might not be trusted, but that every such trust was a breach of that rule by which the state was then governed.' As to the matter itself, he thought it would be settled reasonably, provided the Aleppo factors held out without giving away their money, 'which is then in Hell, irrecoverable'.[39] Later he condemned such actions as Digby's still more forcibly: 'the great licence given or taken by our ships will leave us no friend to relieve us with a drop of water. They fly at all without difference, and shortly we shall have neither trade nor port in the Levant. At Scanderoon the road hath been scandalized by Sir Kenelm Digby, who hath done bravely, if warrantably; but our poor merchants suffer. It is no jesting with the hungry Turk, who like

---

[37] SP97/14, fol. 189: Wyche to Conway, 2/12 July 1628; SP97/14, fols. 204–7: same to same, 26 July / 5 August 1628.   [38] SP97/14, fols. 226–8: 24 September / 4 October 1628.
[39] Richardson, *Roe's Negotiations*, pp. 821–2: 19/29 July 1628.

a sumner lives by scapes...Briefly, if in England better order be not taken, and a bridle put in these seahorse mouths, his Majesty's honour will be offended, and all our trades forfeited. When I come home I will be bold to inform his Majesty and my Lord Admiral [of] necessary truths.'[40]

But Digby had by no means finished. The voyage so far may have gratified his ego, but it had hardly yet filled his purse. The entire length of the Mediterranean once again stretched invitingly before him. For three weeks after leaving Scanderoon he lay on and off the coast southward, hoping to intercept French shipping, but the French were all lying low, so that much time was wasted in chasing sails which turned out to be Greek caramusals. But some of the time was spent more pleasantly. One night, after hunting the wild boar up in the hills, he was stranded ashore: 'wherefore I gave a Turk some money (he leaving his bow and quiver of arrows in pawn for his honesty) to provide us some victuals; who went to one that I had treated well aboard me, and he brought down goats, sheep, hens, milk, eggs, melons and bread baked as thin as strong paper. We made great fires in a grove by the sea side, and roasted the flesh upon the ends of pikes, and passed the night very well.'[41] Eventually, yielding to the entreaties of the English vice-consul, he set course west on 7 July and for the rest of that month and August cruised the waters east of Greece, finding only two or three small prizes.

Coming now to the Archipelago in the heat of summer, Sir Kenelm sought wines and antiquities. He found the island of Milos 'very inconvenient, for it was a place that administered means of such debauchedness that I found by experience I could have no command of my men there', and at Mikonos likewise, though it was not so bad as Milos: 'so that I went with most of my ships to Delphos, a desert island, where staying till the rest were ready, because idleness should not fix their minds upon any untoward fancies (as is usual among seamen), and together to avail myself of the conveniency of carrying away some antiquities there, I busied them in rolling of stones down to the sea, which they did with such eagerness as though it had been the earnestest business that they came out for, and they mastered prodigious massy weights; but one stone, the greatest and fairest of all, containing four statues, they gave over after they had been, 300 men, a whole day about it.'[42] Digby the dilettante, fashionable man of taste, was never far from the shrewd and popular commander. In these idyllic islands he kept his

[40] Ibid., pp. 826–7: Leghorn, 8/18 September 1628. [41] Bruce, *Journal*, p. 44.
[42] Ibid., p. 57.

journal, as always, in the plain prose of a gentleman seaman, but it was at Milos that he composed his 'loose fantasies', taking refuge in romance from the temptations of that place. Nor did Digby the courtier lose the chance to present the king and his friends at Court with these antique trophies.[43]

When the fleet reached Zante its reception was unsurprisingly cold. Within a few days Digby retreated to a harbour on the Greek coast, fortifying himself against a threatened galley attack while he caulked, careened and tallowed all his ships, burned and pitched their bottoms, emptied their holds of ballast and cargo and re-stowed the same, hooped over a hundred tons of cask, repaired and replaced sails, and took in six months' wood. Knowing the Venetians would not allow him to victual in any of their ports, he had to resort to Patras, where the Turks beat up and imprisoned several of his men before exacting excessive port charges as well as handsome 'presents' and permitting him to trade on most unfavourable terms for provisions. 'All the time of my staying in this port', he complained, 'I had continual vexation and trouble through the injustice and tyranny of the Turks', but he had no alternative but to grin and bear such treatment now that the boot was on another's foot. Nevertheless he found the Morea an attractive country, rich in silk and (he heard) in mines; the Turks had no strength there and the Greeks 'would infallibly take part with a Christian invader and would soon become a belliguous nation'. Digby, however, should not be confused with Byron. In fact it was the dominant commercial and shipping presence of the English on and off the western shores of Greece that inspired such covetously liberating notions. When he moved on to nearby Cephalonia Digby met there 'the fleet of currant ships homewards bound, consisting of 8 English and 5 Flemings', among whom Captains Driver and Trenchfield had the temerity to try to interfere with a prize Digby regarded as rightfully his. Sir Kenelm of course put them in their place, but such men were not unused to exercising in such waters a cumulative and pervasive form of sea power more characteristic of that age than the kind postulated by A. T. Mahan.[44]

At length, weary of inhospitable Turks and Venetians, Digby shaped his course homewards on 11 November. A month later, off the coast of Sardinia, he took two large prizes: a 500-ton Hamburger, the *Jonas*, and a 400-ton Ragusan, the *St Michael*, both laden with goods Digby claimed as Spanish.[45] Passing Gibraltar on 1 January 1629, the fleet of

[43] Petersson, *Digby*, pp. 81–2. [44] Bruce, *Journal*, pp. 59–67; Mahan, *Influence of Sea Power*.
[45] Bruce, *Journal*, p. 78.

five, beaten by storm and hampered by the wallowing but rich *Jonas*, came up the Thames to anchor by Woolwich on 2 February. The next day Sir Kenelm 'went ashore and received gracious entertainment from the king and a happy welcome from all my friends'.[46] The year-long voyage was over, but Digby had months of trouble ahead, months of political and legal struggle to retain such spoil as he had managed to haul home. Already in August 1628 the Venetian ambassador, Alvise Contarini, had complained to King Charles about Digby's conduct in the Ionian Islands on his way to the Levant, asking for his recall or punishment. Charles listened sympathetically, but referred the matter to Secretary Conway, who wrote to Sir Isaac Wake, the English ambassador in Venice, telling him to forbid Digby and others to commit acts of hostility prejudicial to the rights and interests of the Republic. Wake was to 'arrange' with the Doge and Senate what this vague formula might mean in practice. Thus the protest was diplomatically smothered.[47]

Next, in October, came the turn of the Levant Company, demanding compensation from Digby's partners for the 50,000 dollars exacted by the Turks at Aleppo. The Privy Council summoned the partners to the Board for questioning, but there is no evidence that they ever paid damages and the only apparent outcome was the eventual prohibition, in June 1629, of privateering within the Straits.[48] In November Contarini had to report that Conway had actually complained to him about the behaviour of the galleasses at Scanderoon, to which the ambassador, finding the initiative thus rudely snatched, could only reply somewhat lamely that Digby's story was untrue and 'rendered him quite unworthy of his Majesty's protection'. Contarini's repeated remonstrances finally elicited instructions to Wake, dated 2 December, to send Digby home, 'out of regard for the Republic of Venice', but not because his Majesty believed he had committed any offence. It was obvious in any case that Digby would be long gone for London before the message was received.[49] In the same month his account of the Scanderoon action was published in England as a pamphlet, and further expostulations by Contarini produced another sop from Conway: the unfortunate printer was imprisoned and his pamphlets delivered to the ambassador, who sent one home. His masters, it may be imagined, were not amused.[50]

---

[46] *Ibid.*, pp. 80–95. Before leaving Italian waters Digby unladed the Ragusan and let her go with her crew, allowing the captain and crew of the *Jonas* to take the *Swallow*.
[47] *CSPV 1628–9*, pp. 209–12: Contarini to Doge and Senate, 7 August 1628.
[48] *APC 1628–9*, pp. 189–90, 222; SP16/121, fol. 137; Marsden, *Law and Custom*, I, 456–7.
[49] *CSPV 1628–9*, pp. 380–1, 437.   [50] *Ibid.*, pp. 443–4, 484, 507–9.

Soon after Digby's return Contarini obtained the sequestration of the *Jonas* and the goods from the *St Michael*, claiming them as Venetian, but it was with little faith or hope that he faced the contest for them. As he reported to Venice, so many Mediterranean traders used the Republic's name as a cover that 'I really believe from what I have seen, that there is much property belonging to those nations [Spanish, French and Genoese] in the ships in question, under the name of Venetian subjects.' Furthermore, 'it is whispered to me that if these ships are declared the property of Venetians and not lawful prize, the merchants of the Levant Company will demand their sequestration as damages for what they paid at Aleppo'. He had been advised by his government to try to get the dispute settled 'by the royal hand, as between prince and prince', rather than leave it to due legal process, but his opponent had the upper hand at Court also: 'Digby is working with all his might, *per fas et nefas*, to keep this plunder, as it forms the chief part of his profit. He has brought presents for all the chief lords of the government. For the king, a stone carved in low relief, brought from Greece, which is said to have belonged to the temple at Delphi, with some ancient statues, according to his Majesty's taste. He distributed a variety of delicacies among the ministers, some receiving wine from Crete, and some other things. I observe that he is well looked on, and some of the ministers told me that they believed, on his return, that my complaints of him would cease, as on this voyage he had become poor, [and that] the cargoes of those two ships belonged to Spaniards and Genoese rather than to Venetians.'[51]

Contarini pressed as hard as he could for the return of the two cargoes by royal command, but Charles did not give way. Proceedings in the Admiralty Court before Sir Henry Marten began in March and went for the most part in Digby's favour. In June Contarini made his last effort to have the case stopped, but in vain. 'I learn covertly from all the ministers', he wrote, 'that the king is extremely anxious to gratify the Republic, but as his subjects appeal to the statutes of the realm founded on their privileges, in virtue of which they very often dare to oppose his Majesty himself, he could not prevent them even if he wished. It would seem farcical to speak thus of the subjects of any other state. I consider it is a weakness, but so great and so permissible are the quarrels between the king and his people, who censure his slightest act, and terrify his ministers, that I do not know what to say...To my repeated remonstrances the only answer has been that even if the king wished he cannot deny justice to those who ask it. In

[51] *Ibid.*, pp. 548–50, 554–5.

spite of this his Majesty himself spoke to Digby and warned him to desist. But he threw himself at the king's feet, with his numerous partners, who share the cost and the plunder, and insists on the matter being left to the ordinary court, so that no one can be wronged.'[52] From this it would appear that the king and his ministers were not above using their political weakness, which was real enough, as a convenient excuse for favouring their friend, though whether Contarini believed them may be doubted.

Marten's sentence in respect of the goods in the *Jonas* and the *St Michael* awarded the greater part to Digby, much to the disgust of Contarini's successor, who estimated the value of that share at 200,000 ducats.[53] Nor did Digby have any difficulty over the rest of his booty. It seems likely therefore that he and his partners managed at least to recover their outlay, though on the other hand it is unlikely to have been a very profitable venture, for his other prize cargoes were not outstandingly rich and the ships themselves would have fetched little. Money certainly mattered to Sir Kenelm, and in that respect the voyage may well have proved disappointing. Yet he did achieve a quite spectacular personal triumph and all the glory he could have wished, for this was the only episode during those wars which the English could celebrate as a victory, albeit a victory over Venice rather than Spain or France, their proper enemies.

[52] *Ibid.*, pp. 568–71, 576–9, 587–8, 597–9; *CSPV 1629–32*, pp. 45–8, 115.
[53] *Ibid.*, pp. 144–5, 152, 164–6, 190–3; SP16/147, fol. 45; SP16/155, fol. 34; HCA 13/48, fols. 131–240.

CHAPTER 6

SHIP MONEY: ITS PURPOSES AND USES

ON 20 OCTOBER 1634 King Charles issued writs for the levy of ship money in the ports, coastal towns and other maritime places of England and Wales. Thereby the local authorities, headed by their respective sheriffs, were commanded to provide the Crown, by March of the following year, with a number of warships of specified burden, fully furnished, armed, manned and victualled for six months' active service. However, recognizing that the outports could not in fact find ships of the kind and size required, his Majesty was graciously pleased to lend them ships of his own. Thus by a convenient fiction the maritime parts of the realm, instead of contributing private shipping to supplement and work alongside the king's, as they had done in the past, now directly supplied the funds for setting forth a royal fleet. London alone equipped armed merchantmen in the traditional way, though it also accepted the loan of two royal men-of-war. The first ship-money fleet, which eventually put to sea under the earl of Lindsey in May 1635, consisted of nineteen royal ships and six others, fifteen of the former and five of the latter at the charge of subjects, while the Crown paid for the rest, as well as for the preparation of a reinforcement of ten vessels which in the end took no part in the operations.[1]

So was launched what his closest advisers called 'the king's great business'. Charles himself had directed the devising of the scheme, which was prepared, on the advice of his lawyers, with great care to ensure its acceptance by the public. Its chief authors, Lord Treasurer Weston, earl of Portland, and William Noy, the Attorney General, were among those who already in 1634 thought in terms of extending

[1] Gardiner, *Constitutional Documents*, pp. 105–8, prints a 1634 writ. On the loan of royal ships: *CSPD 1634-5*, pp. 559–60; SP16/283, fol. 239; SP16/284, fols. 1–5; BL, Additional MSS, 9295, fols. 89–90. Gordon, 'Ship money', p. 154, notes that the charge of the 1635 fleet, including the ten reinforcement ships, was reckoned at about £114,000, to which the Exchequer advanced about £23,000, while some £8,000 was met out of the returns on the 1635 writs.

the levy to the entire realm and were most anxious that this first, limited exercise should, in Noy's words, 'go on willingly and cheerfully'. It was important, for example, that the people should 'see a real employment and that his Majesty is at charge among them'.[2] Whereas the money was to be raised to maintain a fleet, work had to be found for the fleet, it seems, to justify the levy and, even more, its future development into a national tax. Not all those concerned in the shaping of ship money – probably not Charles himself – regarded it as a purely fiscal device, but that financial advantage was a principal object was suspected from the first and came to be generally accepted as a fact, in spite of the government's elaborate efforts to present its policy in another light. To this end as well as to secure efficient administration of the levy, the king and Council decided in February 1635 that 'the government and direction of all things concerning the ships which are to be furnished and set out by virtue of his Majesty's writ shall depend upon his Majesty's commandment and the order of the Council Board, and to be distinguished and kept divided from other services of the Navy'. Although the Navy Officers were to handle the furnishing and setting forth of the ships, they were to keep separate books for this service, while the returns of the levy were to be sent to the Treasurer of the Navy, who should employ them solely for this service and should account to the Council and its auditors directly.[3]

By such means ship money was emphatically demonstrated to be a special charge for a special purpose, 'not a business which concerned the officials of the Treasury and Exchequer as such'.[4] Indeed the Exchequer continued throughout the years of ship money to fund the Navy Office for its ordinary outgoings. The £41,570 for 'the Navy ultra surplusage and extraordinary fleets' in 1635 constituted one of the largest items in Exchequer payments totalling £636,536 for that year.[5] The average amount so paid in the six years of ship money amounted in fact to little less than what the Navy had received in the previous six years.[6] Meanwhile the ship-money levies, which were applied to all the shires in 1635 and yearly thereafter down to the last writs of 1639, generated large sums which were spent almost exclusively on the annual fleets, providing in effect an independent revenue for current naval operations. The details of this revenue and expenditure were established beyond dispute by M. D. Gordon in 1910. They show that the amount

[2] BL, Additional MSS, 32093, fol. 55: William Noy to Sir John Coke, 21 June 1634; Alexander, *Charles I's Lord Treasurer*, pp. 209–17.
[3] BL, Additional MSS, 29975, fol. 117: Council minutes (the king being present) of 1 February 1635.   [4] Gordon, 'Ship money', p. 141.   [5] BL, Harleian MSS, 3796, fols. 75–6.
[6] Gordon, 'Ship money', p. 144.

required in the first year from the maritime districts was about £80,000, nearly all of which was collected. In subsequent years the national assessment amounted to about £200,000, which again was nearly all realized, until the 1638 writs, which claimed only about £70,000, of which over a third remained unpaid. The writs of 1639 demanded over £200,000, of which only about £43,000 was paid.[7]

As the figures themselves suggest, all these strenuous endeavours of the government to persuade the nation that ship money was strictly for ships failed in the end to achieve their purpose. As Clarendon much later observed, 'imminent necessity and public safety were convincing persuasions' at first, but eventually ship money was perceived to be a regular, national and unparliamentary tax, designed 'for a spring and magazine that should have no bottom, and for an everlasting supply of all occasions'.[8] But was this perception, which Clarendon endorsed, right? If imminent necessity and public safety were convincing persuasions at first, why did they cease to be so later? It was apparently not until 1639, when the collection to meet the 1638 writs was attempted, that resistance made an important impact upon revenue, by which time the government was obviously unpopular for other reasons. Was it then unjustly condemned for pursuing a necessary build-up of naval power, using the only financial means available in the existing political circumstances? Had it not excellent reasons, arising from considerations of maritime security and foreign policy, for striving to create and exercise a modicum of sea power? Or were these reasons and considerations merely camouflage for the maintenance of a force to be employed on unpopular and secretly pro-Spanish courses smacking of Popery? Since it is the naval significance of ship money which concerns us here, it is tempting to dismiss such political questions, particularly because they are difficult – indeed impossible to answer definitively. But they are relevant, and although it is neither necessary nor desirable here to examine the domestic controversy which is naturally the chief interest of political historians, it is important to discuss the motives and intentions of Charles and his ministers in respect of ship money. Finance, defence and foreign policy cannot realistically be treated as separate matters, nor is it realistic to expect a simple answer.

The justification for the first ship-money levy, as formulated in the 1634 writs, was 'that certain thieves, pirates, and robbers of the sea, as

[7] *Ibid.*, pp. 143–4.   [8] Clarendon, *History*, I, 85.

well Turks, enemies of the Christian name, as others, being gathered together, wickedly taking by force and spoiling the ships, and goods, and merchandises, not only of our subjects, but also the subjects of our friends in the sea...have carried them away, delivering the men in the same into miserable captivity...also the dangers considered which, on every side, in these times of war do hang over our heads.' The king had therefore to provide for the defence of the kingdom and the security of his subjects and their shipping, as well as for the preservation of his princely honour as hereditary master of the sea.[9] Here the pride of place and emphasis given to piracy, and especially to the Barbary corsairs, is misleading, and was presumably meant to mislead. In 1634 neither the 'Turks' nor other pirates caused as much loss and distress as they had done in 1625–6 or were to do in 1635–6. Nor was it appropriate to summon up a great fleet of heavy warships to deal with them. As the naval experts of the day – Knott, Butler, Monson, Mainwaring, Gifford among them – reiterated *ad nauseam*, and as the experience of the ship-money fleets themselves depressingly proved, his Majesty's ships could not catch pirates, except in port or disabled. When Lindsey finally put to sea in May 1635 his instructions said little about pirates, and the hectoring orders he received from Secretary Coke during that summer were equally reticent on that subject. Both harped rather on the 'insolencies' of the French and Dutch and on the sovereignty of the sea.[10] The writs of later years continued to refer to piracy and the Barbary corsairs as if they were the main concern, but they clearly were not. Rainborowe's expedition of 1637 was a side-show. In 1635 neither the Privy Council's instructions to the sheriffs concerning ship money nor the Lord Keeper's address to the Assize judges on this matter so much as mention piracy, dwelling rather on the safety of the realm 'against those dangers and extremities which have distressed other nations, and are common effects of war, whensoever it taketh a people unprepared', and on the need for a powerful fleet to show foreign nations 'that England is both able and ready to keep itself and all its rights' and so gain peace through strength.[11]

Ship money was not about piracy, but its promoters were clever enough politicians to realize that maritime England, the target in 1634, would respond 'willingly and cheerfully' to an appeal which gave prominence to the feared and hated Moor. Conversely, no grounds must be given for any suspicion that the fleet might be employed for

[9] Gardiner, *Constitutional Documents*, pp. 105–6.
[10] Fulton, *Sovereignty of the Sea*, pp. 259–65; Manwaring and Perrin, *Mainwaring*, I, 228–30; *CSPD 1635*, pp. 154–5.   [11] Rushworth, *Collections*, II, 259–64, 294–8.

Spain's benefit, though in fact the first levy was closely associated with secret negotiations for an Anglo-Spanish alliance. Upon the nature of this connection Secretary Windebank instructed Sir Arthur Hopton, the English agent in Madrid, in a letter of 16 February 1634:[12]

> In the meantime, their [viz. the Spaniards'] affairs in Flanders growing every day into more desperate estate, his Majesty, considering in his princely wisdom how much it concerns him, in his own interest, to carry a jealous and watchful eye over the growing greatness of the States, by whose insolencies he is every day much awakened, hath been pleased to direct the Lord Treasurer to call the Lord Cottington and myself unto him, and to confer with Necolalde [the Spanish agent in London] upon some course to be held for giving alliance to the king of Spain; such as may stop the current of the Hollanders' conquests, and peradventure draw them to a peace, yet not plunge his Majesty into a sudden, dangerous and untimely war with those people. To do this, it is of both sides thought fit that his Majesty should put a strong and powerful fleet to sea, that may open the ports, prohibit all kind of depredation in those seas, and secure even the coasts of Flanders. And this to be done upon pretence of suppressing and punishing the great liberty which hath of late been taken, both by the States and those of Dunkirk, to commit hostilities one upon the other, even within his Majesty's safest harbours, both in England and Ireland. And, when his Majesty is so armed at sea, it is conceived it will not be unseasonable for him to call upon his neighbours to accept good conditions of peace from the king of Spain; which, if they should refuse, he may peradventure speak louder than is yet fitting for him to do.

In exchange for this promise of naval assistance, Windebank added, 'it will be necessary for the king of Spain to furnish money toward it'. In the protracted negotiations which followed, money was the stumbling block. Articles drawn up in the summer specified a loan of 200,000 crowns (about £50,000) to subsidize the setting forth of twenty ships, repayable only if Charles failed to carry out his promise. But Olivares in Madrid and Necolalde in London were deeply sceptical about English intentions and unwilling to advance hard cash for measures Charles could not afford to risk.[13] Windebank wrote to Hopton in October that 'Necolalde gave us great hopes of it that

---
[12] *Clarendon Papers*, I, 74–7.
[13] English versions of the articles are in *Clarendon Papers*, I, 109–11, and BL, Additional MSS, 32093, fols. 72–5. A Spanish version is printed in Alcalá-Zamora, *España, Flandés y el Mar del Norte*, pp. 510–13. The articles set out in some detail how the English fleet would convoy Spanish ships to Dunkirk, counter Dutch hostilities, etc. Spanish reactions may be read between the lines of Hopton's dispatch of 7 April 1634 in *Clarendon Papers*, I, 81–5.

moneys should have been presently furnished by the king of Spain, and that our fleet, which is in a readiness upon a month's warning, should have been put to sea by the beginning of this last September' (here both sides were blatantly lying). Now they would have to work to effect the plan next spring, 'which his Majesty will not fail to do if these articles may be yielded unto by you there, and moneys sent over hither accordingly'.[14] Necolalde in December, noting what little could be expected from English promises, said he had known from the beginning 'that they wish to put these ships to sea for their own security and to win respect, and to operate against your Majesty's ships and those of his subjects more than against the Dutch, and to maintain the freedom of Dutch and English trade with these [Flemish] coasts and canals', fearing as they did the onslaught of the Dunkirkers and Biscayners.[15] The upshot was that the articles were agreed by both sides but never became effective because Spain never paid the money and probably never intended to, being more interested in keeping Charles on a string and out of the arms of Richelieu.

Necolalde and his masters were certainly right to distrust English promises. Charles and his three agents in this affair were inclined to favour Spain for various reasons, but others, inside as well as outside the Privy Council, were not. Far from speaking with a single voice, the government embraced men of widely differing views and, as Peter Paul Rubens had observed in 1628, policies were neither persistent nor consistent. The Spanish negotiation was conducted by Portland, Windebank and Cottington without the knowledge of the rest of the Council. As Cottington informed Hopton in February 1634, 'you will perceive that Secretary Coke is ignorant of these businesses; therefore you must address your dispatches to Secretary Windebank, yet write also to the other as hitherto you have done, so as he may suspect nothing'.[16] At this very juncture Coke sent Hopton a long and angry protest about the disorderly and hostile behaviour of Dunkirkers and Biscayners in English waters and ports, telling him to bring it to the notice of the Spanish government.[17] The alliance proposals were pursued in secret because Coke and some other councillors would have refused to stomach them. What realistic prospect could there be of putting such a policy into effect? Charles and his three allies cannot seriously have contemplated carrying out, in the teeth of general opposition and without anything like the financial resources necessary,

[14] BL, Additional MSS, 32093, fol. 64: 16 October 1634.
[15] Alcalá-Zamora, *España, Flandés y el Mar del Norte*, p. 513; and pp. 350–1 on Spain's failure to pay.   [16] BL, Egerton MSS, 1820, fols. 325–6.   [17] *Ibid.*, fols. 321–3.

a course of action which would bring the country into open conflict, if not outright war, with Holland and France. It is mistaken, therefore, to infer a pro-Spanish plot from these deceitful parleys. One article, it is true, states 'that the pretext of this arming shall be to secure the coasts of Great Britain and Ireland and to free them from pirates and others who commit disorders and hostilities there', and the writs did spell out that pretext, doubtless with a view to showing Spain that Charles meant what the articles said about the employment of the English fleet in Spain's service. But the Spaniards reasonably concluded that as a declaration of intent the articles were no more reliable than the writs. For their part, as Hopton reported to Windebank, they 'intended only to entertain him [Charles] in his present neutrality', assuming correctly that ship money was 'a business whereon his Majesty had set his resolution, which, whether they entered therein or no, would take effect'.[18]

While one secretary thus pursued the forlorn hope of a Spanish subsidy, the other steered a different course. On 8 June 1634 Sir John Coke reported to the king and Privy Council on the unsatisfactory state of relations between England and various foreign countries, referring to outrages committed against his Majesty's subjects in Turkey, Tunis, Sallee, Savoy and Spain. Nearer home all free trade was interrupted and within the king's own chambers squadrons of men-of-war from Biscay and Flanders took not only Hollanders but Frenchmen and others, even English ships, ruining the trade of Ireland, for example. The French were trying to drive our trade out of their country and the Dutch, with their intrusion upon our fisheries and their claim to *mare liberum*, were worst of all, pursuing and taking prizes in British ports and rivers. He concluded by advising the immediate reinforcement of the king's guards to recover his undoubted right of sovereignty in all his seas.[19] Although it has long been argued and generally believed that Coke was duped by Charles into presenting this heart-felt plea in order 'to cloak the nefarious scheme' to help Spain destroy the Dutch, the far-fetched notion that one councillor could thus have been used, without his knowledge, to 'hoodwink' the rest is merely a nineteenth-century inference, based on nothing more than suspicion, whereas there is a mass of evidence – even cited by the same authorities – that Charles was intensely concerned about the increasing infringement of what he

---

[18] *Clarendon Papers*, I, 100–2: Hopton to Windebank, 7 July 1634. The fact that ship money and the naval build-up went ahead with neither Spanish money nor any commitment to assist Spain argues strongly against Gardiner's view of this affair: *History of England*, VII, 366–72.
[19] *CSPD 1634–5*, pp. 68–9; SP16/269, fols 97–100.

regarded as his sovereign rights by foreign men-of-war, whether Dutch, French, Spanish or Dunkirker.[20]

Recent years had seen a rapid escalation of maritime violence in the North Sea, the English Channel, the Irish Sea and waters southwards. While the Barbary corsairs continued their aggression against Christian shipping and professional pirates preyed upon all and sundry as usual, the Thirty Years War was waged at sea by increasingly powerful forces on either side. Maritime trade and the North Sea herring fishery, Holland's main resources, were under constant attack by raiding warships from Dunkirk, squadrons of state-built as well as private men-of-war, designed for speed and strength. These and their Spanish allies from the Biscay ports wrought havoc in northern waters and had few scruples about interfering with neutrals, especially since they might well be carrying Dutch cargoes.[21] Nor did they balk at chasing their prey into English ports and anchorages. During 1634–5 Dunkirker raids on the numerous herring busses were resisted by Dutch warships and the fighting spilled into Yarmouth, Scarborough and Blyth harbours and even ashore.[22] On the other hand Dutch privateers and States men-of-war plied the Channel and the Flemish coast for prize, seeking to cut the vital life-line between Spain and the army of Flanders, a sea-link of increasing strategic importance as the 'Spanish road' overland was endangered and finally became untenable. Anti-Dutch feeling in England, aroused long since by bitter disputes in eastern and Arctic seas, focussed above all on the North Sea fishery. Here Secretary Coke, backed enthusiastically by Charles and his Council, had striven for some years to oust the Hollanders by setting up a grand national fishery association to monopolize the herring, vehemently proclaiming English sovereignty over British seas and all that swam therein. By 1634 he had succeeded in forming a Fishery Society, but not yet in catching any considerable amount of herring. Something more forceful seemed to be required.[23]

The claim to sovereignty over neighbouring waters was not new. It

---

[20] 'Hoodwink' was Gardiner's word: *History of England*, VII, 356–7, but his interpretation was subtler than some of the glosses later put upon it, for example by Fulton, who used the phrase quoted: *Sovereignty of the Sea*, p. 254. Most other historians have bowed to Gardiner's authority in this – even Coke's latest biographer in his otherwise excellent book: Young, *Servility and Service*, pp. 239–40.
[21] Stradling, 'Spanish Dunkirkers'. On the Thirty Years War at sea, see Israel, *Dutch Republic*; Alcalá-Zamora, *España, Flandés y el Mar del Norte*; Boxer, *Tromp's Journal*; Stradling, 'Catastrophe and recovery'. On Biscayner spoil of English shipping: *CSPD 1634–5*, pp. 147, 191–2, 212–13.
[22] *CSPD 1634–5*, pp. 31–2, 46, 63, 95, 226–7; *CSPD 1635*, pp. xv–xvi, etc.
[23] Fulton, *Sovereignty of the Sea*, pp. 209–45.

was at this time traced back, on good evidence, to those Plantagenet kings who had asserted a right to maintain the ancient supremacy of the Crown over English seas. In Elizabeth's reign the great magus John Dee had proposed a 'petty navy royal', financed by taxing foreign fishermen and English property, to establish jurisdiction over all shipping in British waters for the security of international trade.[24] King James had publicly forbidden hostilities within his ports and havens and his High Court of Admiralty had produced a chart defining twenty-six 'king's chambers', lying between various headlands, within which no foreigners would be permitted to fight. James also prohibited unlicensed fishing by foreigners in British seas, a measure directed against the Dutch, and tried to develop a national fishing company. Whether for lack of resources, resolution or sea power, these claims were not enforced, and Dutchmen were found increasingly to grudge even the traditional 'homage to the flag' – the striking of top-sails or flags in the presence of the king's ships.[25] But frustration only served to fuel English resentment as the Dutch presence in the North Sea loomed larger than ever and foreign men-of-war disregarded the king's chambers, interfering with English merchantmen and even repeatedly plundering the Dover packet carrying the king's mail. In the early 1630s a sense of outrage developed, following the humiliations of the wars with France and Spain and borne upon the rising tide of maritime disorder. The result was an assertion of sovereignty which went far beyond former claims and implied some ambition to impose a supreme and far-flung dominion.

Such was the so-called 'Reglement for the Narrow Seas', drawn up by the Attorney General and the Judge of the Admiralty in February 1634. This strictly prohibited violence between ships of any nation in the king's chambers, forbade ships of war entry to his sea-roads and havens except for victualling, repair or refuge from storm and offered protection to merchant shipping throughout 'the four English seas' (the North and Irish Seas and the Channel). It also contained an explicit assertion of sovereignty over those seas and thus erected a legal platform for the licensing of foreign fishing in that area.[26] Meanwhile Charles had inspired research by Sir John Boroughs, keeper of the Tower records, to substantiate his claims, work which, begun in 1631, resulted in Boroughs's treatise of 1633 on 'The Sovereignty of the British Seas'. This was superseded by John Selden's great *Mare*

---

[24] Dee, *General and Rare Memorials*.
[25] Fulton, *Sovereignty of the Sea*, pp. 30, 99–104, 118–208.
[26] Marsden, *Law and Custom*, I, 484–90; Fulton, *Sovereignty of the Sea*, pp. 251–2, 759–61.

Clausum, written long before in James's time but now re-cast at Charles's request and published in 1635, providing the legal and ideological underpinning for his master's royal pretension to command the sea.[27] What else was necessary but a fleet to enforce that pretension and the money to create the fleet? Here indeed was a major root of ship money.

Immediate naval and strategic considerations were also important. As we have seen, the combined sea power of Spain and Dunkirk was pitted against that of the Dutch, backed and finally in 1635 joined openly by Richelieu, in a titanic struggle for command of the sea-route to and from Flanders, the route which bore Spain's troops and bullion to her forces there, supplying not only the army of Flanders but also the squadrons of Dunkirk. The state navies and privateering forces of these Continental powers had developed progressively since about 1620 as victory came to depend more and more upon this theatre of the war. Spain had totally reconstituted her navy in the years 1617 to 1623, seventy new ships being ordered then by the Crown, and in spite of losses Peninsular sea power continued to mount until 1639, when the great armada of 47 Spanish and 21 Flemish warships (apart from transports and others) sailed under Don Antonio de Oquendo to its destruction in the Downs.[28] Meanwhile the Flemish royal squadrons and privateers in the 1630s numbered some 25–30 and 60–70 respectively.[29] A detailed report of 1631 on the naval resources of the United Provinces listed 98 men-of-war apart from pinnaces, frigates and boats.[30] Tromp, when he attacked the Spanish armada in 1639, had 96 warships, manned with nearly 10,000 men, off the English coast, a force built up from some 30 ships in the space of two or three weeks.[31] As for France, Richelieu, taking control of maritime and naval affairs in 1626, created almost from scratch, with Dutch help, a substantial Atlantic fleet numbering some 39 men-of-war great and small in 1636. In 1639 Admiral de Sourdis commanded an offensive force of 40 warships, 21 fireships and 12 transports against Coruña.[32] France also, like Spain, maintained a powerful presence in the Mediterranean. Alongside such forces the naval strength Charles could afford to put to sea in the early 1630s was pitifully inadequate: Admiral Pennington in 1633 and 1634 guarded the Narrow Seas with two major and two minor warships, while Captain Plumleigh attempted to maintain order in Irish waters with one of each.

---

[27] Fulton, *Sovereignty of the Sea*, pp. 364–74.
[28] Thompson, *War and Government*, pp. 198–200; Alcalá-Zamora, *España, Flandés y el Mar del Norte*, pp. 430–3; Boxer, *Tromp's Journal*. [29] Stradling, 'Spanish Dunkirkers', p. 549.
[30] SP84/149, fols. 65–84. [31] Israel, *Dutch Republic*, p. 270.
[32] SP78/101, fols. 146–7; Boxer, *Tromp's Journal*, p. 7.

It may be argued, of course, that England, being neutral, needed no more ships than these on active service. She had, in case of war or serious emergency, a Royal Navy of 42 warships, apart from numerous powerful merchantmen, to call upon. That no emergency existed in 1634 has always been an essential point in the opposition case, and behind it lies the thought that Charles's foreign policy, consisting in single-minded and futile efforts to recover the Palatinate for his nephew, was purely dynastic and unworthy of the nation's support. This typically Whig view, however, does violence to the complexity of foreign affairs and less than justice to Charles's policies. A neutrality based on impotence could only harm the national interest, which lay essentially in preserving as much the Netherlands from Spanish or French domination as England's commerce from Dutch domination. For both strategic and commercial reasons the English government did not wish to see any one power supreme in that region, but to maintain the equilibrium the island kingdom had to be made safe from attack and had to have some considerable weight to throw into the balance. To exert any influence a positive neutrality was essential, and in the circumstances sea power was the only means available to achieve it. The doctrine of neutrality was freely canvassed in government circles in 1634 and 1635, when Charles himself expounded it to the Dutch ambassador.[33] If his policy appears vacillating, it vacillated with rational intent. Nor is it true, as critics gleefully allege, that it failed. The balance of power at sea in this decade was such that the ship-money fleets were strong enough to tip it either way, and the powers concerned were well aware of this. The policy worked and served the nation's interests – especially her maritime interests – well until 1639, when the national and international situation plunged into crisis.

It is mistaken, then, to seek any simple explanation of ship money. It was certainly designed for financial advantage in the sense that it would enable the Crown to pursue a credible foreign policy without bankrupting itself, and would thus help substantially to make the régime independent of Parliamentary taxes. To the same end the government no doubt hoped to make the fleets show a profit. Perhaps eventually by such means ship money might become, as Clarendon thought was intended, 'an everlasting supply for all occasions'. Although the writs gave undue prominence to piracy, the government did regard checking the tide of disorder at sea, whether created by belligerents or Barbary corsairs, as an important objective, and asserting

---

[33] *CSPV 1632–6*, pp. xx–xxi. On the rationality of Charles's foreign policy see also Edmundson, *Anglo-Dutch Rivalry*, pp. 5, 105–31.

the king's sovereignty over British seas was a cause dear to Charles's heart. In terms of strategy it is unlikely that even Cottington and Windebank, let alone Portland or Charles himself, thought seriously of committing the Royal Navy to the Spanish side: their aim was rather to obtain the money and hence the sea power necessary to defend the interests of the realm in neighbouring seas and countries. Differing motives and attitudes were at work in the planning of ship money and naval re-armament, and they converged rather than conflicted precisely because this was 'the king's great business'. Even so, intentions and expectations do not entirely explain ship money. Other reasons for the choice of this particular method of funding the desired access of sea power lay in the past: specifically in the political and naval problems which had come to a head in the recent wars.

Down even to Cromwell's time Englishmen looked back upon the Elizabethan war with Spain as an age of naval glory, when their seafaring forbears had dominated the ocean. This legend was not without a basis in fact. The queen's ships and their auxiliaries did defeat, though natural forces actually destroyed, King Philip's armada in 1588. After that, Spain's invasion threats came to naught and English forces commanded the waters from the North Sea southwards to the Canary Islands and the Azores and roved almost unmolested the Mediterranean and Spain's own Caribbean Sea. But in this long sea war England had special advantages. She had the advantage of a well-organized and technically advanced Royal Navy, unrivalled at the time as a specialized fighting force. She had no great, rich merchant marine in need of protection, but plenty of merchants and gentlemen prepared to set forth ships in quest of prize, so that after 1588 this became essentially a privateering war. The English were well placed in every way to take the role of predators against the rich and vulnerable shipping of the Iberian nations and any neutrals who ventured to assist them as carriers or suppliers of merchandise. In this incessant campaign of commerce-raiding the queen's ships themselves took the lead and were indeed expected to pay their way. Collaboration between them and merchant men-of-war in ocean cruises or great amphibious expeditions like those to Lisbon in 1589 and Cadiz in 1596 was usual. The queen's admirals and captains promoted and often commanded privateering ventures; she herself, her Lord Admiral and her Navy Treasurer led what onlookers from abroad often described as a national business of maritime predation. Elizabethan sea power thus depended upon the effective amalgamation of a small, but efficient Royal Navy and a large number of voluntary ships, together making up a genuinely national navy. This characteristically hybrid force was on the whole successful, but its performance was in certain significant respects disappointing, to say the least.

In the nostalgic afterglow men forgot the disgraceful corruption and indiscipline which attended those great expeditions in which large numbers of private ships, commandeered or volunteered for hire, took part, spoiling the Cadiz raid of 1596, for example, and ruining the Portugal voyage of 1589 and the Islands voyage of 1597.[34] They forgot the protests, wrangling and excuses of most of the coast towns which were asked to subscribe to the cost of ships required by the queen from the outports in 1588.[35] They forgot how in 1596, when the government demanded ship money from inland towns in maritime counties to provide auxiliaries against the renewed threat of invasion that year, it met widespread resistance on the part of towns and individuals, even counties. The Council charged Norfolk justices with wilful disobedience and the justices and people of the West Riding with 'dilatory, frivolous and framed excuses' amounting to the same. When London, at the end of that year, actually refused to subscribe ten ships for a new expedition, the Council quietly dropped the demand.[36] Above all they forgot the ravages of the Dunkirkers upon English merchant shipping during the later 1590s and early 1600s, when those raiders mounted an increasingly successful campaign in the North Sea and the Channel, threatening to drive smaller merchantmen and fishing craft off the sea altogether. The outports' cries of distress assailed the ears of the Council, their burgesses complained in Parliament about the failure of the Navy to protect trade and finally the government responded with an extraordinary proposal, the implications of which throw an interesting light on the later history of ship money.[37]

In February 1603, a few weeks before her own death and the end of the war, the queen wrote to her Privy Council in the following terms:

> We have determined that there must be some proportion of shipping wholly assigned to guard our merchants from what parts soever they set forth and return, which being a matter no way for our own ships to attend, the uncertainty of their trade requiring sudden and changeable going to and fro, it shall be most necessary to appropriate some other

[34] Wernham, *Portugal 1589*; *Monson's Tracts*, I, 344–95; II, 1–83.
[35] Laughton, *Defeat*, I, 129–65.
[36] Lewis, *Elizabethan Ship Money*; Tawney and Power, *Tudor Economic Documents*, II, 128–30.
[37] Corbett, *Successors of Drake*, pp. 299–303, 359–62, 397–9; Lewis, *Elizabethan Ship Money*; Swales, 'Ship-money levy', pp. 165–6.

ships for that purpose. And therein we make no question but all our loving subjects will conclude that these important actions wherein our own fleets be still engaged being well considered, and the charge thereof daily multiplying more and more, this burden of expense (whatever it shall amount unto) must be for the most part raised and maintained by the voluntary contributions of our subjects, whereof whosoever at the first shall least apprehend their own interests will, upon those reasons which we have given you to express in your letters, plainly see that general inconvenience to be imminent in consequence which is not so visible at the first appearance. For which purpose, because there may be many particular incidents to persuade and order this levy, for which it is reason that you have our warrant how and with whom to deal, we have thought good by virtue hereof to command and authorize you to direct your letters to such effect as you may procure a speedy collection and disbursement of all things necessary for the providing and furnishing of ten or twelve ships wholly and only to attend that service. Authorizing you also to promise that the charge of all manner of munition for that service shall be borne by ourselves, that they shall be free from paying any customs, tenths or other duties for all things which they shall take being lawful prize, [and] lastly that when they have tried what charge they shall be at and see the success thereof, they may then advise how to continue or give over the course...[38]

Accordingly the Council wrote to the authorities in the counties, inland as well as maritime, calling upon them 'to draw the rest of her Majesty's loving subjects... to a voluntary contribution' and to set the example themselves since, if 'by their refusal it should still be left to her, that would be found too heavy for her to bear, which being assisted by many hands will be found easy and profitable to all'. They were particularly to allay any suspicion that private profit might be intended, 'but that all the moneys shall be converted to their use that gave it'. The money was therefore to be conveyed by deputies, appointed for each county, to Sir Paul Bayning, a leading London merchant and financier with a major interest in shipping, who was to act as treasurer and to consult those deputies in the disbursement of funds so raised. Thus the West Country, with Sussex and Wales, was to subscribe about £8,700 for a fleet of some 1,000 tons to protect the waters from Beachy Head to Milford Haven, while other parts should provide similar squadrons for the North Sea and for the Thames and eastern Channel.[39]

---

[38] BL, Harleian MSS, 703, fol. 129; another copy SP12/287, fols. 36–7. 'Success' here (as always at that time) means outcome.

[39] BL, Harleian MSS, 703, fols. 130–1; SP12/287, fols. 9–10. Contributions were to be requested only from the well-to-do: people with lands worth £20 a year or money and goods worth £200 a year.

Elizabeth thus anticipated Charles's extension of ship money to the inland counties, but eased the demand by calling the subscription voluntary, in tacit acknowledgement of the resistance encountered in 1596 and of the protests only to be expected from the inland counties at least. It was hardly necessary for her councillors to indicate how her Majesty would make her displeasure felt by those who refused. At the same time she took care to demonstrate, as Charles did later, that the money would not come to her Exchequer, but would be handled separately and spent only on its proper purpose and in the interests of the subscribers, who would be enabled to monitor its expenditure and terminate the scheme at will, with the clear implication that this would not become a permanent tax. However, the similarity between this and Charles's ship-money plans is less important than the difference. Elizabeth in effect refused to take responsibility for the defence of merchant shipping. As the Council put it, her Majesty's ships were 'not so proper' for this service, being 'not aptly built for this purpose' and having other duties. Their letters made clear that 'divers persons, and especially the merchants... do show themselves very willing to undergo any reasonable charge whereby some convenient number of ships may be maintained', meaning undoubtedly Bayning and some partners, who owned merchant men-of-war and ran the syndicates which dominated the privateering business in London and elsewhere.[40] The government was happy, in this as in many other spheres, to leave powerful interests to look after their own affairs. If the privateering interest thought it could manage the defence of trade to its own benefit – or at least thought it worth trying, the scheme being terminable – the Crown would be relieved of the expense and the queen's ships could pursue their work of waging war unimpeded. Sea power consisted in the partnership of the Royal Navy and private shipping, just as the realm was a partnership between the queen and her subjects. In 1625 Charles found his subjects thinking along similar lines, but was unable to share their opinion, for reasons to be considered hereafter.

The naval problems encountered by Charles I were indeed not merely immediate symptoms of his political and financial difficulties, but had deep roots in history. Traditionally sea power had been vested in the stronger sort of merchantmen, armed for trade or war, some of which would be bought or hired by the king when needed, many more

---

[40] Andrews, *Elizabethan Privateering*, pp. 100–23. The idea of using officially sponsored private enterprise to deal with the Dunkirkers was typically Elizabethan, and may be compared with the earlier commissions for setting forth ships to capture pirates.

of which would operate against enemy shipping for booty, serving themselves as well as the king. Henry VIII added to these resources a state-built force in which the major units, prototypes of broadside sailing warships, were more powerful than any merchantman. Royal dockyards and storehouses and a regular naval administration – the Navy Board – came into being. But this impressive and expensive force was not a modern state navy. It was too small to undertake even the task of national defence. The 34 vessels of 12,000 tons actually commissioned in 1588 formed the core of a fleet comprising 140 units, including some 60 effective fighting ships. For other purposes the Crown depended still more on private shipping. Whilst it could not, as the government freely admitted, protect the merchant marine, and did not even regard this as its duty, it employed merchantmen as auxiliaries and relied on private shipping voluntarily to undertake a continuous campaign against enemy commerce as well as a large part in officially organized expeditions.

By the end of Elizabeth's reign the tension inherent in this system of dual sea power was already evident. The Royal Navy, though not significantly larger than in 1588, was becoming a more regular, professional force. Some of its leading officers, like Sir William Monson, made no secret of their contempt for privateersmen, with whom they had to compete for manpower. Merchants on the other hand had cause to complain that the queen's ships offered them no protection though their ships might be commandeered or their men pressed for the queen's service. With the ending of the war these problems faded into the background, along with the 1603 scheme for an alternative navy, but the process which created them continued, for the former interchangeability of warship and merchantman was passing away. After 1600 the gap widened as the tonnage and fire power of royal warships increased. Phineas Pett (thanks to his autobiography the best known of the king's master shipwrights) set the pace with the *Prince Royal* in 1610, a ship of 1,200 tons and 55 guns.[41] Merchant men-of-war still had an important part to play in distant seas as armed traders or privateers and in time of war the Crown would still require their help, but they could no longer match the king's ships for fighting purposes, while alongside them a mass of vulnerable merchantmen sailed unprotected. For the Royal Navy remained a small force under James and was even less fit than formerly to assume the responsibilities of a fully fledged state navy.

[41] Quinn and Ryan, *England's Sea Empire*, p. 217.

Nor did the naval reform of 1618 tackle these structural problems. The moving spirit in this was Sir Lionel Cranfield, who came to it fresh from his successful overhaul of the king's household. Cranfield's aim was retrenchment: the royal finances urgently required economy in the spending departments, among which the Navy was one of the most demanding and wasteful, notorious for corruption under the lax rule of the earl of Nottingham, Lord High Admiral, Sir Robert Mansell, its Treasurer, and Sir John Trevor, its Surveyor. The detailed work of the inquiry, the drafting of the reform programme and the subsequent administration of it were carried out by Sir John Coke, whose passion for economy matched his untiring industry.[42] The Commission accordingly concerned itself chiefly with 'the charge of the Navy' and the means to reduce it. James and Buckingham, who now succeeded Nottingham as Lord High Admiral, certainly wanted a stronger Navy, but that meant little more than its restoration to its former strength. The objective now proposed, to be reached in five years, was a Navy of thirty ships amounting to 17,110 tons, compared with the 11,070 tons of serviceable shipping to which Elizabeth's force had decayed by 1618. The annual ordinary charge to the king over the past seven years, averaging £53,000, would be cut to £30,000 approximately for the next five years (including the cost of building ten new ships) and after that would stabilize at just under £20,000. On the other hand the Commission took a pernicious view of the character and function of the Royal Navy:

> The number of small vessels built in former times were a means to draw on many needless employments and charges, and withal neither able to perform service nor give reputation to the state, whereas these greater ships will not so easily be sent out and when they are abroad will carry with them more power and honour, and keep the seas with more respect and command, and when there is need of small ships they may be had from merchants.[43]

The concern for prestige and presence thus dovetailed neatly with the concern for economy, but at the expense of effectual sea power. The greater ships were intended for reputation rather than regular service, while the need for lighter men-of-war – those nimble and prime sailers for which the king's commanders continually cried out – was scorned. This was false economy. In the pursuit of prestige Charles's *Sovereign of the Sea* was to cost over £40,000 without her guns,[44] and the Navy's

[42] Prestwich, *Cranfield*, pp. 211–19; McGowan, *Jacobean Commissions*; Young, *Servility and Service*.
[43] McGowan, *Jacobean Commissions*, p. 288.   [44] Oppenheim, *Administration*, p. 260.

lack of light warships in the years to come proved even more costly, contributing heavily to the failures and losses of the wars with France and Spain. Above all, this policy led directly, given the maritime circumstances, to that excessive dependence on merchant auxiliaries which Charles and his commanders would have cause to regret. Not only might small ships be had from merchants: as the report added, 'the common building of great and warlike ships to reinforce the Navy, when need shall require, may well contain his Majesty's number and charge within these bounds.'[45]

The 1618 Commission did make a notable effort to reform the naval administration, pointing out the direct responsibility of the Principal Officers for the waste, peculation and neglect which had prevailed since 1603, and proposing certain measures (though in the event these were insufficient) to check venal office-holding, the chief source of corruption. Moreover its suggestion that the Commissioners themselves should take over the management of the Navy was adopted, effectively putting Coke, an excellent peace-time administrator, in charge, backed by all the power and good intentions of the new Lord Admiral. As a result the reformed administration achieved its stated objectives in respect of the ordinary upkeep of the Navy.[46] Unfortunately it did not achieve the creative reform which the changing maritime situation demanded. It failed to recognize the need to develop the Navy's real capability and to change the relationship between the state force and the rest of the nation's shipping. On the other hand it can scarcely be censured for such omissions since it was instituted to save money. In this sense at least lack of money was a major cause of the inadequacy of England's sea forces in the wars which soon followed.

Nor is it unreasonable to attribute the disastrous course of naval operations during these wars in large measure to the financial chaos produced by Charles's failure to win the support of Parliament.[47] Shortage of funds in 1625 delayed the departure of the Cadiz expedition and thereby prejudiced its chances of success. The poverty of the Crown was responsible for the bad victualling, pay arrears and mutinous conduct which attended this enterprise and those to the Ile de Rhé and La Rochelle. In 1628, after three years of such misery, even the faithful Coke was in despair, writing from Portsmouth: 'give me leave

---

[45] McGowan, *Jacobean Commissions*, p. 288.
[46] Quinn and Ryan, *England's Sea Empire*, p. 225.
[47] An adequate analysis of the naval aspect of these wars has yet to be written. Gardiner's cursory account is subordinate to his narrative of domestic politics (*History of England*, vol. VI) and Penn's *Early Stuart Navy* is poor and unreliable. The best modern account, by Ryan in Quinn and Ryan, *England's Sea Empire*, is excellent but necessarily brief.

to say freely that not only my abode here will be of no use, but that every day while the fleet stayeth in this harbour it will be less ready and worse provided to set to sea'.[48] Yet as an explanation of the naval failure financial weakness cannot stand alone: it was enmeshed with other weaknesses, both political and naval.

Charles's impecuniosity was itself due in part to the difference between his own and Parliament's concepts of the war and naval strategy. In 1624 Parliament had enthusiastically supported the breach with Spain, looking forward to a sea war to be waged against Iberian shipping and colonies in the Elizabethan tradition. In 1625, however, this euphoria faded. The money granted the previous year was wasted on the expensive and fruitless expedition led by Count Mansfeld, a misguided attempt to intervene in the Continental war. The Cadiz venture was in preparation, but the Crown's war aims and strategy remained obscure, and its demand for supply met a cold reception in a sceptical House of Commons. In 1626 the difference became obvious. An influential group headed by Sir Dudley Digges, Sir Benjamin Rudyerd, Sir Nathaniel Rich (the earl of Warwick's cousin) and John Pym proposed the establishment of a joint-stock company to finance and direct the sea war so that 'the subject will make the war against the king of Spain, and his Majesty shall have no more to do at sea but to defend the coasts'.[49] This proposal, reflecting the West Indian interests and ambitions which found a vehicle in Warwick's Providence Company after the war, was of course unwelcome to Charles and Buckingham, who thought rather in terms of European objectives and of mobilizing the resources, including the shipping, of the realm to achieve them. Confusion and disagreement about the function and organization of the nation's sea forces thus underlay (along with other political problems) the rift between king and Commons which now developed with the impeachment of Buckingham, Parliament's refusal of supply and its dissolution.

In the event the conduct of the war at sea was based neither upon voluntary collaboration between the Royal Navy and private shipping in the Elizabethan style, nor upon the formal division of labour advocated by the Warwick interest, but on fleets of commandeered merchantmen led by royal ships on the one hand, and random, small-scale privateering, having no connection with official operations, on the other. Numerous but unwilling, the merchant auxiliaries made a poor

[48] Quinn and Ryan, *England's Sea Empire*, p. 233.
[49] Rudyerd's speech, cited in Appleby, 'West Indies', which clarifies the significance of these proposals. See also Thompson, 'Middle group', on the Parliamentary context.

showing in these wars.[50] At Cadiz in 1625 and again at La Rochelle in 1628 they behaved badly, showing no stomach for the fight and deplorable indiscipline. The capital itself set an example to the rest of the country. When asked in January 1626 to contribute five ships towards a fleet of ten to defend the Thames, the City replied that the service was 'not such as concerned them otherwise than the whole kingdom, the defence of which is a regal work'. Later the same year the Council summoned coastal towns to furnish ships, specifying its requirements from each. Nearly everywhere the assessments were resisted by local officials and in the end the government had to make substantial concessions.[51] London, called upon to provide twenty ships, again objected, alleging itself unable to comply, though making clear that many merchants would willingly set forth their ships as privateers. The Council eventually overcame this opposition, but then the City found its own citizens recalcitrant. Finally it placed at Admiral Pennington's disposal the disgraceful force he thus described to Buckingham:

> But every ship wants a good part of their men, and the greatest part of those they have are poor things or skullers, land men and boys... all the ships that are here except three or four are very mean things and such as are not fit for men-of-war... and those few ordnance they have for the most part very mean... wondrous poorly fitted with munition.

Half the three months' service of these ships was spent in idleness, the masters as much as possible steered clear of the French coast, where they were ordered to operate, and several of the crews turned to mutiny, which their captains condoned.[52]

Meanwhile the losses of the English merchant marine from 1625 to 1630 rose to disastrous proportions. It was estimated already in 1628 that 390 ships had been lost to the enemy or by storms, of which 260 alone were worth almost £200,000. Although exhaustive analysis has shown that prizes and prize goods taken by English ships in the course of these wars far exceeded those losses in number and value,[53] most of the captors were powerful merchantmen or private men-of-war, the losers being by and large a different set of people from the winners. Complaints by the former led Parliament to blame Buckingham, as

---

[50] The Cadiz expedition contained 12 king's ships and 73 merchantmen; the Ile de Rhé expedition 14 and 82 respectively: Oppenheim, *Administration*, pp. 251–2.
[51] Alexander, *Charles I's Lord Treasurer*, pp. 110–11.
[52] Wren, 'London and the twenty ships'.
[53] Kepler, 'Ships gained and lost'; the gains figures are corrected in Appleby, 'Privateering', I, 260–88. This estimates between 737 and 1,000 prizes worth £800,000 to £900,000 approximately between September 1625 and November 1630.

SHIPS, MONEY AND POLITICS

Lord High Admiral, but the inability of the Navy to deal with the predators was hardly his fault, as we have seen.[54] At the same time, in 1626, Buckingham lost patience with the Navy Commissioners and appointed a commission of inquiry into the state of the Navy. This body found fault with the ships, the dockyards and the administration. Nineteen of the thirty ships were in need of substantial repair and the ten new ships built since 1618 were particularly criticized. William Burrell, the shipwright responsible for these, became the chief scapegoat, but eventually in 1628 the Commission which had governed the Navy since 1618 was scrapped and the old régime of Principal Officers restored. No doubt the Navy had fallen into a sad state in the last years of the Commission's rule, but to lay the blame on them was all too convenient.[55]

It was left to one of the members of the commission of inquiry, Captain Richard Gifford, to offer a more penetrating and constructive analysis of the ills and needs of the Navy. His 'proposition touching the number etc. of ships for the guarding of the Narrow Seas', submitted in February 1627, argued:

> First, his Majesty's navy, which are 34 sail of ships little and great, must be speedily repaired and made strong, the most of them being at this present very insufficient to be employed in any service, to the great danger of England's safety. And whereas the most part of the said navy are ships of great burthen, though of great strength, yet they are not fit for any offensive service: as to suppress the Dunkirkers, Turks, pirates, etc., or to offend the enemy any way, without having with them some lesser ships of burthen from 300 to 400 tons or thereabouts, the which to be built and made of purpose to be excellent of sail. And to take up merchant ships and colliers, they are as unfit as his Majesty's great ships, in regard they are built altogether for merchandizing and for burthen, yet good for defence but not to offend, because they are not good of sail, as ships of war ought to be, so as by them no service can be performed or expected. And to take up merchants' ships for war may be great hurt to the commonwealth, and unprofitable charge to the king: a discouragement to all men that would build ships, and in conclusion the ready way to decay all shipping, which is the strength of the kingdom.

Thirty ships of 200 to 400 tons should be added to the Navy immediately, he proposed, and more later, in addition to twenty pinnaces of 80 to 100 tons and thirty 'tartans' of 12 to 15 tons, equipped with oars and sail. His Majesty would then have seventy ships of force

---

[54] Gardiner, *Impeachment*, pp. 9–17.
[55] Manwaring and Perrin, *Mainwaring*, I, 146–60; Oppenheim, *Administration*, pp. 259–60.

and thirty small pinnaces, and 'shall have no occasion to be served with merchants' ships and others, except it be upon some defensive or offensive invasion'.[56] To those who argued that merchantmen might serve as well now as in Elizabeth's time, he answered admitting that they were now of greater strength than they were then, 'but not to offend', for the nobility, gentry and merchants then 'did apply themselves much to sea affairs and did set forth ships purposely built for those employments, by which the enemy was much weakened and impoverished, as by the infinite number of prizes which they daily brought into England...But we have no such shipping, nor such affection to sea affairs; neither have we such seamen to put in execution, and few that know the right way to perform any royal service.' Even if merchantmen were good sailers, he added, they would cost as much for a year's hire as the proposed royal vessels would to build, and besides 'many confusions and exclamations would come thereof, as there hath done and still will do till this course be taken'.

Others in the government and the Navy shared Gifford's evident disgust with merchant auxiliaries, as well as his appreciation of the need for a much larger and better balanced Navy, well provided with light warships and pinnaces capable of outsailing or at least matching the Dunkirkers and corsairs. The great problem facing them, however, was to raise the large sums any such programme would require. A year later, in the first quarter of 1628, the government was urgently seeking funds to meet even more pressing demands, and it was in these circumstances of financial crisis that the Council had recourse to a ship-money levy which should be both national in scope and compulsory in form. The demand was not for ships but for money, to be levied on all the counties under the direction of the sheriffs. A yield of £173,411 was expected and was to be used to provide a fleet for the defence of the realm. This scheme thus anticipated in important respects the ship-money levies of 1635 to 1639, though the fiction by which the latter called for actual ships was not employed in 1628. However, the procedure for the levy was almost immediately aborted. The Council having sent letters to the sheriffs and others on 12 February, four days later a proclamation declared the scheme abandoned. Instead, the government now hoped that Parliament, recently summoned for March, would provide. There had hardly been time for opposition to manifest itself in popular protest, but the Council appears to have been

---

[56] SP16/54, fols. 14–30. In addition to the 70 'ships of force' and the 30 small pinnaces, his Majesty would have had the twenty larger pinnaces, which Gifford overlooked in his summary.

unsure how best to deal with its financial difficulties, while events abroad may have induced it to prefer the conventional course to such a hazardous emergency measure.[57]

The pressure of war did bring about some shift in the size and composition of the Royal Navy by 1630. In 1627-8 ten small warships of 180 tons each – the so-called Lion's Whelps – were added to the fleet, which incorporated also a number of prizes. As a result the second La Rochelle expedition of 1628, led by the earl of Lindsey, counted 29 king's ships and 31 merchantmen, a better balance than had been achieved in the earlier fleets. In 1629 the royal force consisted of 53 serviceable and 13 unserviceable vessels totalling 24,388 tons.[58] But this access of strength was in part temporary, in part illusory. By 1632 the total had fallen to 38 ships of about 21,000 tons,[59] and the 10 Whelps, though often in service during this decade, proved disappointing in performance and troublesome to maintain in good repair. The significant legacy of these wars consisted not in *matériel* but in understanding. Those responsible for the Navy, including above all the king, recognized now the need for a more powerful and professional force, less dependent upon auxiliary merchantmen, though regard for prestige kept it still top-heavy with sluggish and over-gunned capital ships. The unsatisfactory performance of ships, commanders and men during the wars had demonstrated the importance of continuous or at least regular service. This must entail large extraordinary expenditure above the routine charges of the Navy and it was unlikely that Parliament would supply such funds unless it also controlled their disposal. This left ship money as a potential source. Charles and his advisers knew well enough how unpopular this had been in the past even when manifestly warranted by war-time need. They would not resort to it without careful preparation and studied presentation, but that they kept in mind the scheme of 1628 is a reasonable assumption. The old form of ship money, involving the contribution of ships by the ports, had caused more trouble than it was worth, whereas the alternative, of imposing the burden on the whole country and using the proceeds for a regular fleet of the king's ships, must have seemed – indeed actually was – fairer and more efficient.

The years of ship money were not happy years for Charles's Navy. Its

[57] Swales, 'Ship-money levy', discusses the circumstances and terms of the 1628 scheme, refuting Gardiner's view that opposition in the country forced its withdrawal. He also argues that the 'fiction' of the 1630s, that ship money was not a tax accountable at Westminster, was not required by a government as yet unhampered by the Petition of Right. [58] SP16/138/73.
[59] Manwaring and Perrin, *Mainwaring*, I, 223.

task – to exercise sea power while avoiding conflict with the belligerents – was difficult and of necessity inglorious, while it inherited chronic problems from its ill-managed and underfunded past. It is not surprising that the administration, the ships, the men, the victuals and the performance of the fleets came in for severe criticism at the time by Charles's own admirals, the men best placed to judge and to express their opinion openly. Their strictures cannot be refuted, but should properly be evaluated in their historical context rather than used as evidence to condemn the current naval régime and its political master. As for the fleets' achievements, historians ought to know better than to repeat uncritically the ignorant or politically motivated complaints of contemporaries that the service did little or nothing to justify the tax.[60]

When the earl of Northumberland, commander of the second ship-money fleet in 1636, reported the defects of the king's ships that year, he protested, first, that some of them were too old and decayed to be of considerable service; secondly, that others required girdling (external double-planking to improve their stability); thirdly, that many were leaky and badly masted; and fourthly that all were furnished with much poor cordage. Of these charges, substantiated in detail by Pennington and others, the last two suggested recent negligence, but the first two concerned a heritage of neglect.[61] Of seven ships said to be beyond repair at any reasonable cost, five had been built for Queen Elizabeth. At least four of these had been 'rebuilt' since, but whatever this meant in practice, the results were apparently unimpressive.[62] Another Elizabethan warship, the *Merhonour* (800 tons), rebuilt in 1612 and the earl of Lindsey's flagship in 1635, was among those described as fit for girdling in 1636. Most of the ships singled out for this treatment, which would render them even more sluggish, had already been faulted as weak, 'crank' (liable to heel over excessively) or otherwise badly built in the inquiry of 1627.[63] Some of the vessels added to the Navy in the last ten years had serious structural defects. The Navy Officers declared in 1637, 'we have had sufficient experience of all the Whelps, which occasioned extraordinary charge to maintain them this long'. The ten Whelps had been built in haste in 1627–8 'of

---

[60] Gardiner's dismissive comments on the results of Lindsey's and Northumberland's cruises, in *History of England*, VII, 390, and VIII, 158, are outdone by Fulton's sarcastic review of operations from 1635 to 1639 in *Sovereignty of the Sea*, pp. 265–74, 295–313, 319–36.
[61] Manwaring and Perrin, *Mainwaring*, I, 246–51; Tanner, *Hollond's Discourses*, pp. 361–406.
[62] The *Assurance* (610 tons) 1603; the *Due Repulse* (764 tons) 1610; the *Defiance* (875 tons) 1612; the *Dreadnought* (450 tons) 1612: Oppenheim, *Administration*, p. 202; Tanner, *Hollond's Discourses*, pp. 361–2; Manwaring and Perrin, *Mainwaring*, I, 234–5.
[63] Manwaring and Perrin, *Mainwaring*, I, 156–7.

mean, sappy timber' and were frequently unfit for service.[64] The *Charles*, built in 1632, required girdling in 1636, and when Pennington tried out the new warship *Unicorn* in 1634 he found her a disgrace to her builders and so dangerous as to be unserviceable unless girdled.[65]

What difference did ship money make to the *matériel* of the Navy? It clearly did not, nor was it intended to create a larger force. In 1634 the king had 42 ships totalling 21,000 tons and in 1642 the figures were 42 and 23,000.[66] The increase is largely accounted for by the addition of the purely prestigious *Sovereign* (1,522 tons) in 1637. Otherwise the royal fleet was improved by the acquisition of 5 very useful pinnaces ranging from 45 to 300 tons, including the *Nicodemus*, a Dunkirk prize whose speed and nimbleness long continued to amaze the rest of the fleet.[67] Ship money did not pay for these additions, but its contribution to the improvement of the king's ships was valuable because it made possible that continuity of operations and experience which exposed the deficiencies and indicated the requirements of the fleet. The inquest demanded by Northumberland, 'these things passing for some years unquestioned', was thus a by-product of ship money.[68] As Oppenheim observed, 'although relatively weaker as regards other powers, England, as far as ships and dockyards were concerned, was stronger absolutely in 1642 than in 1625'.[69] The performance of the Parliamentary Navy amply confirms this judgement, but it is obvious that the advance had not occurred by 1636. It too was a by-product of ship money.

Other major naval problems were less amenable to treatment. The appalling quality of the victuals supplied in 1636, roundly denounced by all the officers questioned, was doubtless bettered in later years, when no similar outburst of complaint on this score appears in the records, but this cannot be taken to imply general satisfaction. As for corruption in the administration and the dockyards, it could not have been appreciably reduced by anything other than a transformation in naval finance and in attitudes to office. As the best modern authority

---

[64] *CSPD 1637*, pp. 350–1. In July 1641 five of them were unfit: BL, Additional MSS, 9300, fol. 64. [65] *CSPD 1634–5*, p. 13.
[66] Manwaring and Perrin, *Mainwaring*, I, 223–5; Powell and Timings, *Documents*, pp. 7–8 (1642 survey).
[67] The new pinnaces were the *Providence*, *Expedition*, *Greyhound*, *Roebuck* and *Nicodemus*. The captain and company of this last reported her 'the most absolute sailer in the world. She runs from every ship she sees as a greyhound from a little dog': *CSPD 1636-7*, p. 498. The *Swan*, another Dunkirk prize, also much admired, was lost in 1638: Oppenheim, *Administration*, pp. 254, 258. [68] Manwaring and Perrin, *Mainwaring*, I, 251.
[69] Oppenheim, *Administration*, p. 295.

on such matters has said, 'there is little to show that Northumberland succeeded in stamping out the long-standing abuses which he and earlier critics had remarked. Indeed, disillusioned by the Admiralty commissioners' tepid response to his efforts, he told Wentworth that: "This proceeding hath brought me to a resolution not to trouble myself any more with endeavouring a reformation unless I be commanded to it".'[70] Soon after he became Lord High Admiral in 1638 his secretary, Thomas Smith, was busy with the traffic in naval jobs.[71]

In respect of manning, the ship-money fleets encountered difficulties worse than the usual because these were, at least until 1640, years of remarkable prosperity for England's merchant shipping, while the demand for seamen by foreign navies was also very strong. The king offered wages well below the rates paid by private owners, and seamen had not forgotten the miseries of the recent wars, when deprivation of clothing, food, pay and health had taught them to hate the royal service. Called upon to provide large numbers of men, the prestmasters were only too ready to accept tips from able mariners, replacing them with poor, unskilled men whom captains had often to dismiss as useless. Northumberland's commanders in 1636 complained bitterly of this: 'I never saw a ship so meanly manned as the *Unicorn*', Sir Henry Mainwaring reported; 'scarce a seafaring man except the officers; men of poor and wretched person, without clothes, or ability of body, tradesmen, some that were never at sea.'[72] Captain Carteret said that nearly a third of the men in the *Entrance* had never been to sea in a ship, and that among 150 of them there were not twelve, apart from the officers, capable of taking a turn at the helm.[73] Others reported in the same vein. During the following years, however, there is no evidence that the ship-money fleets faced manning problems of the same order, and it may well be that until the yield of the levy declined in 1640 the flow of funds helped the Navy to crew its ships more adequately.

Judgements of the ship-money Navy have too often rested more or less exclusively on the evidence of the 1636 inquiry. The period from 1635 to 1641 as a whole gives the impression, rather, of a force gradually gaining in efficiency in spite of those old evils which would continue to plague the Navy for generations to come. Regular active service encouraged the emergence of a corps of professional com-

---

[70] Aylmer, 'Attempts at reform', pp. 238–9.
[71] Ibid., and compare *CSPD 1637–8*, pp. 356, 609; *CSPD 1638–9*, pp. 21, 465, 491–3. Oppenheim, *Administration*, p. 286.   [72] Manwaring and Perrin, *Mainwaring*, I 248–9.
[73] Tanner, *Hollond's Discourses*, p. 381.

manders and ships' officers, and above all the state fleets depended now far less than formerly on the aid of merchantmen. Lindsey's fleet in 1635 consisted of 19 royal warships, 5 large Londoners and a ketch; Northumberland's in 1636 of 24 royal ships and 3 Londoners; in 1637 he commanded a fleet of 19 royal ships and 9 merchantmen, while Rainborowe sailed for Sallee with 2 royal warships and 2 Londoners, to be reinforced later with the 2 royal pinnaces built for the occasion and 2 men-of-war from Northumberland's fleet. The 1638 fleet under Pennington comprised 24 royal ships and 7 merchantmen, and in 1639 he began with 18 of the former and only one of the latter, to be reinforced belatedly by 10 more of each in September and October, the extra merchantmen being stayed in the Downs for service there. The following year 21 royal ships were commissioned and in 1641 Pennington commanded a force of 15 of the king's men-of-war and 10 merchantmen.[74] In addition to these 'summer guard' fleets a skeleton 'winter guard' kept the seas from October to March.

In their appraisal of the services rendered by these forces, naval authorities who have studied the matter have for the most part declined to endorse the derogatory phrases of Whig historians.[75] Contemporaries were of course divided and critics were to be found even in the Navy. Pennington, for example, confided to his friend Nicholas in August 1635 his hope that next year's fleet 'may do more than the present fleet has done, or the money were as well saved as spent'.[76] This, however, he probably meant to imply criticism of Lindsey, whom he held in low esteem, rather than of the government's naval policy, for he greeted the choice of Lindsey's successor with enthusiasm for both the man and the service.[77] Pennington in any case acknowledged himself a plain sailor and no statesman.[78] On the international importance of the Royal Navy at this time Sir Kenelm Digby was better qualified to judge: 'in all which', he wrote to Sir John Coke from Paris in September 1635, 'our master will have a power to keep the balance even, if he keep a fleet at sea and his Navy in that reputation it now is in; for I assure your honour that it is very great, and although my lord of Lindsey do no more than sail up and down, yet the very setting of our best fleet to sea is the greatest service that I believe hath been done the king these many years'.[79] Lindsey's

[74] Manwaring and Perrin, *Mainwaring*, I, 231, 234–5, 254–5, 262–3, 269, 280, 288, 291–2.
[75] 'No doubt the English ship-money fleets were taken very seriously abroad, and so far justified their existence': *Monson's Tracts*, III, 273. See also Manwaring and Perrin, *Mainwaring*, I, 233, 246, 263–4, 292–3; and Quinn and Ryan, *England's Sea Empire*, p. 238: 'they seem to have done a real service'. [76] *CSPD 1635*, p. 316. [77] *CSPD 1635–6*, p. 259.
[78] *CSPD 1637*, p. 519. [79] *Cowper MSS*, II, 95.

cruise was certainly no 'fiasco'.[80] The aim of Dutch and French operations in 1635 was to take control of the Narrow Seas with a view to blockading or even capturing Dunkirk, cutting the sea-route between Flanders and Spain and so threatening to overrun the Spanish Netherlands. The English fleet effectively prevented this by keeping the French out of the Channel. Latter-day Whig historians chose to ridicule Lindsey and his fleet because they deplored its political objectives.

Neither Lindsey nor his successors could do much to check piracy and the disorders of Dutch, French, Dunkirker and Biscayner raiders in the waters over which Charles claimed sovereignty. The fleets they commanded were neither large nor flexible enough to cope with the widespread and rising spate of depredations by ships designed for marauding. In this respect Rainborowe's expedition was the only considerable success. Otherwise the main functions of the Navy were to demonstrate English sea power by showing the flag and exacting the salute and, more practically, to exert its strength and return a profit to the king in two specific ways: by imposing licences upon Dutch herring busses in the North Sea, and by convoying shipping, particularly ships carrying bullion, troops, munitions of war and other supplies, to the Flanders ports.

To assert sovereignty over British seas in respect of fishing rights was from the first an important object of the ship-money fleets. The nationalistic sentiment that the Dutch should be made to pay for their insolence in virtually monopolizing that rich resource was reinforced by the Crown's hunger for revenue. Lindsey had no opportunity to implement this policy, but in 1636 Northumberland was instructed to compel the busses to take and pay for licences, and had some success in doing so. The financial yield of his North Sea operations – a mere £500 – made but a trifling contribution to his Majesty's income, but the Dutch were duly alarmed by the prospect of having in future to pay regularly and much more heavily for the harvest which sustained their entire maritime economy. The issue thus at once became an important bargaining counter in Anglo-Dutch relations. With a fleet in being, Charles could threaten to inflict the toll or graciously refrain from inflicting it. In 1637, however, in his anxiety at that juncture not to offend the Dutch but at the same time to have their money, he ineptly threw away his advantage by sending a solitary merchantman to sell licences to six or seven hundred busses convoyed by twenty-three Dutch men-of-war. The unfortunate English commander was sent

---

[80] Davies, *Early Stuarts*, p. 217, repeating Fulton's description of the first ship-money fleet.

SHIPS, MONEY AND POLITICS

packing and Charles's claim to sovereignty of the sea suddenly appeared unreal.[81]

The truth is that Charles did not lack considerable sea power: what he lacked was the will to use it decisively, because he could not afford war. After 1637 this became still more evident as he became embroiled in the Scottish troubles, leading to the rebellion of 1639, while simultaneously other powers stepped up their maritime strength, leaving the Royal Navy relatively weak. The intensification of the struggle for control of the Narrow Seas in 1638 and 1639 on the other hand magnified the opportunities and importance of England's shipping in the supply of Spain's Netherlands and provided the ship-money fleets of those years with a useful income from convoy duties, since the Dutch for their part forbade their blockading men-of-war to challenge the king's ships.[82] The States had to be careful at this juncture to avoid presenting Charles with a *casus belli* and so aligning the Royal Navy with Spain, which was now preparing its great offensive to achieve mastery in northern waters and to reinforce the army of Flanders. Yet equally they could not ignore the increasingly valuable role of English merchantmen as carriers in Spain's service. In the summer of 1639, therefore, as part of the campaign to counter Spain's impending assault, they deployed a strong fleet off Portland and thereabouts to intercept the expected armada and incidentally to check neutrals for contraband, particularly Spanish troops. Pennington, recalled from the Scottish coast to the Downs with only part of the fleet, heard in June from Smith that 'the Hollanders begin to be bold in our seas, and lie about Portland with 50 sail, examining and searching all English ships'.[83] The English admiral knew that with his small force he could do nothing to stop this, and when M. H. Tromp, commanding the Dutch fleet, removed over a thousand soldiers from certain English merchantmen, politely leaving aboard large sums of money allegedly consigned to English merchants, Pennington pointed out to Charles's indignant mouthpiece, Windebank, that Tromp was fairly exercising a reasonable belligerent right. Furthermore, he added, 'before we seek reparation of that which is so ill resented, it behoves us to have a mastering strength for fear of a greater loss and dishonour, for they are very strong here in the Narrow Seas at present'.[84]

The drama which then unfolded, culminating in the destruction of the Spanish armada in the Downs in October, has been well told

---
[81] Fulton, *Sovereignty of the Sea*, pp. 291–324; Edmundson, *Anglo-Dutch Rivalry*, pp. 108–18.
[82] Israel, *Dutch Republic*, p. 267; *CSPD 1638-9*, pp. 21, 465, 492; *CSPD 1639*, pp. 273, 275.
[83] *CSPD 1639*, p. 292.   [84] *CSPD 1639*, p. 390.

elsewhere. No shame should attach to the king's ships for the part they played in it. As the best authority on this affair has declared, 'no impartial reader can peruse the accounts...without coming to the conclusion that the English admiral did his best under very difficult circumstances'.[85] After bruising engagements with Tromp in the Channel in mid-September, Oquendo's armada limped into the Downs to seek refuge, soon to be followed by the relentless Hollander, determined now to blockade and finally to crush the enemy. During the next four weeks, while Tromp built up an overwhelming superiority preparatory to his onslaught, Pennington took pains to warn him to respect the neutrality of the road. His own force consisted of a mere ten royal ships and a similar number of merchantmen detained *ad hoc* in the Downs, much against their will. Like his men, who cheered the Dutch sailors on when battle broke, Pennington was no friend to Spain, but he kept the foreign fleets apart and strictly ordered his captains to attack any ships which broke the peace in the king's chamber. Nor was his thankless task made easier by King Charles, who decided to use the Spaniards' predicament to extort money – to the tune of £150,000 – and support for his nephew's Palatinate claim as the price for saving them from Tromp's guns. At the same time Smith advised Pennington that, since Northumberland could not get his Majesty to declare his resolution, 'I doubt not but you will do your best, but if you be opposed by a greater power, I know not what you can do...And for your opposing them by way of defending the Spaniards, very able men are of opinion that no man can expect it from you, but you should seem to make a show of assisting them.' He went on to warn Pennington to expect 'some check for neglecting their preservation, but that will be quickly taken off'.[86]

A week later Northumberland himself instructed the luckless admiral that when the Dutch attacked he should come to the aid of the Spaniards if they put up such an effective defence that his help might 'make their party good...Otherwise you must make as handsome a retreat as you can in so unlucky a business. More particular instructions than these I cannot get for you.'[87] Events turned out much as these gentlemen expected: Tromp routed the armada and Pennington offered a token resistance by firing a few shots at the Dutch, who ignored them. In fact Oquendo had managed before this to get his squadron of thirteen Dunkirkers away with some third of the infantry and all the bullion, to be joined after the battle by some more of the

[85] Boxer, *Tromp's Journal*, pp. 53, 63, *et passim*.   [86] *CSPD 1639*, p. 538.
[87] *CSPD 1639–40*, p. 19.

armada vessels and eventually by many more soldiers shipped over from England, so that Tromp's triumph was not quite such a disaster for Spain as it seemed at the time.[88] Pennington of course took the blame for allowing to happen what he could not have prevented, but survived to recover his Majesty's favour, as Smith had predicted.

This episode damaged the king's reputation more than that of his Navy. It certainly exploded Charles's pretension to sovereignty of the sea, but it did not disgrace the fleet, which served him better than he served it on this occasion as on others before. The need for naval rearmament and reform was widely recognized in his reign. It was forced onto the financial and political agenda in the first half of the seventeenth century by the development of the capital warship on the one hand and the expansion of the merchant marine on the other, changes which were not peculiar to England but international in scope, producing a race for sea power which would continue throughout this century and beyond. The naval disasters of the 1620s made the matter urgent at a time when the government was least capable of dealing with it, for the race required not simply ships, guns and seamen, but great financial resources and solid political strength. Charles's lack of these was so conspicuous that he found it difficult to exploit even the limited power he managed to create, for his feet of clay were clearly visible to those he sought to impress. He took immense trouble to produce the ship-money fleets, juggling together a variety of motives and arguments, good, bad and indifferent, driving ministers, judges, sheriffs and the rest with uncharacteristic persistence and energy to provide the money. Those fleets did win the nation a significant role in Europe until the political collapse of 1639 and, although they never came near imposing sovereignty over British seas, they notably assisted the remarkable success of England's merchant shipping in those years. When finally in the Downs this naval strength was put to the test the immediate circumstances and Charles's discreditable conduct produced an impression of impotence which did not fairly reflect the prevailing balance of sea power.

Ship money provided the king with a fleet which was more emphatically royal than the Navy had been since the days of Henry VIII. By dispensing to a large extent with merchant auxiliaries it gave the Navy a more distinct identity and professional pride, while associating it closely with the person of the monarch. Charles personally directed not only the devising and administration of ship money, but also the employment of the fleets and the appointment of commanders.

[88] Stradling, 'Catastrophe and recovery', p. 213.

SHIP MONEY: ITS PURPOSES AND USES

The effects of his princely control and intervention were manifest in lamentable episodes such as the attempt and failure to license the Dutch herring fleet. They were felt in the social snobbery which divided his officers and surfaced, for example, in Rainborowe's expedition. They contributed to the unfriendly attitude of many ships' masters to the royal service. It would of course be unfair to attribute these unfortunate events and developments to the king's influence alone, but it undoubtedly aggravated them. Moreover it was in considerable measure Charles's fault that his treasured creation depended upon a deeply unpopular tax, the resistance to which came to express all the various discontents, reasonable or unreasonable, of many of his subjects. It must not be forgotten that the ship-money fleets, whatever their naval merits and usefulness abroad, were equally if not more valuable to Charles at home, since they enabled him to pass on to his subjects the greater part of his necessary defence expenditure without recourse to Parliament – at least for several years. Such was the fundamental ambiguity of ship money from its inception in 1634 until its abolition in 1641.

Nevertheless this Navy, so much the king's own instrument, fashioned and wielded by him, may be seen in perspective as a significant step in the direction of a state Navy. The provision and exercise of substantial operating fleets over a period of seven years produced a real revival of England's sea power, even though this was overshadowed by Dutch dominance and Dunkirk's offensive capability. These, after all, were forces mounted with extreme effort in a maritime struggle for survival, whereas the modest progress of the Royal Navy occurred in peace-time, when even the maintenance of a fleet in being was a remarkable achievement. Above all, ship money made possible an advance in the structure of the nation's maritime forces, quickening the evolution of a regular state service apart from the merchant marine, more efficient and fitter to respond to a variety of needs. This was a gradual process and the decisive step was yet to come, under the Commonwealth and Protectorate, but Cromwell's Navy was a development of the Navy Parliament inherited from Charles.[89]

[89] Capp, *Cromwell's Navy*.

CHAPTER 7

WILLIAM RAINBOROWE AND THE SALLEE ROVERS

THE EXPEDITION to Sallee in 1637, led by William Rainborowe, has usually been accepted as standing to the credit of the Caroline Navy, providing at least some justification for the ship-money levies, since it was a tolerably well-conducted attempt to realize their ostensible purpose – the security of English shipping. It failed of course to stem the rising tide of public resistance to what was regarded as an illegal tax, and in the political storm which followed it was soon forgotten, seldom thereafter to be recalled and never adequately explained.[1] It was after all a side-show. Its obscure commander could claim no glorious victory and within a short time the plague of Sallee piracy raged worse than before. In the long history of the Barbary corsairs and the vain efforts of European powers to repress their continual depredations it was only a passing episode. Yet this is a story worth telling because in various ways it typifies the long-term difficulties of North African piracy for European seafarers and their governments, bringing home the grim reality experienced by numerous seamen and their families, and illustrating the tangled web of commercial, naval and political constraints and pressures which affected the determination and execution of royal policy.

Major changes occurred in the scale and character of piracy in the first quarter of the seventeenth century. Single vessels or units of two or three, which prevailed before, now gave place to fleets of marauders, while not only in the Mediterranean but in the Atlantic as well the so-

[1] Among modern authorities Gardiner, *History of England*, v, 270 and Oppenheim, *Administration*, pp. 277–8, deal briefly with the episode. Chaplin, 'William Rainsborough' is valuable on the personnel but brief and inaccurate on the events. R. Coindreau, *Corsaires* is good on the context but quite brief on Rainborowe's expedition. Two fine studies of Sallee may be found in Castries, *France*, III, 187–98: 'Les Moriscos à Salé et Sidi el-Ayachi'; and *Pays-Bas*, v, i–xxviii: 'Les trois républiques du Bou Regreg'. The Barbary corsairs have been the subject of a large, and largely indifferent, literature, but there is a good bibliography of more serious works in Julien, *North Africa*.

160

called Barbary corsairs came to dominate the sea. The English experience of piracy changed dramatically at the same time. Formerly predators rather than prey, they now became victims acquainted with suffering and grief. In the transition period of twelve years or so following the Anglo-Spanish peace of 1603 Englishmen played a leading part in the expansion of piracy, operating from bases in Ireland and Atlantic Morocco, and some of them turned Turk, taking their skills to Algiers, Tunis, Mamora and other North African centres. In doing so they transformed the offensive capability of the Barbary corsairs by enabling them to employ sailing ships and ordnance.[2] By 1620 the Algerines were regularly invading the Atlantic in fast, well-armed ships, snapping up small merchantmen and fishing craft of all European nationalities, and even before that date they were joined by a new breed of pirates from the Moroccan Atlantic harbour of Sallee.[3]

By the beginning of Charles's reign Salleemen constituted the main threat to English shipping, haunting particularly the westerly waters of the English Channel, the Scillies and the Bristol Channel throughout the spring and summer months. At the end of April 1625 the governor of the Scilly Isles reported the presence of a Sallee man-of-war of 230 tons and 32 guns, accompanied by eight lesser vessels operating off the West Country coasts, and warned that at Sallee twenty more were ready to reinforce them.[4] A week later from St Ives came news of thirty Salleemen on that coast, taking from their prizes only men: 'we have been affrighted by them, fearing their landing by night among us... we have the greater cause to fear because we hear of no defence present, the king's majesty's ships being not upon the coast to fear them'.[5] At the same time an English mariner described how he had been captured from a Dutch vessel (the Dutch crew being allowed to proceed), taken to Sallee and forthwith compelled to join a Sallee rover under an English master with four other Englishmen, five Flemish renegades and thirty 'Turks and Moors'. They operated as slave-raiders, taking the 'choicest' seamen only and planning to 'fetch Christians from the shore'.[6] Later in May the mayor of Weymouth informed the Privy Council that Sallee pirates lay so ordinarily off Land's End and the Scillies that 'our shipping dare not to pass that way', divers ships and barks of late having been taken and their men removed 'into most

[2] On English piracy in the early years of the seventeenth century, see Senior, *Nation of Pirates*.
[3] The most common English form in the seventeenth century, though 'Sally' and 'Salley' occur often.
[4] SP16/1, fol. 134.   [5] SP16/2, fol. 78.
[6] SP16/2, fol. 82.

miserable captivity', being treated 'worse by much than they were wont to be used in Argier' and held for impossibly high ransoms.[7]

The depredations continued throughout that summer. In August the mayor of Plymouth wrote in desperation to the Council about 'the daily losses which we and our neighbours have received by the Turkish ships of Salley, who have taken from us within one year now last past, besides ships and goods, to the number of 1,000 mariners and sailors at least...and we do much fear, if there be no other course taken than there is as yet, that his majesty will shortly have very few mariners and sailors left in these parts to do him service'. In the last ten days Looe alone had lost eighty mariners bound on fishing voyages, while the enemy had taken twenty-seven other vessels and two hundred men. Sir Francis Stewart, the admiral recently sent to protect the coast, had dispatched five ships to chase them, 'but could not come near them, the said ships being far better sailers'.[8] Such complaints had already reached the House of Commons, where Buckingham, as Lord High Admiral, was held responsible, to whom the luckless Stewart penned his lengthy excuses, blaming the weather, 'thick and hawsey', sickness among his men, leaky ships, Flemish freebooters who supplied the rovers with men, munitions, victuals and stores, and even the fishermen themselves, who 'go scattering both outwards and homewards bound by twos and threes and single to make the best of their market as they term it'. 'These picaroons', he concluded, 'will ever lie hankering upon our coast and the state will find it both chargeable and difficult to clear it or secure the Newfoundland fishermen from them, unless it be directly resolved to sack Salley.'[9] In effect, he had been assigned inadequate means for a virtually impossible task. Others later were to find similar reasons for advocating the alternative course of action.

During this campaign of slave-raiding the Salleemen held Lundy Island for a fortnight and landed in Mounts Bay on a Sunday to take seventy men, women and children from a church.[10] Towards the end of the year, two separate sources estimated that British prisoners in Sallee numbered 1,500, and similar figures occur in further independent reports in May and August 1626.[11] After some investigation Trinity House considered there were 1,200 to 1,400 in March of that year, when a petition of seamen's wives pleaded for the redemption of 'near 2,000 poor mariners' held there.[12] Even allowing for the usual element

---

[7] SP16/2, fol. 150.   [8] SP16/5, fol. 78.
[9] SP16/5, no. 49, printed in Gardiner, *Impeachment*, pp. 9–12.   [10] SP16/5, fol. 143.
[11] Castries, *Angleterre*, II, 592–4; SP16/27, fols. 127–8; SP16/34, fol. 111.
[12] Harris, *Transactions*, no. 261; Castries, *Angleterre*, III, 1–3.

of exaggeration, it seems likely that at least 1,000 English captives remained at Sallee during the winter of 1625–6. One of them, Robert Adams, wrote to his father describing the conditions: 'my patron made me work at a mill like a horse from morning until night with chains upon my legs of 36 pounds weight apiece, my meat nothing but a little coarse bread and water, my lodging in a dungeon underground, where some 150 or 200 of us lay together...here are some 1,500 Englishmen in as bad case as myself'.[13] Others reported similar treatment, as well as the use of torture to extract ransom.[14]

Adams put the number of Sallee men-of-war at forty and upwards. Rainborowe twelve years later reported forty to fifty, of which twenty had from ten to twenty pieces of artillery. An English sailor who was captive there in 1635 thought Sallee then had thirty-six.[15] Apart from a few so-called great ships, which were large, well-armed caravels of 100 to 200 tons or more, the majority were small, light caravels and similar craft, carrying few guns. All were very shallow, as they had to be to negotiate the entrance to their own harbour, and consequently nimble and fast, combining sails and oars. These 'picaroons' were crammed with men armed to the teeth with scimitars, pistols and other hand weapons, for these were boarding parties. Fighting men, distinct from the sailing crew, they comprised not Turks but Moriscos of Spanish origin and some native Moroccans. The sailing crew on the other hand consisted for the most part of unarmed Christian slaves, led by a handful of renegade seamen, whose services as masters and craftsmen of the sea remained indispensable. Among these the most notorious were the Dutch *raïs*, Claes Gerritz Compaen and Jan Jansz, pirate admirals and organizers. The commanders and ships' officers were usually European renegades unlikely to desert, while the slaves were chained together before any engagement.[16]

Salleemen did not normally operate in the Mediterranean, but confined their attentions to the Atlantic, where they appeared in the 1610s as newcomers alongside the more numerous Algerines. At first they concentrated their attack upon their Spanish enemies, behaving like true corsairs rather than pirates, but in the early 1620s they widened their range, moving north to prey upon French and English shipping and especially to ravage the western Channel. Here since the late sixteenth century the West Country ports had been flourishing on the Newfoundland fishery trade, which by 1625 was employing some 250

---

[13] Castries, *Angleterre*, II, 591–2.   [14] Harris, *Transactions*, nos. 213, 228.
[15] Castries, *Angleterre*, III, 282; *CSPD 1635–6*, p. 303.
[16] Coindreau, *Corsaires*, pp. 56–68; Castries, *Pays-Bas*, v, xiii–xiv.

vessels and 5,000 fishermen yearly.[17] By this time too Salleemen outnumbered Algerines in these waters, where they could rove extensively, even across the Atlantic to raid the fishery, for they managed to subsist on very little and could on occasion pick up provisions in Holland. In the Newfoundland fishing fleet of the West Country the Salleemen found their ideal prey: defenceless, small vessels well manned with experienced seafaring men. The return ladings of fish were doubtless welcome, but men constituted the main target, both as manpower for cruising and as bargaining counters. Individually they might yield ransom and collectively they might be exchanged for arms, trade agreements and so forth. These were men England could ill afford to lose. The wars with France and Spain from 1625 to 1629 plunged the West Country fish trade into chaos as the main markets collapsed, sailings were stayed and seamen conscripted for the disastrous expeditions to Cadiz and La Rochelle. The loss of hundreds of seamen to the corsairs in 1625 and again in 1626 came as a body blow to an industry stricken with multiple adversity. But the Crown's own demand for seamen for the wars was an even more serious matter for the government, which was often reminded that the potential as well as the actual captives were particularly precious and useful subjects of his Majesty, above all at this critical juncture, though the argument retained some force in later years.[18]

West Country seamen, merchants, mayors and MPs had reason to complain to the Council and to the Commons that the Lord High Admiral provided them with no effective defence against the raiders. The Royal Navy had indeed been reformed and strengthened since Sir John Coke and Buckingham took charge in 1618, but neither the old nor the new generation of king's ships was built to chase pirates. As Nathaniel Knott observed in his 'advice' of 1634 concerning the Barbary corsairs, 'he that knoweth the Turks' ships can tell you that they are the chosen sailers of Europe...Our English built are indeed strong and well enough contrived for fight, but so bound with timbers that they are but indifferent sailers the best of them. If the worse be chosen, as soon may you catch a hare with a caber (as the vulgar adage is) as surprise as Turk.'[19] The Admiralty was slow to recognize the protection of merchant shipping as its proper duty and reluctant to address the widely appreciated need for faster, handier men-of-war, those 'lighter ships and nimble and prime sailers' for which Nathaniel

---

[17] Cell, *Newfoundland*, pp. 100, 107.
[18] Richardson, *Roe's Negotiations*, pp. 572–4: Roe to Privy Council, 20/30 November 1626.
[19] BL, Harleian MSS, 6893, fols. 20–1.

Butler called.[20] The naval commission of 1618 feebly advised that 'when there is need of small ships they may be had from merchants'.[21] When at last in the later 1620s something had to be done to check the onslaught of Dunkirkers and Barbary corsairs, the Navy produced the ten so-called Whelps, which proved by and large inadequate for those purposes. English shipbuilders were evidently unable to match the Dunkirk privateer or the Sallee pirate. Patrols of the western Channel and Irish Sea became more or less regular from around 1620, but the few and cumbersome vessels assigned to these duties could achieve little, even when the Navy acquired direct and generous funding in the form of ship money.

Sallee, the source of all this trouble, lay at the mouth of the Bou Regreg, where stand today the cities of Sale on the north bank and Rabat, capital of Morocco, on the south. In the seventeenth century also there were two distinct cities: the ancient foundation of Old Sallee to the north, and the twelfth-century city of Rabat, often called New Sallee, to the south. The former was an ordinary Moroccan town, staunchly Moslem, strong in tradition. The latter was dominated by a magnificent castle, the Kasba, guarding the mouth of the estuary, but at the beginning of the century the grounds of this imposing citadel were occupied only by a royal governor and a score of soldiers, overlooking an almost empty town. Sallee had a barred harbour, protected by a great sandbank, behind which dangerous shoals made entrance to the port virtually impossible for ordinary ships without a pilot. Once inside, however, ships could find deep water and anchorage by the south bank. It was a ready-made nest for pirates, but little used as such until the arrival of those who proved themselves worthy of the site – the Hornacheros.[22]

They came from Hornachos in Estremadura, an extraordinary clan of Moriscos, faithful, in defiance of all edicts, to Islam and Moorish custom, fierce and unscrupulous in resisting interference and in dominating their neighbours, Christian or Moslem. Already before the official expulsion of the Moriscos from Spain in 1609 they emigrated to Morocco, taking their weapons and gold with them, and were encouraged by Mulay Zidan, the ruling sherif, to repair and garrison the Kasba of Sallee. Soon they gathered to their stronghold many of the other Moriscos who had found refuge in Morocco. These, generally

[20] Butler, *Dialogues*, pp. 250–6.   [21] McGowan, *Jacobean Commissions*, p. 288.
[22] See p. 166 for a contemporary chart of the Bou Regreg. The frequently cited Dan, *Histoire*, though strictly contemporary, is sketchy and inaccurate on Sallee.

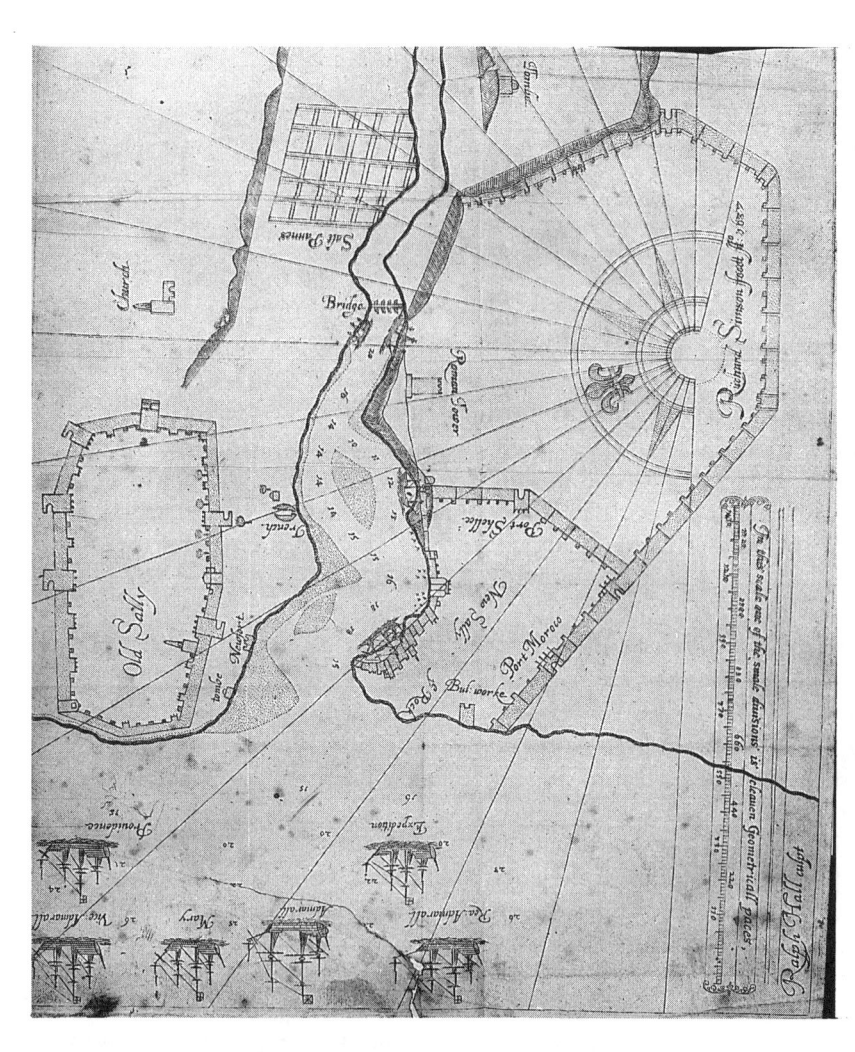

Richard Simson's chart of Sallee, 1637, printed in John Dunton, *A True Journal of the Sally Fleet* (1637) from the copy in the British Library.

called Andalos, were Spanish-speaking, unlike the haughty Hornacheros, and hispanized in varying degree. Despised by the masters of the Kasba, poor and inferior, they settled below them in the town of New Sallee, where they were joined by a motley collection of pirates ousted from nearby Mamora by the Spaniards. New Sallee was thus an alien enclave, surrounded by distrustful and hostile tribes, an exotic and composite society of discordant elements united only by their common interest in piracy.

For a time the Hornacheros deferred to the sherif, grudgingly paying the 10 per cent he claimed on their prizes and captives. But since the death of the great Mulay Ahmed al-Mansur in 1603 the kingdom of Morocco had fallen into anarchy. At Marrakech his son and chief heir, Mulay Zidan, reigned with declining authority over a country divided, a prey to warring factions, insubordinate local governors and upstart marabouts, self-appointed and ambitious champions of the Holy War. Among the latter stood out the impressive figure of Sidi al-Ayachi. The most dedicated and respected of the *mujahedin*, he had at his command many thousand fighting men and scarcely concealed his contempt for the sherif whose interests he pretended to serve. It was with his support that the Hornacheros, already wealthy and powerful from the management of piracy, finally in 1627 expelled the sherif's governor and constituted themselves a virtually independent republic. With their governor and council the English agent in Morocco, John Harrison, negotiated terms of peace in May of that year, a month after their *coup d'état*.

Charles and his government had little room for manœuvre. They had hoped in 1625 to have Moroccan co-operation after taking Cadiz, but the ignominious failure of that expedition ruined English prestige. The Anglo-Moroccan alliance had been meaningful in the days of Queen Elizabeth and Mulay al-Mansur, two strong rulers with compatible anti-Spanish aims. The flourishing sugar trade conducted by the Barbary Company reinforced the common interests of the two states and provided convenient cover for a substantial trade in arms.[23] Now the sherif wielded so little power in his own country that his alliance was as worthless as the ruined sugar industry, while the king of England, at odds with his own people and desperately short of money, waged disastrous wars with Europe's two great powers. The anarchic condition of Morocco contributed much to the rise of the Sallee rovers, just as English vulnerability at sea presented them with startling gains.

[23] Willan, *Studies*; Castries, *Angleterre*, III, 31.

In 1627, when the Hornacheros asserted their independence, Sallee became an Atlantic power which others had to treat as such, however distasteful this might be.

But treating with such a piratical power was no easy matter. Concessions made from weakness would certainly encourage renewed threats and attacks designed to win more concessions, unless England could emulate the Dutch, gaining exemption at the expense of others by becoming the pirates' friend. Even so, could the corsairs be trusted to keep their side of such a bargain? The answer was obviously no, but Charles was under pressure from domestic interests to reach some accommodation. The seamen and their clamorous women might have small influence, but they were backed by a considerable shipping interest represented by Trinity House, which had both mercantile and naval affiliations, and by the fishing interest, which carried the entire West Country with it. These elements wanted action to arrest the growing spate of shipping and manpower losses, which also directly sapped the state's own naval resources. Protests resounded in Parliament and when Buckingham was impeached one of the charges brought against him was that he had failed to guard the sea.[24] Nothing much could be done in existing circumstances to repress or eliminate the pirates; the only feasible course was that of appeasement, which might bring not only some respite from the intolerable raiding, but some sorely needed advantage in the European struggle. The state was not in principle averse to bargaining with pirates: had it not so bargained again and again with men like Henry Mainwaring, offering pardons – and even in his case preferment – in exchange for little more than repentance?[25]

When, therefore, Harrison, who had undertaken repeated missions to Morocco for the Crown since 1610, brought overtures from al-Ayachi and the Hornacheros in 1626, these were well received. Initially, indeed, Harrison was commissioned not only to exchange arms for prisoners, but to convey royal goodwill and to offer trade in return for the cessation of hostilities. In the event objections by Sir Henry Marten, Judge of the Admiralty, to such compromising terms caused all specific reference to trade and hostilities to be dropped, but the general purport remained the same. Harrison duly reached Sallee in the spring of 1627 with guns and munitions and secured the release of about 190 captives. In a draft treaty each side agreed to permit the other's ships to trade and revictual in its ports and to refrain from molesting them at sea, though

---

[24] Gardiner, *Impeachment*, pp. 9–17.
[25] Manwaring and Perrin, *Mainwaring*, I, 1–34; Senior, *Nation of Pirates*, pp. 40–1, 70–2.

the English conceded the right of Salleemen to remove 'enemy' goods from English vessels. Each side was to assist the other against its enemies.[26] This treaty was not ratified by Charles, for Sir Henry Marten again objected, pointing out that Sallee was in rebellion against the recognized ruler of Morocco and that an alliance with pirates was dishonourable to his Majesty. Charles's letters to Sidi al-Ayachi and the governors of Sallee were accordingly evasive, but their essential message was one of accord.[27]

Appeasement continued to be the government's policy so long as the war with Spain lasted. In 1628 Barbary protests against allegedly hostile acts by certain English ships evoked a proclamation promising condign punishment to anyone offering violence to vessels of the Barbary ports, including Sallee, and for the remainder of the war English privateers were required to give bonds not to harm such ships.[28] As the war petered out, however, peace being finally concluded in November 1630, relations deteriorated. From Sallee in August of that year came strong complaint about 'the many offences committed by vessels of your Majesty's subjects against those of this port', referring to the demands of the aggrieved for arrest of English merchants' goods in reprisal.[29] Matters came to a head in May 1631 when Captain John Maddock in the *William and John* of London captured a Sallee man-of-war and sold her with her crew in Cadiz, the men being enslaved. Fury raged in Sallee when the news broke and Harrison, sympathetic as ever to the corsairs, was horrified. He had apparently issued this pirate (and presumably others) with a certificate of protection referring to the proclamation of 1628, but 'Maddock took my certificate and wiped his tail with it...I am afraid but too many will have cause to curse Maddock; I am sure some do already, sold for slaves as heretofore, and ships preparing as fast as can be to bring in more, and yet but little care, for aught I see, on our part to prevent.'[30]

What Harrison described as Maddock's 'mad act' was deplored and denounced by many who suffered the consequences in due course, but it expressed an attitude common among those who sailed England's more powerful merchantmen. These, equipped during the wars with letters of marque or venturing forth as men-of-war, deferred only to the king's ships, and not always to those. They were neither afraid nor enamoured of Barbary corsairs who made a habit of enslaving their fellow seamen. Normally corsairs steered sufficiently clear, but as the

[26] Castries, *Angleterre*, III, 10-13, 16-20, 30-57.   [27] *Ibid.*, III, 58-64.
[28] *Ibid.*, III, 80-1; Larkin, *Stuart Proclamations*, II, 209-11; Marsden, *Law and Custom*, I, 407; *APC 1628-9*, p. 144.   [29] Castries, *Angleterre*, III, 91-2.   [30] *Ibid.*, III, 164-5.

war drew to a close Sallee had cause to complain and the English government was no longer disposed to listen. Harrison's efforts to save or patch up his so-called peace failed. Merchants' goods were arrested, the maritime offensive resumed, captives again taken in considerable numbers, maltreated and held to ransom.[31] Civil conflict between the Hornacheros, the Andalos and Sidi al-Ayachi during 1630, 1631 and 1632 hampered the development of this new onslaught, but by 1636 it was in full spate once more.

Late in that year the merchants and shipowners of Devon, Dorset and Hampshire jointly petitioned the Council: 'that there are a great number of Turkish pirates from Algiers, and especially from Salley in Barbary, which of late years have so infested both this and the Irish coasts that they have within these few years taken from your petitioners four score and 7 sail of ships; that the said ships and their loading were worth £96,700; that they retain in miserable captivity 1,160 able seamen taken in the said ships, besides almost 2,000 others of his Majesty's subjects taken in other ships; that your honours petitioners the last summer did not dare to trade into foreign parts'.[32] That summer indeed the mayor of Plymouth had reported the coast to be full of Turkish men-of-war, causing damage greater than for many years past, especially to the Newfoundland fishermen. He had heard that in April (1636) 200 Christians had been brought into Sallee in one day.[33] The marauders had sailed right into the River Severn and all the terror and outrage of a decade before were repeated with interest. Such reports were perhaps less concerned with accuracy than with impressing upon the Council the gravity and urgency of the matter, but that it was serious and rapidly deteriorating can hardly be doubted. In July 1635, according to a Plymouth mariner then a prisoner there, Sallee had held 150 British prisoners and early in the next year Edmund Bradshaw reported still only 250. But in September his figure was 1,100 or 1,200, while Giles Penn in August declared that Salleemen had taken a thousand English and Irish captives in the past six months.[34]

Ten years before, faced with such losses, the government had sought

---

[31] *Ibid.*, III, 179–81, 184–8.
[32] SP16/536, fol. 251 (the transcript in Castries, *Angleterre*, III, 259–62 is inaccurate).
[33] *CSPD 1636*, p. 72.
[34] *CSPD 1635–6*, p. 303; *CSPD 1636*, p. 86; Castries, *Angleterre*, III, 233, 250; Coindreau, *Corsaires*, p. 182; Castries, *France*, III, 196. The higher figures may be exaggerated, but the fact that Rainborowe delivered only about 300 (including some not British) does not prove them grossly so, for their owners clearly had time and incentive enough to send large numbers to Algiers and Tunis, as indeed they were said to have done.

to appease the marauders, but now the circumstances were different. Ship money, which had been instituted in 1634 for the express purpose of protecting the country's shipping and asserting the Crown's sovereignty in home seas, now made it possible to set forth substantial fleets year after year in peace-time, something never achieved and seldom even contemplated before. Good relations now prevailed with Spain, which of all the European powers had most interest in suppressing the corsairs, and especially those of Sallee, led as they were by embittered Moriscos. On the other hand experience proved that measures against the pirates at sea could, given the pirates' nautical superiority, make little impression. The alternative was to attack them in their lair. This was no new idea: Sir Robert Mansell's expedition against Algiers in 1623 set a precedent and the French had already sent successive expeditions to Sallee in 1629, 1630 and 1635. None of these ventures achieved anything like the success expected of them. At best they inflicted some damage on the pirates' shipping, delivered some Christian captives and obtained a short-lived truce.[35] It is hardly to be supposed therefore that the English government anticipated some crushing and conclusive victory, but it did have some reasons at this juncture for hoping to teach the rovers a lesson and to gain some commercial concessions in Morocco at the same time. Such reasons, together with practical advice, were persuasively expounded by Giles Penn, the brain behind this enterprise.

Penn, father of Admiral Sir William and grandfather of William the Quaker, was a merchant and sea captain of Bristol. Now nearing 60, he was an old Morocco hand, speaking the language, experienced in the trade, acquainted with the people who mattered and on good terms with Sidi al-Ayachi, known to the English as the Saint.[36] His project for an expedition to Sallee came to the government's notice in June 1636 and, being well liked, was remitted to the Admiralty for action.[37] Preparations were already in hand when he submitted to the Admiralty Commissioners in December a memorandum urging certain particulars he regarded as important.[38] As he explained, 'now the time offers to good purposes for his Majesty's service', for the pirate base was now vulnerable as never before. The deep-seated enmity between the Morisco factions in New Sallee – Hornacheros and Andalos – had flared once more into civil war in 1636 and now the Andalos, having

---

[35] Coindreau, *Corsaires*, pp. 178–82.
[36] Wildes, *Penn*, pp. 7–8, 388; Powell, *Bristol Privateers*, p. 86; HCA 13/54, fol. 59. He had traded in Morocco since at least 1622, was appointed consul in Sallee in December 1637 and died before 1645: Castries, *Angleterre*, III, 85, 389. [37] *CSPD 1636*, p. 19.
[38] Castries, *Angleterre*, III, 263–70.

by a ruse driven their hated masters out of the castle, commanded both castle and town. But to the Saint, who had long striven to bring Old and New Sallee alike under his power, these new occupants of the Kasba were among the worst enemies of the faith, crypto-Christians ready to betray the stronghold to Spain. Indeed at this time they were in secret communication with the Spaniards of Mamora, who hoped thus to win Sallee.[39] With the Saint now gathering all the strength he could muster to attack the Andalos, the time was ripe for 'procuring the Saint with his forces to besiege the castle by land as his Majesty's ships doth by sea, and then I doubt not to bring all to a period'. In a three months' campaign New Sallee could be starved into submission. Meanwhile all Penn required was a royal letter to the Saint 'in that form as, under correction, I shall give some directions, knowing him and his condition as I have of long time'. Time would show this to be a shrewd appraisement of the prospects.

Again time was the key to checking the corsairs' offensive: 'the principal matter on this voyage is expedition to send the ships for Sallee to be there, by God's leave, by the end of February next, and to be ready to set sail from hence by the twentieth or last of January at furthest, for if the ships are not in the road of Sallee to keep them in from coming forth the river from the first to the last of March, there will be a great prejudice and main hurt to his Majesty's royal design', since fishing vessels would then be setting forth for Newfoundland and elsewhere. Penn was also much exercised about the equipment of the expedition. Two pinnaces were being built especially for this venture, but they would not be ready to sail with the first ships; another pinnace should be provided in the meantime. Here he mentioned certain particular vessels which would be suitable, but this piece of advice unfortunately produced no effect, though the Admiralty did apparently heed his suggestion that instead of their usual long-boats the ships should carry Biscay shallops for sixteen oars, fitted with masts and sails, to watch the channels at the river mouth at night.[40] He thus put his finger on what was to be the main difficulty of the operation. He further tendered excellent advice concerning the victualling and clothing of the crews, though this was certainly beyond the capacity of those responsible to implement, even perhaps to comprehend.

Finally Penn came, like any projector, however worthy, to his

[39] Coindreau, *Corsaires*, pp. 44–5; Castries, *France*, III, 195–7.
[40] Secretary Nicholas noted on 19 December 1636 that two such vessels had been ordered for the Sallee expedition, but nothing more is heard of these. If they were taken they evidently failed to serve their purpose. *CSPD 1636*, p. 237.

personal interest. Having spent a great deal of time and money on this business already, having been its 'first motioner' and having thirty years' experience of the country, he recommended himself for the command, which, like sea fighting, would be 'no new thing' to him. In addition he asked to be appointed surveyor of such prize as the venture might yield, with responsibility for moneys disbursed during the voyage. He calculated, no doubt correctly, that the combination of command and financial control should produce adequate compensation, but his appeal fell upon deaf ears. Instead the Admiralty in its wisdom chose a less entrepreneurial candidate – William Rainborowe.

Rainborowe (1587–1642)[41] was an Elder Brother of Trinity House, having been Master thereof in 1633–4. Eldest son of a successful shipowning master of Whitechapel, he inherited his father's shares in several London ships and followed in his footsteps as a prosperous master and part-owner of London merchantmen, notably the 500-ton *Sampson*, employed in the Levant trade in the later 1620s. Rainborowe resided in Wapping, at the centre of the Thames-side shipping world, a prominent and influential figure in the network of families which dominated that business. He married the daughter of Rowland Coytmore, a Wapping master of similar stature in the previous generation,[42] and was for some years in partnership with Nehemiah Bourne, the Wapping shipbuilder who later served Parliament and Cromwell as a naval commander.[43] In the Short and Long Parliaments Rainborowe shared the representation of Aldeburgh with Squire Bence, another successful shipping master. As one of the most capable seamen of his time, he was appointed flag-captain under the earl of Lindsey in the first ship-money fleet of 1635 and retained that position in the 1636 fleet under the earl of Northumberland, who selected him to command the Sallee expedition. Northumberland's confidence in him must have grown out of personal knowledge of his performance as flag-captain, a most demanding and responsible position, but other naval officers may have disliked his preferment.

[41] He signed himself thus, though his name was frequently spelled otherwise by contemporaries. Biographical details are specified in Chaplin, 'William Rainsborough', and Keeler, *Long Parliament*.
[42] Elder Brother of Trinity House, died 1626: Harris, *Trinity House*, p. 275. Master in Mediterranean voyages and in Drake's last voyage: Andrews, *Last Voyage*, p. 43.
[43] Son of Robert Bourne, Wapping shipbuilder; emigrated to Massachusetts in 1638 in the *Confidence*, in which he and Rainborowe had shares, returned to serve in the Parliamentary Navy and rose to the rank of rear-admiral in 1652, when he was appointed a Navy Commissioner; a strong Independent. He and Rainborowe were both interested in North American trade: Firth, 'Sailors'; Dewar, 'Naval administration'; Chaplin, 'William Rainsborough'.

Admiral Sir John Pennington, doyen of the new generation of gentlemen commanders, was certainly one of Rainborowe's critics, and his criticism is redolent of the antipathy prevailing in the Navy between officers of Pennington's breed and the captains associated with the merchant service, whom Rainborowe represented and from whom he chose the leaders of this venture.[44] Apart from George Carteret, his vice-admiral,[45] all these were London masters. Brian Harrison of Wapping, an Elder Brother of Trinity House related to Nehemiah Bourne, commanded the *Hercules*. George Hatch, another Elder Brother, formerly a shipowning partner of Rainborowe's, commanded the *Mary*. Edmund Seaman of Wapping commanded the pinnace *Providence*. Thomas White of Deptford commanded the pinnace *Expedition*. Thomas Trenchfield, captain of the *Mary Rose*, which came to reinforce Rainborowe, was also an Elder Brother. Though describing himself as 'gent. of St Mary Gray, Kent', aged 58 in 1638, he had in fact been the part-owning master of a London merchantman in the 1620s. The *Roebuck*, which accompanied the *Mary Rose*, sailed under one Mr Broad of Rotherhithe. Apart from White and Broad, all these are known to have served as commanders in the Parliamentary Navy,[46] but in the 1630s men of their background could hardly expect preferment in competition with gentlemen. When employed in the Navy they usually served as masters or as captains of hired merchantmen.

Their exceptional dominance in this expedition reflected the special interest of Trinity House in the redemption of captive seamen. The House, officially representing seafaring men, regularly played an important part in such matters, raising funds for ransoms and for Mansell's expedition, and providing the Crown with relevant information and advice. Thus on 6 December 1636 it advised the Admiralty that four ships and two pinnaces would be sufficient for the proposed enterprise, naming suitable ships and recommending that they should be ready by mid-February or the beginning of March to forestall the corsairs' assault on the Newfoundlandmen, and should be victualled and revictualled so as to lie on that coast until 5 October. At the same time they supplied specifications for the pinnaces to be built: they should be 90 feet by 25 or 26, having 15 or 16 oars on each side

---

[44] Kennedy, 'Naval captains'. [45] *Ibid.* and Chaplin, 'William Rainsborough'.
[46] Kennedy, 'Naval captains'; Chaplin, 'William Rainsborough'; Powell and Timings, *Documents*. Harrison described himself in June 1638 as of Wapping, sailor, aged 50, having used the sea thirty-three years, twenty of them as a master, and having been part-owner of the 400-ton *Scipio* of London for ten years: HCA 13/54, fol. 139. Trenchfield's daughter married Gregory Clement, the London merchant, shipowner, Irish adventurer, rumper and regicide: HCA 13/54, fol. 22.

and carrying 14 pieces of ordnance. They should be ready by the end of February.[47] In the light of this, it is not surprising that the Admiralty nominated the House's most eminent seaman to the command, nor that he was allowed to choose his own men as captains.

Penn was predictably one of those who did not approve, though he had reasons of his own: 'those now placed never went step nor spent penny therein, but are good able seamen within full sea-mark all the seas over. But for matter on land for those parts, in knowledge of the people, their language, to read or answer their letters, or acquaintance with them, in all this they come short, for more belongs to conclude with them in the way of peace... than these captains know.'[48] Personal interest aside, this was fair comment. Rainborowe was not equipped to deal with the political jungle that was Morocco, but he could hardly avoid it, for this was essentially a political operation, not simply a naval one. The mouth of the Bou Regreg was a dangerous place not only for ships, but also for political novices.

It is unfortunate therefore that the terms of Rainborowe's political instructions remain unknown, nor do we know whether he was accompanied by any political adviser or expert in Moroccan affairs, though we may reasonably infer from later developments that he had authority to form an alliance with the Saint and to secure the release of captives, but not to conclude any treaty with the sherif. As for his operational instructions, they were simple enough: to repair directly with his Majesty's ships *Leopard* (515 tons) and *Antelope* (c. 350 tons), the merchantmen *Hercules* (400 tons, chartered at £160 a month) and *Mary* (400 tons) and the two oared pinnaces *Expedition* and *Providence*, each of 250 tons, to Sallee, there to do his best to suppress the pirates, bring away the captives and apprehend or sink any rovers wherever encountered.[49] He duly departed on 21 February 1637, but without the pinnaces, which were far from ready and sorely to be missed until they finally joined the ships in Sallee road in June, no less than two and a half months late.[50]

On this voyage Rainborowe took as master of his flagship one John Dunton, who attained this post in a manner unconventional even by the lax standards of the Caroline Navy. Bound out for Virginia in the *Little David* of London under John Hogg master with a cargo of

---

[47] *CSPD 1636–7*, pp. 227–8.   [48] *Ibid.*, p. 363.
[49] SP16/347, fols. 32–3, printed in Castries, *Angleterre*, III, 276–8.
[50] The dates here are in Old (English) Style with the years modernized. The Admiralty contracted the building of the pinnaces to Robert Tranckmore and John Graves of Bermondsey. Tranckmore, aged 63, was then master of the Company of Shipwrights and a leading shipbuilder: Shilton and Holworthy, *Examinations*, nos. 292, 312; SP16/16 and 17 *passim*.

servants, Dunton and his 9-year-old son were captured along with the rest and sold as slaves in Sallee. Later his owner sent him as pilot of a Sallee pirate manned by five Dutch renegades, one of whom went captain, and twenty-one 'Moors', including eighteen Moriscos. Dunton's story (uncorroborated in this particular) was that they had instructions to take English women, 'being of more worth than other', but in the event they captured some fishermen, with whose aid he and the renegades, having previously agreed on revolt, took over the Salleeman and brought her with eleven Moors (only) to the Isle of Wight. In the ensuing trial the surviving Moors were convicted of piracy while Dunton and the Dutch were honourably acquitted. As a 'lusty man' our hero was at first recommended for pressing into his Majesty's service, but, coming to the notice of Sir Henry Vane and claiming close acquaintance with Sallee, found himself a more comfortable berth. He afterwards dedicated to Sir Henry an artless and misleading account of the events, redeemed only by an excellent chart drawn by someone else.[51]

Rainborowe arrived off Sallee on 24 March with the *Leopard*, *Antelope* and *Mary*. The *Hercules*, having spent her mainmast in a storm, put into Lisbon and rejoined on 17 April. The following day Rainborowe reported that so far he had been 'able to do little good'. New Sallee refused to parley and 'their small carvels do row out in the dark night; do what we can, we are all heavy ships and cannot follow them so near the shore as they go'. An attempted boat assault on the pirate vessels in harbour 'came off well beaten'.[52] Three weeks later he wrote to Vane in frustration: 'it is not possible in this place to take or destroy any of them without pinnaces...and I am so much grieved that they do not come that I am almost out of heart'. Hopes of recovering the captives seemed at this stage remote, but at least the Saint had now begun his offensive against the new town and had formally entered into alliance with the English.[53] On 20 May Rainborowe sent his first dispatch to the Admiralty, recapitulating the events since his arrival. Again deploring the absence of the pinnaces, he described how a

---

[51] Dunton, *Sallee Fleet*. For the chart, by Richard Simson, see p. 166. Senior, *Naval History*, pp. 13–25, examines the trial of Dunton, the other seamen and the Moors, who were apparently bought in order to be exchanged for English captives. Harrison had taken captured Moors to Morocco for exchange in 1627, when he protested against the conduct of Samuel Vassall, who at that time bought a number of Moorish captives for shipment to Leghorn and sale as slaves: Castries, *Angleterre*, III, 35–6.   [52] Castries, *Angleterre*, III, 281–3.
[53] *Ibid.*, III, 284–94. In this letter Rainborowe mentioned that he had heard nothing of 'the galleys out of Spain', referring to the (vain) hope that Spain might assist the English blockade.

Salleeman with eight pieces had managed to enter despite their bombardment, adding that 'there hath gone out and in seven or eight small carvels of one and two guns apiece'. Nevertheless 'we have kept in all their great ships, not one of them hath gone out this year', and he expressed the hope that 'they will never arrive at their former greatness', for those ships confined to port must become worm-eaten. The Saint was pressing his siege with 20,000 men and had burned all the corn around New Sallee. Having no ordnance he would not be able to take the town, but with the pinnaces the blockade by land and sea would starve them out. As for the captives, he was informed that only 300 remained, the rest, about a thousand in number, having been sold at Algiers and Tunis.[54]

Since Rainborowe did not send another dispatch until 8 August, it must have been this of 20 May to which Pennington referred when he wrote to Nicholas on 10 July: 'you will find that all things is not true that Rainsbrowe writes'. Rainborowe probably had understated the number of minor vessels which had entered and left the port, but he had made no attempt to conceal the inadequacy of the blockade, nor had he distorted the position in any other respect. Pennington's damaging remark was evidently based on a report from Carteret, which he forwarded to Nicholas with the equally damaging comment, 'I perceive he neither dares to write to you nor me but covertly, for these letters were consigned to a friend at London, and from thence to me.' Carteret's letter cannot be traced, but he had in fact written another directly to Nicholas and was to write again later, without in either letter offering the slightest hint of disagreement or mistrust between Rainborowe and himself. Pennington went on to tell Nicholas that one Captain Lewis Kirke had refused to go under Rainborowe's command and had 'to his great discontent' been placed under Trenchfield in the *Mary Rose*.[55] Here Pennington seems to be retailing the sort of bickering snobbery which was all too common in the Caroline Navy and betraying some prejudice of his own against the admiral from Trinity House.

In his next dispatch of 8 August Rainborowe had better news to

[54] *Ibid.*, III, 309–13.
[55] SP16/363, fols. 181–2. Carteret and Fulke Powell both put the number of vessels evading the blockade higher than Rainborowe, whose own journal confirms their figures: Castries, *Angleterre*, III, 306–8, 314–18, 343–54. William Brissenden, purser of the *Providence*, wrote scathingly to Nicholas about 'many reports of our actions, taking of ships and many other wonders' (SP71/13, fol. 25), but his account does not actually contradict anything in Rainborowe's letters. Brissenden had been charged on a former occasion with uttering 'contumelious speeches' against his commanding officer, the captain of the *Fifth Whelp*: *CSPD 1629–31*, p. 484.

report.[56] At the beginning of June in the old town, occupied by the Saint, his sailors planted a culverin and bombarded the men-of-war in the harbour, seven or eight of which 'great ships', he claimed, were damaged beyond repair. Soon after this the pinnaces arrived and the blockade at last took effect. They chased and drove ashore with heavy loss three strong Salleemen seeking entrance, and so bottled up the port that the Andalos, deprived of supplies from the sea and the land alike, grew desperate. Facing the prospect of starvation, their only hope was to come to terms with one of the interested powers: the English, the Saint, the sherif or Spain. Factions now emerged among them favouring different courses, and while Rainborowe's ships stood by there occurred ashore a confused sequence of twists and turns beyond their reach.

First the Andalos made overtures to both the English and the Saint, but the former refused a separate peace and the latter set unacceptable conditions, demanding reparations, half of all future prize and the return of the Hornacheros to the Kasba. Then on 22 June the Andalos rose in rebellion against their governor, a man especially obnoxious to the Saint, and sent him to the sherif.[57] Those responsible for this coup hoped thereby to placate Sidi al-Ayachi, while others hoped to be rescued by the sherif, who at this juncture was marching upon Sallee with a large army, intent upon preventing it from falling into the Saint's hands, for the latter's power overshadowed his own. The Saint, however, frustrated this move by burning the crops for many miles around Sallee. The sherif's troops accordingly melted away and rather than risk humiliation he withdrew. At this point the hapless Andalos, despairing of the sherif and dreading the wrath of the marabout, resolved to surrender the Kasba to Spain, but before the Spaniards at Mamora could take advantage of this offer the former governor of New Sallee returned with the sherif's blessing in an English merchantman, accompanied by one Robert Blake, factor in Morocco for William Cloberry and Sir Brian Janson.[58]

Blake, who was in high favour at Marrakech, now arranged matters between the sherif, the Andalos and the English. The governor was reinstated, the Andalos pardoned and some 300 Christians delivered to

---

[56] Castries, *Angleterre*, III, 322–7. The following summary of events is based also on Carteret's report of 21 September and Rainborowe's journal (*ibid.*, pp. 339–42 and 343–54), as well as Castries, *Pays-Bas*, V, and *France*, III.

[57] Mulay Mohammed ech-Cheikh, who succeeded Mulay al-Oualid on 22 February 1636 (New Style dating).

[58] Castries, *Angleterre*, III, 247. According to Powell, *Blake*, de Castries was mistaken in identifying this merchant as the Cromwellian admiral.

Rainborowe's ships.[59] The Andalos for their part promised obedience to their sherif and peace to the English. Only the Saint was displeased. Thus in the last days of July and the first days of August came a swift *dénouement*. The Saint, it is true, continued to besiege the castle, but Rainborowe was satisfied. On 8 August he dispatched Carteret in the *Antelope*, together with the *Hercules* and the two pinnaces, to hunt Algerines off the Spanish coast and decided to sail south to Safi himself 'to settle the peace with the king of Morocco'. Then, as he prepared to leave the road of Sallee, reinforcements arrived: the royal ships *Mary Rose* (290 tons) and *Roebuck* (80 tons).

Rainborowe of course expected to receive fresh supplies in order to continue the blockade as planned, but the decision actually to send them arose out of a curious muddle. At the end of July the government in England received information by way of Spain that New Sallee was about to fall to the Saint and must by now be his. Thereupon Secretary Windebank wrote to Rainborowe conveying the king's congratulations and ordering him to hold the castle, should it surrender, for his Majesty. Three days later, however, on 4 August, Northumberland from his flagship in the Downs advised Windebank that, even with the reinforcements the government now proposed to send, Rainborowe would not have sufficient strength to hold it. In any case, he argued, 'sending more ships to Sallee would be to little purpose, for we judge that the work there is already done, and that Captain Rainsborough will be come away before they can get to him'.[60] While Windebank and Northumberland were equally misinformed, the latter's opinion seems the more sensible. Nevertheless the government chose, for whatever reasons, to send the ships, which in those uncertain circumstances was probably the safer course after all, even though in the end they were not needed.

Departing then for Safi on 20 August, Rainborowe believed, or at least claimed, that he had done remarkably good service: 'we did not only redeem these, but kept a great many from being taken this summer in not suffering them to go out with any good shipping. And what we have sunk without and within their harbour, they have not the one third of the ships remaining that they had the year before, and few of them they have that are serviceable... And although they be as

---

[59] Dunton lists 299 English, including 11 women, adding 25 French, 8 Dutch and 7 Spanish, totalling 339; another list mentions 272 only, which corresponds closely to Carteret's estimate: Castries, *Angleterre*, III, 325, 341, 352, 377.
[60] SP71/13, fol. 17 (Windebank to Rainborowe, 1 August 1637); *CSPD 1637*, pp. 341, 351 (Northumberland to Windebank, 31 July and 4 August 1637).

wicked fellows as any be, and nothing else but a den of thieves, yet I am persuaded they will keep the peace with us. First, because we have brought them to such extremity and they now see what we can do upon any other occasion, and our ships are terrible to them. And secondly they fear, if they perform not, that the king of Morocco may besiege them by land, and that his Majesty's ships should again besiege them by sea, so I doubt not but there will be much quietness upon his Majesty's coasts.'[61] This may exaggerate the immediate impact of the operation, but by no means grossly. The corsairs' wings were clipped and when Carteret came to Sallee the following year he found they had only four serviceable men-of-war left.[62]

On the other hand, Rainborowe's assessment of the prospects was hardly realistic. The corsairs could quickly and easily recover their strength unless their opponents renewed the blockade regularly every spring, which in the circumstances was scarcely conceivable. Nor did the English ships inspire such terror as he imagined. Until the arrival of the pinnaces the pirate caravels freely pursued their usual business and even after that the Kasba was reduced to extremity only by the close combination of powerful land and sea forces. In fact Rainborowe owed his success, such as it was, entirely to the alliance of the Saint, without whose co-operation he could not have mounted the land-based artillery attack on the men-of-war in harbour, nor have cut off the defenders' food supplies. What the English admiral apparently failed to understand, or at least to admit, was that the success of any expedition of the kind undertaken in 1637 depended on the internal situation in Morocco, and that he had been peculiarly lucky in that respect.

His expectation that the sherif would prove an effective ally in controlling the pirates or in repressing them if necessary was unfortunately ill-grounded. The terms of the accord he negotiated with the sherif, providing for freedom of trade, good behaviour of the shipping of both countries and the release of all captives, amounted at best to an avowal of good intentions.[63] In reality, as Giles Penn pointed out in his report from Morocco in November of the same year, the sherif had not the strength to impose his will upon Sallee. Penn doubted the place would continue in obedience to the sherif 'unless hostages of some great consequence or a governor put into the castle by the king

---

[61] Castries, *Angleterre*, III, 325–6.
[62] *Ibid.*, III, 447. Carteret, *Barbary Voyage*, contains two near-contemporary views of Sallee, but the account of the 1637 episode in the foreword is unreliable.
[63] Castries, *Angleterre*, III, 328–55. These terms were not accepted in London and the text of the 1638 treaty differed in important respects: *ibid.*, III, 400–4.

of Morocco with 500 men to command both the shipping and the new town'. He likewise doubted 'if occasion were offered again by the castle against us, we should get the Saint to do as much as he hath done already', whereas the sherif, with forces inferior to those of the Saint, could not be expected to afford effective assistance in a siege.[64]

In the event the restored governor did not send the hostages he had promised to the sherif, nor did the latter's troops occupy the Kasba until after the governor was murdered in January 1638. When Carteret returned a few months later with the king's *Convertive* and the pinnace *Expedition*, anarchy still reigned in Morocco and turmoil in Sallee. In the Kasba the sherif's men and the Andalos, hotly besieged by revengeful Hornacheros, were on the verge of starvation and contemplating surrender to Spain. Carteret's arrival brought relief and encouraged the sherif to assert his authority over the Bou Regreg, but in the attempt his army was intercepted and destroyed in October 1638. The victor in this decisive battle was Sidi Mohammed al-Hadj, the Berber marabout of Dila, who then dominated a great part of Morocco and in 1640–1 took possession of both Old and New Sallee. Under his stronger rule the internecine conflicts there were for a time quelled, and piracy, which was already by then recovering from its temporary depression in 1637–8, flourished more than ever.[65]

In large measure the difficulties of the Caroline government with Sallee piracy resembled those of European governments with Barbary corsairs throughout the early-modern era. As at other times, the powers of Europe failed to co-operate. Spain, France, Holland and England were all actively interested in Moroccan affairs and especially in Sallee. Each endeavoured, by means of more or less ineffectual demonstrations of sea power and commercial cajolery, to bargain with the pirates, who were of course willing to deliver captives for some kind of price: this after all was the point of taking them in the first place. Trading arms openly or covertly for hostages and promises of preferential treatment, however worthless, was the standard practice. What it implied was plainly stated by Sir Thomas Roe in reference to a 'peace' with Algiers in 1624: 'it little concerns us to leave the French for a prey: cormorants and wolves must have some food, else they will seize on anything'.[66] Charles was content a few years later to have such a peace at Spain's

---

[64] *Ibid.*, III, 358–64. In December 1637 Penn was appointed consul at Sallee: *CSPD 1637–8*, p. 42.
[65] Coindreau, *Corsaires*, p. 183; Castries, *Pays-Bas*, v, xxiv–xxv; Castries, *Angleterre*, III, 445–8. The dominance of the Dila chief was finally assured by the assassination of Sidi al-Ayachi in April 1641.
[66] Richardson, *Roe's Negotiations*, p. 316: Roe to Sir Dudley Carleton, 27 November 1624.

expense, and when Anglo-Spanish relations were better, in the 1630s, the rival ambitions of the two powers in Morocco meant that collaboration remained only a talking point. But even a united Europe would have found it hard to deal with North African piracy by any means short of war, because the corsairs were not effectively subject to any reliable authority. Like the Ottoman sultans, the sherifs exercised at best a certain remote and intermittent control over their pirates and maintained towards them an ambiguous attitude compounded of impotence and cupidity. In this respect the Morocco of the 1620s and 1630s was an extreme case, and the efforts of Harrison, Penn and Blake to manipulate local politics could never win their sovereign more than a fleeting advantage, particularly because the pirate base itself was a cockpit of intrigue and convulsive instability.

On the other hand, divisions among Charles's own subjects tended to complicate his task. The seafaring community itself was split between appeasers, led naturally by the wives and families of prisoners in captivity, and aggressive captains like Charles Driver, Squire Bence and John Maddock, who wanted no truck with Barbary corsairs. In 1631 a group of the former petitioned the king against Maddock and his chief shipowner, William Wye, asking for redress and the punishment of the culprits. A suit for damages followed.[67] English merchants interested in the Barbary trade were also divided. The royal agent Edmund Bradshaw complained to the Council in 1635 that he was unable to recover a debt from the sherif because certain other English merchants traded with Moroccan rebels in Sallee and elsewhere. Furthermore, he alleged, this illicit trade was responsible for the sherif's refusal to release the captives he held. The group thus accused, led by Sir William Courten, admitted trading with the rebels, but pointed out that all Barbary traders did the same, since most of the Moroccan ports were in rebel hands. They could not be held responsible for the sherif's retention of captives, nor for his failure to repay Bradshaw.[68] The dispute continued, but Bradshaw was finally undone by the machinations of another royal agent, Robert Blake, who not only ruined him but managed, by dint of exploiting the favour of both sovereigns, to obtain a monopoly of English trade with Morocco for a new Barbary Company, chartered in 1638. Unhappily for Blake, the company was

[67] *CSPD 1631–3*, p. 219; HCA 13/50, fols. 129, 132.
[68] Castries, *Angleterre*, III, 215–44. Courten's partners were John Dike, Thomas Ferrars, Humphrey Onby and Thomas Briggs. Courten's ships did trade at Sallee: *ibid.*, III, 167 (the *Peter*, 1631); *ibid.*, III, 307, 345, SP16/17, no. 86, SP71/13, fol. 19 (the *Hester*, 1637). Peter Courten of Middelburg, Sir William's younger brother, was allegedly trading with Sallee in 1625, and 'grows by unlawful ways rich': Castries, *Angleterre*, II, 584.

soon overthrown by those it aspired to exclude, headed by William Courten the younger.[69] Since corruption was a way of life in Marrakech, it was only to be expected that royal agents would use — and in these cases abuse — their position for private advantage, but the commercial squabbles they thus promoted did not help the Crown to hold a steady course in its Moroccan policy.

For all these reasons Sallee piracy was a problem the Caroline administration could not reasonably hope to solve. That it did nevertheless manage to mount an expedition which substantially relieved the pressure for two or three years is some measure of the country's sea power at this stage. Rainborowe, it is true, was greatly assisted by the uproar in that hornets' nest, but it was the success of ship money which gave the government the resources and the confidence to seize this opportunity and exploit it. As for Rainborowe, he played his part well. Sent initially without the shipping necessary for the task, he stuck doggedly to it for five months — an extraordinary achievement in the circumstances: a bad anchorage, a dangerous lee shore, constant exposure to the heavy Atlantic swell. During all this time, moreover, there was no mention of the sickness and disorder which usually attended such expeditions to warmer climes, where victuals rotted, beer went bad and men grew ill and discontented. Rainborowe was too optimistic about the prospect of holding down or repressing the pirates in future, but his own success did demonstrate what could be done in favourable circumstances. It would not be bettered for many a year.

[69] Blake and Bradshaw: *ibid.*, III, 385–8. Barbary Company charter: *ibid.*, III, 408–23. The merchants named were William Cloberry senior, George Fletcher, Humphrey Slany senior, John Fletcher, Thomas Fletcher, William Geere, Henry Janson, Samuel Crispe, Ellis Crispe, John Wood, Edward Russell, Humphrey Slany junior, William Cloberry junior, Oliver Cloberry junior and Robert Blake junior. Dispute over the monopoly: *ibid.*, III, 515–39. In a recapitulation of the dispute written in January 1641 Sir John Coke suggested that those who traded with the rebels opposed the new Barbary Company in 'the interest of Spain', adding, 'I fear the pirates will return to their haunt and perhaps these and other merchants bemoan themselves when it will be too late': *ibid.*, III, 542–6. He was right about the pirates, if not the rest, for they had in fact already returned to their haunt.

CHAPTER 8

PARLIAMENTARY NAVAL ENTERPRISE

WHEN, IN the summer of 1642, Parliament seized control of the fleet, it accomplished a naval revolution. Not only the political and physical means employed, but also the effects in terms of leadership, organization and policy, were revolutionary. Nevertheless the state-owned and state-hired ships and the sailors who manned them changed but little and the Parliamentary Navy exhibited a strongly traditional character, appearing in important respects more old-fashioned than the ship-money Navy. It was not new-modelled until 1649, when it came under a different and more revolutionary management. The English revolution of the 1640s occurred, in this respect as in others, in two stages.

Clarendon's account of the first of these makes clear that Parliament's naval coup of 2 July 1642 was well prepared: so well in fact that it took the form of a repulse of the king's belated attempt to recover command of his own fleet.[1] Earlier that year he had accepted Parliament's vetting of the commanders for the summer guard, including their rejection of Sir John Pennington, his choice for admiral of the fleet, and had allowed his Lord High Admiral, the earl of Northumberland, to appoint the earl of Warwick to that vital post instead. This 'he thought it not then seasonable to resent' because although 'he had long too much cause to be unsatisfied and displeased with the earl of Northumberland', he did not wish to drive him completely into the arms of the opposition and realized that without Parliament's money there would be no fleet that year. Charles, Clarendon added, had confidence in the affection and fidelity of his captains and in the devotion of the common seamen, failing to perceive that they might be seduced from their loyalty.

Early in June, however, the king's ship *Providence*, coming from Holland with arms for the royal cause, was chased into the Humber by

[1] Clarendon, *History*, II, 214–26.

Warwick's ships, saving herself only by running ashore, and it was this affront which decided Charles to revoke Northumberland's patent, to dismiss Warwick from the command and to appoint Pennington in his place, with orders to take charge of the fleet. Accordingly, on 28 June letters were dispatched to Northumberland and Warwick and instructions were drafted forbidding each captain individually to obey them and commanding him instead to repair to Burlington Bay on the Yorkshire coast to receive the king's further orders. But at the last moment these arrangements were changed at the instance of Pennington, who offered to go to the Downs himself to take command and had the instructions to the captains altered, requiring them only to observe such orders as they should receive from him on his arrival. But according to Clarendon's *Life*, Pennington 'had no mind to expose himself in the first shock to dispossess the earl of Warwick, and prevailed with the king (who suspected no such thing) to give him leave, if he found any indisposition of health, upon so long a journey in so short a time, to rest at the seaside, and to send Sir Henry Palmer, who was Comptroller of the Navy, and of unquestionable loyalty to the king, to take possession of the fleet and to observe his directions till he could himself come to him'. This, said Clarendon, 'was absolutely the ruin of the service', for in the event, while Parliament acted swiftly to appoint Warwick admiral of the fleet by its ordinance (after failing to persuade Northumberland to continue in office), Pennington 'made no such haste' and when he finally arrived at the Downs 'upon pretence of indisposition concealed himself at land', sending the king's revised instructions to the captains and leaving it to Palmer to go aboard 'to feel the pulses'. Since at this juncture Warwick was ashore, enjoying 'a jolly dinner' some five or six miles inland, Pennington, had he been present, might in Clarendon's judgement 'have carried all the fleet whither he would', for he had a greater influence with the seamen than any other person and many of the captains had welcomed the king's orders.

In the *History*, Clarendon stressed that the misfortune which followed could not in justice be imputed to Pennington, 'a very honest gentleman and of unshaken faithfulness and integrity to the king', but also pointed out that he was anxious about his own security, lest 'instead of taking the fleet from the earl of Warwick, he was not himself taken by the earl and sent to the Parliament', which already had 'a great arrear of displeasure against him'. Usually the *History* is to be preferred to the *Life* as a source, but in any case Clarendon clearly thought that the business was bungled. The result was that Warwick,

SHIPS, MONEY AND POLITICS

with all his authority as Parliament's admiral, retained the initiative. William Batten, vice-admiral commanding the fleet in Warwick's absence, sent for the earl immediately upon receiving the king's letters. Warwick then summoned the captains to a council of war aboard his flagship, the *James*, where, as he reported to Pym two days later, on 4 July:

> all of them unanimously and cheerfully took the same resolution, excepting the rear-admiral, Sir John Mennes, Captain Fogge, Captain Burley, Captain Slingsby and Captain Wake: all which five refused to come upon my summons, as having no authority over them; and got together, round, that night, to make their defence against me: only Captain Burley came in and submitted to me. Hereupon in the morning I weighed my anchors and caused the rest of the ships so to do, and came to an anchor round about them and besieged them; and when I had made all things ready I summoned them. Sir John Mennes and Captain Fogge came in to me, but Captain Slingsby and Captain Wake stood out. Whereupon I let fly a gun over them and sent them word I had turned up the glass upon them; if in that space they came not in, they must look for me aboard them. I sent to them by my boat and most of the boats in the fleet. Their answer was so peremptory that my masters and sailors grew so impatient at them, that (although they had no arms in their boats at all) yet God gave them such courage and resolution as, in a moment, they entered them, took hold of their shrouds, and seized upon those captains, although armed with their pistols and swords; struck their yards and topmasts and brought them both to me. The like courage and resolution was never seen among unarmed men, so as all was ended without effusion of blood, which I must attribute to the great God of heaven and earth only, who, in the moment I was ready to give fire on them, put such courage in our men to act, and so saved much blood.[2]

In addition to those five mentioned by Warwick, four other captains of the king's ships refused to obey him. Captain Robert Fox of the *Lion* was driven off his course for Newcastle into the Downs and there, resisting the admiral's orders, was arrested. Captain Hill of the *Tenth Whelp* (whether he was Richard or Philip Hill is not clear) was also arrested, while Thomas Kettleby and Henry Stradling, in the *Swallow* and *Bonaventure* respectively, having declared for the king, were captured later with their ships. Thus in all nine of the king's commanders proved unwilling to accept the Parliamentary admiral, whereas eleven acknowledged his authority at the council of war.[3] On this evidence, therefore, the king's commanders appear to have been

[2] Powell and Timings, *Documents*, p. 18.   [3] *Ibid.*, p. 15; Kennedy, 'Naval captains'.

almost evenly divided in their allegiance and only the difference between Parliament's resolute dispatch and Pennington's tardy hesitation seems to have decided the issue.

It may be true that with prompter and more vigorous action and happier decisions the king need not have suffered this wholesale loss. It was at Charles's own request, for example, that George Carteret declined the post, offered him by Parliament, of vice-admiral under Warwick. Had such an able and royalist officer been the acting commander of the fleet at the beginning of July instead of Batten, 'a man of very different inclinations to his master and his service and furious in the new fancies of religion', as Clarendon observed, events might well have taken another course. Yet beneath these immediate contingencies a deeper historical current was at work in Warwick's favour. As we have noted elsewhere and Kennedy has shown in convincing detail,[4] the division in the naval command was social as well as political. The royalist captains were gentlemen who had chosen a career in the king's Navy. Some of these were senior men who had served in the 1620s and since – Mennes, Richard Fogge, John Burley, Thomas Kettleby. Others, younger officers, had gained their experience in the Royal Navy of the 1630s – Henry Stradling, Robert Slingsby, Robert Fox, Baldwin Wake. But most of those who rallied to Warwick had come into the king's service by quite another route, having grown up in merchant ships: Brian Harrison, George Hatch and Thomas Trenchfield, all selected by William Rainborowe for his Sallee expedition, shipowning London masters and Elder Brethren of the Trinity House, a close set, Puritan and Parliamentary in persuasion and natural leaders of the seamen from whose ranks they sprang. Batten, Richard Blyth and Richard and William Swanley had similar backgrounds. All these, like Rainborowe's captains, were, in comparison with the royalists, newcomers to the king's service, in which none of them had held commands before 1637, and their growing strength in the Navy in recent years may be attributed to Northumberland, who certainly brought Rainborowe and Batten to the fore.

Conversely, the strength of the career gentlemen, which had grown with the expansion of the fleet in the later 1630s, was already on the wane before the crisis of July 1642. Along with Pennington, Sir David Murray and Captain Thomas Price had failed to gain the approval of Parliament earlier that year, while Sir Henry Mainwaring, a royal favourite who had served in the ship-money fleets, was obviously out of the running. Carteret, as we have seen, was excluded by a typically

[4] Kennedy, 'Naval captains'.

Caroline mistake. Moreover the gentlemen captains, with the exception of Pennington, lacked that affinity with the common seamen which the merchant masters, according to Clarendon, enjoyed: 'they had been taught to believe that all the king's bounty and grace towards them had flowed from the mediation of those officers who were now engaged against the king'. The sailors who captured the fleet for Parliament, risking their lives unarmed, showed whom they trusted in no uncertain terms, 'so that a greater or more general defection of any one order of men was never known than that at this time of the seamen; though many gentlemen, and some few of the common sort (to their lasting honour and reputation) either addressed themselves to the active service of their sovereign, or suffered imprisonment and the loss of all they had for refusing to serve against him'.[5]

The fleet thus secure in its possession, Parliament proceeded to construct its own Admiralty and naval administration. This was rendered necessary by the king's revocation of Northumberland's patent as Lord High Admiral and by his order to the Principal Officers of the Navy forbidding them to carry out any instructions from Parliament or Warwick not sanctioned by himself.[6] Naturally Parliament took advantage of this opportunity to staff the Navy with politically reliable managers, though thanks to Northumberland it already had certain key men in place.[7] The chief of these was Thomas Smith, Northumberland's secretary, whom Parliament, by an ordinance of 15 September 1642, appointed Secretary to the Admiralty.[8] It was convenient to continue in office a professional 'man of business' who knew the job, but Smith was no political neuter.[9] Until Warwick's appointment as Lord High Admiral in 1643 the functions of that office were performed by a committee consisting in the first place of Northumberland, Warwick and Hollond from the Lords, with Giles Greene, Henry Marten, Sir Robert Pye, the Sir Henry Vanes senior and junior, and John Rolle, all MPs. Alexander and Squire Bence and Samuel Vassall were added in December 1642. As well as directing fleet movements, appointing officers and issuing orders to the administration, the Admiralty exercised wide powers over shipping

---

[5] Clarendon, *History*, II, 225–6. [6] Powell and Timings, *Documents*, pp. 20–1 (7 July 1642).
[7] Dewar, 'Naval administration'; Kennedy, 'Parliament's Admiralty'; Johns, 'Principal Officers'. [8] Firth and Rait, *Acts*, I, 29–30.
[9] His position in the years around 1640 seems to have been similar to Northumberland's. The statement (Powell and Timings, *Documents*, p. 40) that he was appointed secretary to the Navy Commissioners is mistaken. It was probably another Thomas Smith who became a Navy Commissioner in 1646, and this was probably the Elder Brother of Trinity House who survived the purge of 1649: cf. Harris, *Trinity House*, pp. 37–8.

and seamen generally and was especially occupied with the government of privateering and, in the absence of the Admiralty judge, with adjudication of prize.[10]

On 15 September 1642 Parliament also re-organized the administration of the Navy by creating a body of Navy Commissioners to replace the Principal Officers. The place of Treasurer had already been vacated in August by the royalist Sir William Russell, superseded then by Sir Henry Vane junior, who had formerly shared the office with Russell. Palmer and Carteret, jointly Comptrollers, and George Barlow, Clerk of the Ships, were now dismissed, and only Batten, the Surveyor, remained in post. He and Captain Phineas Pett, Captain Richard Cranley, Captain John Morris, Captain Roger Twiddy and John Hollond now became the salaried officials charged with the detailed administration of the Navy in conjunction with Vane and five unpaid Commissioners who, unlike the salaried men, were MPs: Greene, Rolle, Vassall and the Bence brothers.[11] Around the end of 1645 Hollond resigned and about this time a certain Thomas Smith, probably not the former Admiralty Secretary, joined the Commissioners. The Parliamentary committee called the Navy Committee, or more formally the Committee of the Navy and Customs, was quite a different body, concerned mainly but by no means entirely with naval finance. Formed in 1641, it included Alexander Bence and Samuel Vassall and, under its chairman Giles Greene, played an active part in naval policy, appointments and administration as well as finance.[12]

With some minor modifications of personnel, chiefly affecting the Admiralty when Warwick was obliged to give way to a commission in 1645 (the commissioners being Warwick, Greene, Bence, Rolle and two or three less regular members, apart from a few who attended only once or twice) and when he returned as Lord High Admiral in 1648, the government of the Navy changed little if at all in the years from 1642 to 1648. It rested very largely in the hands of a small clique, dominated by Warwick, Giles Greene, Alexander Bence and Samuel Vassall, the last three of whom belonged to all three bodies mentioned, the other key figures being Vane, Batten, Rolle, Cranley, Morris and Twiddy. This régime, invented piecemeal and *ad hoc* to meet the emergencies of revolution and civil war, bore the tell-tale marks of its origin, offering no effective check to misrule or corruption. With the

---

[10] Kennedy, 'Parliament's Admiralty'.   [11] Firth and Rait, *Acts*, I, 27–9.
[12] Dewar's assertion that it was concerned solely with finance is misleading, as the committee's frequent orders to the Navy Commissioners amply show – e.g. *CSPD 1641–3*, pp. 429–34, 554–62.

exception of Warwick, Vane, Smith the Secretary and Hollond, all the governors of the Parliamentary Navy were merchants or masters in the shipping business. Cranley, Morris, Twiddy, Batten, Alexander Bence and Thomas Smith the Navy Commissioner were London Trinity House men. The overlapping membership of the governing bodies concerned endowed these men with great power and responsibility in the management of large sums of public money, while they retained substantial private business interests and connections with each other and with wider circles of London merchants and shipowners.[13] In particular they had been and continued to be associated with the very men who now commanded Parliament's ships: the Swanleys, the Jordans, Trenchfield, Harrison, Hatch, Peter Andrews, Nathaniel Goodlad, Richard Haddock, Thomas Rainsborough, Robert Moulton, Benjamin Cranley and the rest and with the still more numerous company of owners and captains of merchantmen hired for Parliament's service.

It was remarked as early as 1524 that 'it is no more expedient for an owner of ships to bear rule and keep the account of such a costly business (*viz.* the king's Navy)... than it is for a customer to occupy merchandise'.[14] Those who did so were not necessarily guilty of abusing their official positions to help themselves, their relations and friends out of the public purse, but they were continually accused of such practice in Tudor and early Stuart times. Convincing evidence of corruption is always difficult to find, and unless the charges were legally sustained at the time the historian can speak only of possibilities and probabilities. It is, however, generally accepted that corruption was rife in the Jacobean Navy and had not been banished for good by the 1618 reform. 'There is little to show', according to an authoritative judge, 'that Northumberland succeeded in stamping out the long-standing abuses which he and earlier critics had remarked.'[15] The salaries of £100 each granted to Batten, Pett, Morris, Cranley, Twiddy and Hollond in 1642 were significantly lower than those received by the Principal Officers who preceded them and it is not clear whether expense allowances and permitted perquisites were increased to make up the difference. In the century before Parliament took over the Navy the official incomes of the Principal Officers had not changed. In real terms Charles's men were thus paid far less than their Henrician

[13] The shipowning and commercial interests of these men have been described in Chapter 2 above. On Greene and Rolle see Keeler, *Long Parliament*.
[14] Johns, 'Principal Officers', p. 38; Davies, 'Administration', p. 284.
[15] Aylmer, 'Attempts at reform', p. 238.

forbears, though perhaps more than their Parliamentary successors, and it was presumably in recognition of the inadequacy of the Commissioners' pay that Parliament doubled it in 1646.[16] MPs were well aware that low pay encouraged corruption and perhaps took note of the charges which were levelled at the Commissioners at that time. If so, they had more sense than those naval historians who have dismissed the charges out of hand simply on the strength of Giles Greene's published denials.[17] Greene's driving energy and masterful competence in the management of the Parliamentary Navy no doubt deserved the respect they won, but Hollond, his own colleague, suspected his integrity and wrote in scathing terms of the Commissioners:

> The last (though not the least) of those irregularities of the Navy which I shall mention... is that lawless liberty the Commissioners of the Navy assume to themselves to be at the same time Commissioners of the Navy and private merchants... by whose example they indulge and encourage all subordinate instruments to dance after their pipe and to do the same things.[18]

Hollond was referring generally here to peculation in the purchase of materials, provisions and shipping for the state. More specifically he attacked the Commissioners and the Committee of the Navy for exploiting the state's need of assistance from the merchant marine.[19] This was indeed a golden opportunity for the shipowning merchants and masters who now managed the Navy. Since the state's own shipping did not increase significantly before 1649, Parliament, he observed, 'did employ many merchants' ships as men-of-war, and by the treasurer's accounts it is too apparent what great sums of money were issued and paid upon this head'. The Navy Commissioners' account for the years 1643–5 costed the hire, victualling and pay of 124 merchantmen with 9,486 men at £250,184, compared with £451,917 16s 3d spent on setting forth 164 state ships and pinnaces with 16,723 men. Proportionately as well as absolutely the outlay on merchant auxiliaries was far greater than it had been in the ship-money fleets and warranted Hollond's description of it as 'a vast, expensive and eating charge to the state'. Merchantmen were normally hired for six or eight months' service counting twenty-eight days per month, the owners being paid £3 15s 6d per man per month, allowing 30 men to each 100

---

[16] Davies, 'Administration', p. 285; Aylmer, *King's Servants*, pp. 207–8; Dewar, 'Naval administration', p. 425.
[17] For example, Powell and Timings, *Documents*, pp. 225–6, though the matter had already been better examined in the same Navy Records series: Tanner, *Hollond's Discourses*, pp. lix–lxvii.
[18] Tanner, *Hollond's Discourses*, pp. 309–10.   [19] *Ibid.*, pp. 264–70.

tons. At this standard rate a 500-ton ship would cost the state £3,397 10s 0d or £4,530 for the summer guard, and a 200-ton ship £1,359 or £1,812. Out of this the owners would pay their men's wages and victuals and provide the vessel with guns, ammunition and all necessary tackle and furniture. They would be paid the same rate for any extra men employed, and if the ship were discharged before six months they would receive £1 15s 6d per man per month for the period from discharge up to the end of six months.[20]

These were generous terms, as they no doubt had to be because owners, though promised immediate payment in the contract, knew from experience that they might well wait months, perhaps many months, for the return on their investment. But they were especially tempting, as Hollond pointed out, to those who could assign and manipulate the contracts:

> their zeal burnt as hot in another chimney as the state's interest, and this appears too plainly by those many unworthy practices that were used by some that I could name in this particular, who for ends best known to themselves, after they had thrust unserviceable ships upon the state at dear rates, did by their influence (I could tell you where and with whom) keep out those ships at sea, which at first were hired but for six or eight months at the most, by the space of four and twenty, yea thirty months together without any intermission, and in the interim by the same influence received all or the most part of their freight by way of imprest in good money before their ships were called in.

These men, declared Hollond, employed their own ships in ports and places where profit might be made by saving victuals and cordage, preferred their friends' ships for hire, overrated their tonnage and so forth. His indictment is especially valuable as evidence because it was written long after the events and without personal animus: Hollond had no axe to grind with respect to the management of the Navy in Parliament's time and he coyly refrained from naming ships or men. Andrewes Burrell, shipwright and author of a pamphlet of 1646 denouncing the then government of the Navy (apart from Warwick, who appears to have been 'misled' by the 'officers of the Navy' and the 'brethren of the Trinity') did have an axe to grind, being an obvious 'out' trying to get in. For this reason his revelations, like those of

[20] SP16/514, fols. 19–20: Navy Commissioners' estimate of charges for the fleets of 1643, 1644 and 1645 (summer and winter guards). In addition a sum of £15,612 was spent on victuals allowed by the state to forty-eight ships and pinnaces set forth on reprisal by private adventurers, at the rate of 20 shillings per man per month. The total charge, including other expenses on repairs and wages, came to £801,447 16s 3d for the three years. For typical contracts see BL, Additional MSS, 5489, fol. 57 and *CSPD 1641–3*, p. 402.

Hawkins's rivals in the 1580s, must be suspect, but he did name persons and vessels, so that his allegations are open to verification or contradiction in the light of such independent information as may survive. This shows that Burrell, though not invariably accurate, registered some palpable hits and might, with inside knowledge, have registered more.[21]

Ships employed by the Navy in which Navy Commissioners or members of the Navy or Admiralty committees are known to have had an interest were: the *Mayflower* (450 tons, Captain Peter Andrews, brother-in-law of Samuel Vassall, her owner);[22] the *Providence* (271 tons, Captain William Swanley, owned by Richard Cranley, George and William Swanley);[23] the *Marten* (532 tons, Captain George Marten, owner Henry Marten, MP);[24] the *Blessing* (200 tons, Captain Thomas Shafto, owner John Morris, Alexander Bence having a sixteenth share);[25] the *Lucy* (164 tons, Captains Elias Jordan, Elias Drew, owners Thomas Smith and others);[26] the *Angel* (300 tons, Captain Thomas Perry, owners Thomas Smith, Richard Cranley, Mr Reynolds MP and Major Jephson MP);[27] the *Samuel* (90 tons, Captain Matthew Wood, owners Vassall, the Bence brothers and others);[28] the *Messenger* (Captain Ben Trenyman, owner Benjamin Cranley);[29] the *Truelove* (Captain Gervase Coachman, owned by one of the Cranleys);[30] the *Anne Percy* (Captain Thomas Smith, owners possibly

---

[21] Burrell, *To the Right Honourable*; Greene, *Answer of the Commissioners*; Greene, *A Declaration*. The evidence for particular ships and owners which follows is derived from Tanner, *Hollond's Discourses*, pp. lix–lxvii and other sources indicated below.

[22] Employed by Vassall in the American and Mediterranean trades in the 1630s, mainly under Captain Peter Andrews: Hillier, 'Virginia trade'; HCA 13/50, fol. 136; Shilton and Holworthy, *Examinations*, nos. 196, 287, 318, 515; *APC Col. 1613–80*, pp. 205, 293; Powell and Timings, *Documents*, pp. 9, 70, 139, 166, 211, 276.

[23] Hillier, 'Virginia trade', p. 35, referring to a charter-party rating her at only 200 tons; Powell and Timings, *Documents*, pp. 9, 70, 135. Burrell said Twiddy was also a part-owner, but Greene denied this.

[24] *CSPD 1641–3*, pp. 555, 560. Marten, a violent republican and a member of the Admiralty committee of 1642–3, had his ship rated at 700 tons for the 1642 summer guard, though this was reduced to 532 tons the next year: Powell and Timings, *Documents*, pp. 9, 70.

[25] SP16/137; SP16/17, no. 118; Appleby, 'Privateering', II, 14; *CSPD 1644*, p. 550; BL, Additional MSS, 9305, fol. 11. The *Blessing* was at least fifteen years old in 1644: compare ships' ages in Appendix A, Table 3 below.

[26] Powell and Timings, *Documents*, pp. 83, 110, 139, 166, 202, 211, 245; Smith appears to have obtained special terms for her hire.

[27] A prize taken by Thomas Plunkett in 1645 and bought by Smith, Cranley and the two MPs to be set forth as a privateer, she nevertheless appears on a list of hired ships for 1646: *CSPD 1644–5*, p. 590; Powell and Timings, *Documents*, p. 246.

[28] Powell and Timings, *Documents*, pp. 83, 245, 252, 275, 407; *Commons Journal*, III, 76. Despite being in the winter guard for 1648–9, she was then trading to the Canary Islands: Steckley, *Paige Letters*, pp. 1–2. [29] *CSPD 1645–7*, p. 506; Powell and Timings, *Documents*, p. 246.

[30] Powell and Timings, *Documents*, pp. 182, 212, 245, 275; BL, Additional MSS, 9305, fol. 11.

Richard Cranley and John Morris);[31] the *Honour* (359 tons, Captain Edmund Seaman, part-owned by Richard Cranley).[32].

As to the quality of the hired vessels, Burrell maintained that the Commissioners employed 'the worst of merchant ships', a point which Greene predictably denied. Hollond's opinion was that some of them were 'old toads and leeward jades long before they were hired into the service'. One or two of the ships concerned were certainly old, but it is impossible now to ascertain their condition, nor can it be proved that in employing their own or their friends' vessels the managers of the Navy were cheating the state. Nothing illegal, so far as we know, was involved, and the combination of public service with private profit was recognized as part of the natural order of things, even though men constantly castigated each other for taking undue advantage. Hollond, for example, objected when, in 1643, certain merchantmen in Parliament's service owned by members of the Navy Committee were kept in service after the expiry of their contract and their duties at sea because the Navy could not find the money to pay them off. The matter being argued by him and the interested parties before the earl of Warwick, he was overruled, for 'the truth is, there was one then sat in the chair and others that sat by him that could upon such an account easily help a lame dog over the stile': a clear reference to Greene and his colleagues.[33]

On the other hand Burrell accused those in power of keeping the best ships 'estranged from Parliament' for use as privateersmen, instancing Captain Thomas Plunkett's ship the *Discovery*. Plunkett, 'that noted scourge of the Irish at sea', commanded this 380-ton man-of-war with great success in Irish waters in the years 1645 to 1647. Her chief owner, Gregory Clement, MP for Fowey, regicide and a large investor in Irish lands, was a merchant with extensive interests in shipping and assurance. He and Maurice Thompson had promoted the *Discovery* in privateering already in 1636 and again in the 'sea adventure' to Ireland in 1642 (of which more later) and by 1646 they shared her ownership with Warwick, Thomas Smith, Robert Moulton, Plunkett and her alternating captain, Thomas Griggs.[34] The *Constant Warwick*, of some

---

[31] Powell and Timings, *Documents*, pp. 198, 202, 212, 245, 275. Greene denied Burrell's allegation that she belonged to Cranley and Morris, but she is included here on account of the identity of her captain, himself a Navy Commissioner from 1646.

[32] Powell and Timings, *Documents*, pp. 139, 183. Greene denied Burrell's allegation that Twiddy was a part-owner. [33] Tanner, *Hollond's Discourses*, pp. 138–9.

[34] *CSPD 1645–7*, pp. 506, 512. The *Discovery* was accompanied by the *President*, the *Mermaid* and the *Defiance*. Powell and Timings, *Documents*, pp. 9, 214, 246, 275. The *Discovery* is said to have been granted no fewer than twenty-seven prizes between May 1645 and June 1646: Groenveld,

320 tons, famous as prototype of the new frigate class and as a man-of-war of outstanding performance, served as a hired merchantman after her launching early in 1645 until the end of 1647, when she was licensed as a privateer. Built in a private yard by the state's shipwright Peter Pett, she was owned by Warwick, Batten, Moulton, Richard Swanley, William Jessop (Warwick's secretary and effectively Secretary to the Admiralty from 1643), Thomas Turner (secretary to the Commissioners of the Navy) and three others. Warwick and Jessop kindly permitted her use as a privateer and issued the letters of marque on the grounds that 'she may be of special use in scattering and surprising Irish men-of-war, preserving trade, infesting the trade to and from the rebels, and of great assistance to the Irish squadron'.[35]

Much of Parliament's naval effort, and especially privateering effort, was in fact devoted to those purposes. Indeed the most ambitious private expedition of the civil war, launched even before the king raised his standard at Nottingham, was designed to wage war on the Irish rebels and to reap rewards for its promoters in captured shipping, booty and Irish land. Such was the so-called 'sea adventure' financed by a syndicate of London merchants. The better-known scheme of 'Adventurers for Irish Land' had been established early in 1642 in response to the Irish rebellion. It amounted to a joint-stock company for the re-conquest of Ireland, the investors in which, drawn chiefly from Parliament and the City, were to be repaid eventually in confiscated land, the purposes being not only to put down the rebellion and plant English and Scots Protestant colonists, but also to prevent the king from raising for that work an army which he might use nearer home. Instead, Parliament would have armed force at its disposal.[36] Since, however, political and financial difficulties delayed the mounting of any major assault upon the rebels, a group of Londoners offered to take the initiative themselves. Their head in the first instance was Sir Nicholas Crispe, the biggest subscriber to the 'Adventurers for Irish Land', but as a royalist he soon withdrew, leaving the leadership in the hands of the treasurer, Maurice Thompson, whose associates were George and William Thompson, his brothers, William Pennoyer, Gregory Clement, William Willoughby, Samuel Moyer, Richard Hill, Richard Shute, Richard Waring, Thomas Vincent, Thomas Rains-

'English civil wars', p. 551, n. 37, referring to HCA 34/1. When the Spanish ambassador challenged one of these as a Flemish vessel, Clement and Thompson had the gall to refer to letters of reprisal against Spain granted them by Charles in 1636: *Lords' Journal*, VIII, 198–9. See Chapter 2 above on Clement and Chapter 3 on the *Discovery* in 1636.

[35] Johns, '*Constant Warwick*'; HCA 13/61, fols. 392–3, 395.
[36] MacCormack, 'Irish Adventurers'.

borough, John Wood, Thomas Chamberlain and others unnamed.[37] These were for the most part City radicals and commercial connections of Thompson's, Pennoyer, Clement, Moyer, Hill, Rainsborough and Chamberlain having significant shipping interests.

The arrangement proposed by this group to Parliament in April 1642 was that they should provide the money for an expedition of ships, sailors and soldiers to 'do execution' upon the rebels, destroying their defences, capturing their goods and chattels and seizing all vessels and cargoes bound for their supply. All property thus acquired should accrue to the adventurers, to be divided between them and their men. By the end of the month both Houses agreed that the receivers for the Irish land scheme should credit Thompson's syndicate with subscriptions equivalent to their expenditure up to the value of £40,000, payable in the form of Irish land. In June a Parliamentary ordinance defined the scale and terms of the enterprise more precisely, authorizing the adventurers to set forth twelve ships and six pinnaces, 100 horse and 2,000 soldiers, but providing for all prize to be inventoried and for the captains, masters and leading officers of the vessels to enter into bonds in the High Court of Admiralty to answer for the legality of their booty. This was in effect a privileged privateering expedition since the promoters had a promise, albeit no guarantee, of the return of their entire capital outlay, as well as a fair chance of profits by way of prize, for in the circumstances it was unlikely that the Parliamentary authorities would look too closely at the plunder, unless it was claimed by foreign merchants. Moreover the ships, which belonged to the adventurers, were counted as hired by the state at the normal rate with their seamen's victuals and wages, guns, munitions and so forth, so that it was not difficult for the promoters to spend less than the sums with which they would be credited for the final reckoning. These were, after all, businessmen, however hot for the Good Old Cause, and they had enough influence to obtain the loan of ten of the king's shallops, with no mention of payment.[38]

The force which left Dover about the end of June is said to have consisted of ten or fifteen vessels carrying some 1,000 soldiers. It was led by Alexander Lord Forbes, with John Humfry in command of the army, Benjamin Peter being admiral and Thomas Rainsborough (William Rainborowe's son, the future leveller, whose appointment to command the fleet in 1648 was to cause the seamen's revolt) vice-

---

[37] Firth and Rait, *Acts*, I, 9–12.
[38] *Ibid.*; *Commons Journal*, II, 531, 533, 548, 550, 553, 563; *Lords Journal*, v, 29, 34; *CSPI 1633–47*, pp. 360–1; *CSPI (Adventurers)*, p. 288.

admiral. Hugh Peter, the famous New England Puritan, went as chaplain and kept a journal of the proceedings which was published later in the year.[39] Those ships which can be identified were: the *Discovery*, 380 tons, Captain John Brokhaven; the *Ruth*, 400 tons, Captain Robert Constable;[40] the *Employment*, 440 tons, Captain Thomas Ashley;[41] the *Peter*, 270 tons, Captain Peter Strong; and the *Pennington*, 135 tons, Captain Elias Jordan.[42] The summer's operations achieved little against the rebels apart from desultory raiding on and off County Cork and Galway, where Forbes's men ravaged the countryside and were ravaged themselves, chiefly by disease, though five prizes taken at sea, alleged by Peter to be worth £20,000, went some way to reimbursing the adventurers. But for all Peter's raucous trumpeting of the venture's success, the promoters must have been disappointed. They renewed their efforts in October with the dispatch of a fleet of ten ships, but this time they asked to have their expenses met within one year out of subscriptions paid or to be paid into the Irish land scheme. Moreover, though not actually paid by the Navy, these ships were listed as merchantmen added to the Irish winter guard, and the terms on which they served were close to the normal terms of state hire. One third of their prize was to go to the captains and companies of the ships, the remainder being 'received and accounted to the use of the commonwealth for the reducing of Ireland, and for the assurance of freight, victual and wages unto the owners and captains'. Probably, too, the membership of the original syndicate was now changed and broadened, though Thompson evidently remained the moving spirit.[43]

Privateering continued in the following years of civil war, but it seems to have been undertaken for the most part in conjunction with

[39] Stearns, *Strenuous Puritan*, pp. 187–201; Bagwell, *Ireland*, II, 36–42; Powell and Timings, *Documents*, p. 9; Baumber, 'Navy and Ireland'.
[40] Thompson's contract with the Navy for her service: *CSPD 1641–3*, p. 560.
[41] She had belonged to Matthew Cradock and others from 1629: SP16/16/139; HCA 13/49, fol. 550; HCA 13/54, fol. 175. Prizes taken by: *CSPD 1641–3*, p. 557.
[42] A frigate owned by Warwick, Thompson and others: *CSPD 1641–3*, p. 554.
[43] *Commons Journal*, II, 813–14; Powell and Timings, *Documents*, p. 43; *CSPD 1641–3*, p. 402: contracts with Thompson for the *Hopewell* and Thomas Chamberlain for the *George Bonaventure*. Thomas Cuningham, a Scots merchant resident in the Netherlands, was another contributor to the 'sea adventure'. He relates in his journal that he set forth the *Lorne*, a frigate with fourteen guns, thirty seamen and sixty soldiers in 1642 under Captain Andrew Rany of Dunfermline (the same who agreed to go master of Cradock's *Abraham/William* in 1637 – see Chapter 4) to join the expedition, and did also 'animate and excite Captain Louis Dick', commander of the *Golden Lion* of Leith, to do likewise, which two ships, he claims, did valuable service in securing the Isle of Wight for Parliament and in the defence of Plymouth. In 1643 he set forth the *Lorne* again under Captain William Hodges, with the *Guist*, under Captain William Knightsbridge, as her vice-admiral, these being, he alleges, the first ships to be commissioned with letters of marque against the Irish rebels and other disaffected persons in the three kingdoms; Cuningham, *Journal*, pp. 66–8.

the operations of the Parliamentary Navy, which of course included many hired merchantmen. In fact the borderline between official and private naval enterprise became at least as blurred as it had been during the Elizabethan war with Spain. The resulting entanglement of public and private interests in the business of maritime plunder may be seen in the Parliamentary ordinance of February 1644 'for the selling and disposal of all ships and goods taken by reprisal and belonging to the state'. This was concerned with the collection, inventory and sale, on behalf of the state, of those parts of ships and goods due to the state as prize. It did not attempt to define the state's rightful share of prize taken by privateers or jointly by Parliament's ships and privateers, but named the collectors for the state – Thomas Smith esquire (presumably the Admiralty secretary) and John Hill, merchant – and the commissioners to be responsible for the inventory and sale: Thomas Andrewes, alderman, Maurice Thompson, Brian Harrison (the sea-captain), Samuel Avery, William Methold, John Hollond, Richard Cranley, Roger Twiddy, John Morris, Andrewes Burrell and Solomon Smith, gentleman. The issue of this ordinance coincided with the setting forth of a privateering expedition of five men-of-war under the command of Captain John Man, promoted by Richard Cranley, Abraham and Thomas Chamberlain, Roger Twiddy, John Morris, John Dethick and Thomas Cuningham. This force, intended 'for guarding the seas and hindering of supplies sent from foreign parts to the Irish rebels', consisted of the *Achilles*, the *Lorne*, the *Magdalen*, the *Marigold* and the *Scout*, commanded respectively by John Man, William Hodges, John Hosier, Captain Docks and Captain Partridge. All five were listed in the summer guard for 1644 as merchantmen hired for the service of Parliament, for which arrangement Cranley, Twiddy and Morris must have been responsible as Navy Commissioners. Since they were also commissioners for the inventory and sale of prize, they no doubt considered this ambiguous enterprise a sound investment. Cuningham records that the adventurers recalled their squadron in November 1644, 'finding the charge to exceed the benefit' (so much for their motivation), but he himself launched a further venture with the *Lorne* and another frigate, the *Thistle*, under Captain William Halyburtoun.[44]

---

[44] Firth and Rait, *Acts*, I, 392–3; Cuningham, *Journal*, pp. 73–4, 101; Powell and Timings, *Documents*, p. 140. There is need for a study of the privateering of both sides during the years from 1642 to 1648. That there was a substantial amount of it on the Parliamentary side is evident from the list of prizes in HCA 34/1 and from Groenveld, *Verlopend Getij*, pp. 180–2 (I am grateful to my colleague Dr Price for translating this material). Thompson's interest in this activity was evidently very strong: Junge, *Flottenpolitik*, pp. 56–7; HCA 13/60, deposition by John Tayler, merchant, dated 27 April 1645, where he relates that in the winter of 1643–4

In the following year, 1645, it was appropriately Hugh Peter, Thompson's privateering partner, who put before the House of Commons a plan of naval reform which would, if implemented, have carried private interests and enterprise deeper still into Parliament's naval establishment. What he proposed was that all maritime affairs, including the Navy itself and the Court of Admiralty, should be governed by an Admiralty committee of five or seven rotating members and their secretarial staff, with the assistance of admirals of the fleet when available. The Navy's ships should be ordered from private rather than government yards and contracts put out to the lowest bidders. Captains should be made responsible for the financial management of their respective ships, including their rigging, victualling and manning, and should have to submit ships' accounts to the Admiralty committee accordingly. They would, in effect, run their ships for the state much as the more responsible type of master ran his merchantman for his owners. Sailors would not be pressed for service and captains would have to compete with merchantmen, paying wages at the market rate. It was a utopian project of privatization exhibiting a strong belief in the virtues of capitalism, and it would have presented Maurice Thompson and his friends in the City and the Navy with even more opportunities to exploit the state, though Peter presumably saw it as the godly answer to corruption.[45]

His assumption that men of the necessary integrity could be found to direct maritime and naval policy, administer the Navy and adjudicate shipping and prize disputes in the same small committee could hardly have sounded convincing to experienced men like Warwick and Greene, nor could they be expected to accept the notion of trusting captains with the entire management of their ships. In that same year Warwick had occasion to bring official charges against one of his most trusted captains, Richard Swanley. This was the man who had in 1644 secured Milford Haven for Parliament and, having taken various Irishmen prisoner, bound them back to back and threw them overboard 'to wash them to death from the blood of the Protestants that was upon them'. It was not, however, with this crime that he was charged: in fact within a few weeks of it he was summoned to appear at the bar of the House of Commons to be thanked for his services and decorated with a chain of gold.[46] A year later he appeared

Thompson and he and 'some of the adventurers for prizes' hired certain ships (named) 'to go out upon the employment of taking prizes'. On 6 July 1645 Thompson made a deposition (in the same volume) to the same effect. This and other HCA records for the period will yield much more information on privateering. [45] Stearns, *Strenuous Puritan*, pp. 265–6.
[46] Powell and Timings, *Documents*, pp. 115–16, 135–6, 149.

before the Admiralty committee to answer allegations made by his second-in-command, William Smith, and others, to the effect that he had traded with the enemy and taken aboard his flagship certain Irish women who came and went between the ship and enemy quarters ashore. These women were said to have slept in his cabin and to have made the ship 'a water bawdy house abaft the mast', the scandal being such that 'songs were frequently sung up and down the country of the said Captain Swanley and the said Belinda Steele', one of the ladies in question. The committee, in the teeth of the evidence, exonerated him and 'conceived his reputation will best be repaired by a restitution of him to that command', bearing in mind no doubt the reputation of the cause with which Swanley was identified.[47]

No general inquiry into naval abuses was held in the 1640s, though every previous decade of the century had seen one. This contrast does not mean that old evils melted away in the heat of the struggle for liberty. Swindling continued as ever in the Navy Office, the dockyards, the victuals department and the ships, but whereas formerly rivalries, discontents and external pressures repeatedly gave rise to serious attempts at reform, now the cohesion of a close-knit group of like-minded and mutually supportive merchants, officials and captains stifled criticism from men like Hollond and Burrell who tried to rock the boat. No change occurred in Parliament's naval régime until 1649, and then it came in the shape of political purge rather than reform. The 'Act touching the Regulating of the Officers of the Navy and Customs', dated 16 January 1649, ordained that all Customs officers, victualling and dockyard officials, ships' officers and Elder Brothers of Trinity House who had assisted the king in any way since 1641, or had abetted the recent moves for his return to London, or had aided the revolt of the ships in 1648 were to be removed from office. It included in the ban also any officers who had embezzled arms or stores belonging to the Navy, and customers who had taken bribes from merchants. It ordered an inventory of naval stores, an audit of the store-keepers' accounts, the abolition of unnecessary posts in the Navy and the Customs and a rise in salaries with a view to reducing corruption.[48]

This is enough to show that corruption in the Navy and Customs

---

[47] *Ibid.*, pp. 208, 255–6; HCA 13/60, depositions in September, October and November 1645. Richard Swanley, described as of Limehouse, mariner, aged 36 in 1627, had been a master in the East India Company service (Foster, *Court Minutes 1635–9*, pp. 86–8, 102) and commanded the *Sun* in John Weddell's voyage to the East, promoted by Sir William Courten (*CSPD 1636–7*, pp. 528–9). He was an Elder Brother of Trinity House and a part-owner of the *Constant Warwick*. See Baumber, 'East India captain', for his early career.
[48] Firth and Rait, *Acts*, I, 1257–60.

services was recognized to be a serious problem, but in combining an attack upon it with an overtly political purge this measure confused the issue. Did its authors really believe that the corrupt and the malignant were one and the same, Presbyterian traitors battening upon the cause, whereas the Independents were honest men as well as stalwarts of the revolution, or was it merely politically convenient to imply all this? Whatever the answer, the names of those appointed to carry out the purge leave no doubt as to the main purpose, for they were (with the exception of the Commissioners of the Navy, who were collectively and rather anomalously added to the team) Independents: Aldermen Thomas Andrewes and William Berkeley, Maurice Thompson, Richard Shute, William Willoughby, William and Samuel Pennoyer, Stephen Estwick, John Hollond, John Langley, Richard Hill, Robert Thompson, James Russell, Samuel Moyer, Jonathan Andrews and Richard Hutchinson. Nearly all these men are known to have been associates of Maurice Thompson in overseas trade, in shipowning, in privateering or in the financial management of the Customs, the chief revenue source for the huge expenditure of the Navy.[49] They were already deeply entrenched in commerce, shipping, naval finance and sea warfare and constituted a powerful element in the establishment.

The predictable result of their deliberations was a wholesale purge of the Navy. Its real rulers in the civil war – Warwick, Greene, Alexander Bence, Vassall and Batten – either had been already or were now ousted from power. Of the Navy Commissioners, Cranley, Twiddy and Morris were sacked while Peter Pett, Hollond and Smith survived, to be joined now by William Willoughby, a shipowning merchant with New England ties, and Thompson's brother Robert. At Trinity House the government of the Elder Brethren was swept aside by a committee of nine nominated by the new régime and including Maurice Thompson, Samuel Moyer, Smith the Navy Commissioner, Richard Deane, one of the new 'generals-at-sea', and William Badiley, the later naval commander and administrator. The dockyards were likewise purged of known malignants in the upper ranks and the captains of the fleet were largely replaced. Capp finds that twenty-seven of the forty-three summer guard commanders of 1647 were left off the list in 1649 and thereafter, while the 1648 list, already weeded following Batten's dismissal, also included some who were never employed again. Since very few of the senior captains were politically reliable radicals – Robert Moulton being the most notable exception –

[49] Thomas Andrewes, Berkeley, Thompson, Russell and Estwick were collectors of Customs in 1643: *Commons Journal*, III, 2, 19.

the Commonwealth had to call upon experienced masters of the right persuasion from the merchant service.[50]

The new administration did make some effort to improve the honesty and efficiency of naval officials and officers, but since Smith, Moyer, Pennoyer, Thompson, Pett and some others continued to mix public and private business while the scale of naval enterprise increased far beyond anything formerly known, it cannot be said that the Navy was as thoroughly reformed as it was purged. The results and the Navy's subsequent record need not concern us here, particularly because they have been so well examined elsewhere.[51] As for the record of Warwick's Navy, it should not come as a surprise to find it tarred with the same brush as the naval régimes of many generations past and future. It did its job well enough, but both the political circumstances and the power of commercial forces within it tended to favour rather than inhibit the faults and weaknesses it inherited along with the king's ships.

[50] Capp, *Cromwell's Navy*, pp. 48–56; Harris, *Trinity House*, pp. 34–9. Peter Pett appears to have replaced Phineas as a Navy Commissioner before 1649.   [51] Capp, *Cromwell's Navy*.

APPENDIX A

THE SHIPPING RETURNS OF 1582 AND 1629

TABLE 1 represents the information contained in the report of 1582 on the nation's shipping (SP12/156). The last and most elaborate of the Elizabethan surveys, this lists each ship individually, giving in most cases the name and tonnage. It is, however, incomplete, lacking entries for Falmouth, Plymouth, Dartmouth and Wales. Allowing 2,000 tons for Wales and 2,000 tons for Plymouth, Dartmouth and Falmouth, including 4 vessels of the larger sort together amounting to 500 tons, the entire tonnage for the realm may be estimated at 71,040, comprising 46,275 of vessels under 100 tons in burden and 180 larger ships totalling 24,765 tons.

Table 2 represents similar information incorporated in the general report of 1629 (SP16/155/31), which was based on returns made by Bristol, London, the Cinque Ports and various counties. The primary returns survive for London (SP16/137 and SP16/135/38), Bristol (SP16/138/4), Dorset (SP16/138/11), Hampshire (SP16/132/34) and North Kent (SP16/132/19), comparison of which with the general report indicates that the compilation of the latter from the primary material was carried out with only minor errors. Nevertheless the national survey is defective, and more so than that of 1582. It provides no information about Durham, Yorkshire, Cheshire, Lancashire, Somerset, North Devon, most of Sussex and the greater part of Wales, while Leigh, Southampton and Wells are omitted from the lists for their respective counties and the Northumberland section mentions no vessels at all. Moreover the local returns follow no common form either in arranging their material or in classifying their vessels. Thus the great majority of the 166 craft reported by Southwest Wales were boats of 1, 2 or 3 tons such as the major ports did not deign to notice. Judging from other contemporary evidence, moreover, it seems almost certain that Bristol, Dartmouth, Weymouth, Plymouth and Yarmouth understated their shipping resources.

For these deficiencies a compensation of 20,000 tons is suggested, comprising 12,000 tons of vessels under 100 tons in burden and 55 larger vessels totalling 8,000 tons. These aggregates comprise 8,000 and 4,000 tons respectively for Newcastle and Hull, including 22 and 24 of over 99 tons each, representing the

Appendix A: Table 1: *Shipping in the 1582 survey (SP12/156)*

	\multicolumn{6}{c	}{Vessels by tons burden}	
	\multicolumn{2}{c	}{0–99}	\multicolumn{2}{c	}{100+}	\multicolumn{2}{c	}{Total}	Remarks
	No.	Tons	No.	Tons	No.	Tons	
Cumberland	10	141			10	141	
Lancashire and Cheshire	72	1,155			72	1,155	
Gloucestershire	29	556			29	556	
Bristol	20	819	9	1,500	29	2,319	
Bridgwater	8	319			8	319	
Fowey	8	305	3	360	11	665	
Rest of Cornwall	60	2,084			60	2,084	
Exmouth	8	292	1	120	9	412	
Topsham	12	340	1	250	13	590	
Kenton	12	480	2	235	14	715	
Cockington	5	280	2	260	7	540	
Northam	14	492	1	100	15	592	
Rest of Devon	61	2,158			61	2,158	
Poole	12	469	6	710	18	1,179	
Weymouth	17	614	3	410	20	1,024	
Rest of Dorset	23	471			23	471	

204

THE SHIPPING RETURNS OF 1582 AND 1629

	0–99		100+		Total		
	No.	Tons	No.	Tons	No.	Tons	
Southampton	25	1,176	8	1,680	33	2,856	Includes Isle of Wight
Rest of Hampshire	53	709			53	709	
Sussex	65	1,697			65	1,697	
Kent	99	1,283			99	1,283	
Cinque Ports	219	4,212			219	4,212	
London	67	4,018	60	8,280	127	12,298	
Leigh	29	1,700	2	200	31	1,900	
Harwich	8	430	7	740	15	1,170	
Rest of Essex	110	2,448			110	2,448	
Ipswich	18	1,018	8	800	26	1,818	
Aldeburgh	8	591	15	2,140	23	2,731	
Orford	6	208	1	140	7	348	
Southwold	12	488	3	470	15	958	
Rest of Suffolk	29	913			29	913	
Great Yarmouth	57	2,043	4	500	61	2,543	
Wiveton	9	485	4	400	13	885	
Wells	16	726	3	360	19	1,086	
Blakeney	11	519	1	100	12	619	
Cley	8	268	2	200	10	468	
King's Lynn	32	1,452	2	240	34	1,692	
Rest of Norfolk	20	602			20	602	
Lincolnshire	21	921			21	921	
Hull	30	1,270	11	1,480	41	2,750	
Rest of Yorkshire	13	396			13	396	
Newcastle	16	1,127	17	2,590	33	3,717	
Rest of Northeast	113	1,100			113	1,100	
TOTAL	1,465	42,775	176	24,265	1,641	67,040	

Appendix A: Table 2: *Shipping in the 1629 survey (SP16/155)*

	Number by tons burden						Total tonnage			Remarks
	0–99	100–199	200–299	300+	U	Total	0–99	100+	All	U = unknown
Cumberland	12					12	227		227	4 places
Southwest Wales	166		1			167	921	250	1,171	11 places in Pembroke, Carmarthen and Cardigan
Bristol	18	21	9			48	1,200	3,840	5,040	SP16/138/4 agrees
North Cornwall	10					10	241		241	3 places
South Cornwall	68	6			2	76	1,960	890	2,850	
Dartmouth	77	14	1			92	3,900	2,020	5,920	
Plymouth	49	7				56	2,285	820	3,105	
Rest of Devon	50	4				54	1,703	630	2,333	
Lyme	18					18	799		799	
Weymouth	23	3				26	1,125	310	1,435	SP16/138/11 agrees apart from one clerical error
Poole	18	2				20	855	300	1,155	
Rest of Dorset	4					4	115		115	
Hampshire	9					9	277		277	No entry for Southampton
Isle of Wight	57	1				58	1,064	100	1,164	4 places

THE SHIPPING RETURNS OF 1582 AND 1629

	0–99	100–199	200–299	300+	U	Total	0–99	100+	All	U = unknown
Cinque Ports	177	10	3			190	3,881	2,140	6,021	Hastings, Dover, Sandwich, Hythe, Rye, Feversham, Folkestone, Liddy, Walmer, Deal, Ramsgate, Margate, Broadstairs
North Kent	69					69	1,203		1,203	SP16/132/19 agrees. 15 places. 67 hoys and ketches
London	17	34	48	32		131	935	31,320	32,255	SP16/137 agrees. Prizes and east coast ships omitted here
Maldon	3	2				5	120	280	400	The Essex list does not include Leigh or minor places
Colchester	4	6	3			13	160	1,300	1,460	
Harwich	5	11				16	200	1,320	1,520	
Ipswich	4	29	20	14		67	200	13,900	14,100	
Woodbridge	1	6	10	1		18	40	3,150	3,190	
Aldeburgh	17	8	6	3		34	650	3,210	3,860	
Lowestoft	13	2				15	287	240	527	
Southwold	30					30	876		876	
Rest of Suffolk	59					59	950		950	9 places
Great Yarmouth	37	23	3		1	64	2,255	3,470	5,725	
King's Lynn	35	5				40	1,795	540	2,335	
Rest of Norfolk	6				4	10	167		167	No entry for Wells
Lincolnshire	12					12	485		485	Boston, 11
TOTAL	1,068	194	104	50	7	1,423	30,876	70,030	100,906	

Appendix A: Table 3: *Ages of vessels in 1629*

	Age in years	0–99	100–199	200–299	300+	Total
London	1–4		5	6	6	17
	5–9	5	14	16	12	47
	10–14	2	10	7	7	26
	15–19					
	Over 19		1			1
	Unstated	10	4	19	7	40
	TOTAL	17	34	48	32	131
Bristol	1–4	4	2	2		8
	5–9	7	11	3		21
	10–14	4	4	3		11
	15–19	3	3			6
	Over 19		1	1		2
	TOTAL	18	21	9		48
Dorset	1–4	6	1			7
	5–9	24				24
	10–14	18	2			20
	15–19	3	1			4
	Over 19	10	1			11
	Unstated	2				2
	Total	63	5			68
TOTAL	1–4	10	8	8	6	32
	5–9	36	25	19	12	92
	10–14	24	16	10	7	57
	15–19	6	4			10
	Over 19	10	3	1		14
	Unstated	12	4	19	7	42
	TOTAL	98	60	57	32	247

ships which were granted Trinity House certificates in the years 1625 to 1629; 1,000 tons for the rest of the Northeast, 3,000 tons for Leigh, Southampton and Wells, including 6 ships of over 99 tons, and 4,000 tons including 3 such ships for the other missing parts. These putative additions raise the realm total to 120,906 tons, with 403 ships exceeding 99 tons totalling 78,030 tons, while the lesser vessels total 42,876 tons. These are, especially for Newcastle and Hull, deliberately modest estimates, nor do they take account of the probable understatements mentioned above.

Table 3 analyses information about vessels' ages provided by the 1629 returns for the port of London (SP16/137), Bristol (SP16/138/4) and Dorset (SP16/138/11). The east-coast vessels and prizes in the London list are omitted from this table as insufficient samples, but it is worth noting that 9 out of the 22 prizes were over 14 years of age, none of them being under 5. The Bristol and Dorset lists are especially valuable because the former attributes ages to all, and the latter to all but 2 of the vessels included in what purport to be complete lists. In the London list only 69 per cent of the vessels have attributed ages and at least 29 of the 40 of unknown age were ships at sea. Among the Londoners the oldest was 20, among the Bristolians 24 and among the Dorsetmen 30.

In this period tonnages for individual merchantmen were merely approximate estimates, nearly always given in round figures – to the nearest 5, 10 or even 100. Figures for any particular ship tend to vary and inconsistency in this matter was normal. On tonnage measurement in general see Salisbury, 'Early tonnage'.

APPENDIX B

THE TRINITY HOUSE CERTIFICATES
1626–1638

IN THE years from 1626 to 1638 the Master of the Ordnance would issue guns to merchantmen on receipt of a certificate from the Trinity House of Deptford recommending the ship as suitable. This practice may have been motivated in part by the Crown's desire to take up ships for royal service, though in fact only a minority of the ships thus certified were hired by the Crown. Perhaps the official explanation – that the ordnance was for their 'necessary use and defence at sea' (BL, Additional MSS, 37816, fol. 7) – was in this case true. The certificates, however, were required to prevent the sale of the ordnance abroad, an abuse the government had been trying to stop since 1574. In the 1630s, moreover, the authorities were aware that the number of allegedly English ships owned by foreigners was increasing, and were anxious to prevent the issue of ordnance in those cases. The Admiralty Court thus conducted inquiries into the nationality of owners of ships acquired abroad (HCA 13/50, fols. 19, 20, 25, 55, 84, 102, 103, 151, 172, 204, 205, 230, 254, for example).

The Trinity House certificates issued in the reign of Charles from May 1625 to March 1638 are collected in two volumes of the State Papers series in the Public Record Office (SP16/16 and 17). They give information about the name, port and tonnage of the vessel, where and by whom she was built, the names of her master and chief owners, the ordnance to be supplied and the date of the certificate, though not all these details are invariably included. Each certificate relates to a single vessel, except in the case of Hull ships, twenty-six of which (out of twenty-seven in all) are listed in only two certificates. Tables 1 and 2 below summarize data extracted from these documents. In Table 1 the columns headed 'A' refer to certificates contained in SP16/16, covering the period from May 1625 to December 1629 (approximately the war period), and those headed 'B' refer to those in SP16/17, covering the period from January 1630 to March 1638.

Unfortunately these materials do not constitute a reliable guide to the geographical or tonnage distribution of shipping or to fluctuations in shipbuilding. Many ships not mentioned in this record went to sea well armed, especially from the western ports, which obviously did not obtain their guns through Trinity House. Other sources show that by no means all the certified ships were new and that others not here mentioned were built in these years.

THE TRINITY HOUSE CERTIFICATES, 1626–1638

We know also that Trinity House issued some certificates which do not appear in the State Papers collection. English owners probably bought Dutch ships and Dunkirkers more often than these certificates would indicate. In respect of shipowning and shipbuilding they do provide much interesting information, not obtainable elsewhere, concerning particular ships, builders, owners and masters, but in many cases the evidence is clearly incomplete.

The text of a Trinity House certificate is printed in Harris, *Trinity House*, p. 271.

Appendix B: Table 1: *Ports and tonnage of certificated ships*

Ships by tons burden

	0–99 A	0–99 B	100–199 A	100–199 B	200–299 A	200–299 B	300–399 A	300–399 B	400+ A	400+ B	Not known A	Not known B	Totals A	Totals B	Total A+B
Bristol	1												3		3
Plymouth			2	1									2	1	3
Dartmouth			1		1	1							2	1	3
Exeter			1										1		1
Topsham			1		1	1							2	1	3
Exmouth					1								1		1
Lyme	1		2										3		3
Weymouth	2	1			1								3	1	4
Poole	1												1		1
Dover		1		5				3						9	9
Sandwich			1										1		1
Chatham					1								1		1
Rochester			1										1		1
London	8	16	20	39	23	41	10	23	5	6	1	2	67	127	194

THE TRINITY HOUSE CERTIFICATES, 1626–1638

	0–99 A	0–99 B	100–199 A	100–199 B	200–299 A	200–299 B	300–399 A	300–399 B	400+ A	400+ B	Not known A	Not known B	Totals A	Totals B	Total A+B
Colchester			2	3		1							2	4	6
Harwich					1	1							1	1	2
Ipswich			7	2	23	5	3	2	1				34	9	43
Woodbridge					1		1						2		2
Aldeburgh		1	1	2	4	3	2						7	6	13
Lowestoft	1												1		1
Yarmouth	1		8	1	2					1	1		12	2	14
Cley	1												1		1
King's Lynn			4										4		4
Hull	2		21		3	1							26	1	27
Newcastle	1		13		6		2						22		22
Scotland	3		11	2			1						15	2	17
Port unknown						1								1	1
TOTAL	22	19	97	55	68	55	20	28	6	7	2	2	215	166	381
TOTAL A+B	41		152		123		48		13		4		381		

213

Appendix B: Table 2: *Places of building of certificated ships*

	Ships by tons burden				
	0–99	100–299	300+	Unknown	Total
Otterton (Devon)		1			1
Dartmouth		1			1
Weymouth		1			1
Poole	1				1
Basseldon Ferry (Hants)		1			1
Southampton	1				1
Shoreham		8	4	1	13
Strood (Kent)		1			1
Deptford			1		1
Rotherhithe			1		1
St Saviour's	1	3	1		5
Horseydown		6	2		8
Limehouse		4	8		12
Ratcliffe	4	3	2		9
Shadwell	1				1
Wapping	1	13	3	1	18
Blackwall		2			2
Leigh	1				1
Colchester	1	7			8
Harwich		1	1		2
Ipswich		32	8		40
Woodbridge		4	6		10
Aldeburgh		9	1		10
Yarmouth	2	20	1	1	24
King's Lynn		1			1
Selby (Yorks)		1			1
Whitby		3			3
Scotland		1			1
Foreign		21	3		24
Prizes	3	4	1		8
Total	16	148	43	3	210
Place unstated					171

APPENDIX C

CHARTER-PARTIES

THE RECORDS of the High Court of Admiralty include a box (HCA 15/4) which contains exhibits in HCA causes, consisting chiefly of charter-parties and bills of sale for parts of ships. The former have dates from 1628 to 1640 and number 59 in all: 18 time charters in which the charterers agreed to victual and pay wages; 12 time charters in which the owners agreed to victual and pay wages; 23 tonnage charters; and 6 lump-sum charters. These are summarized in Tables 1–4 below. Charter-parties normally included the names of the chief owners and charterers; the ship's name, tonnage burden, ordnance and manning; details concerning the voyage; terms agreed in respect of port charges, average, primage, petitlodmenage, freight charges and demurrage (payment for days spent in port in excess of those agreed); time limits for payment of freight charges and penalties for breach of the agreement. Time charters would indicate the duration of hire and the extra time allowed if required. Chartering in general is discussed in Davis, *English Shipping Industry*, pp. 166–7, and the business significance of this particular set is further considered in Chapter 1 herein. In all cases listed except two (the *Adventure* and the *Bride*, for which the dates are here shown) the charter-parties have dates from 1630 to 1640. Other charter-parties made in this reign can be found in HCA 15/5 and the HCA 24 series.

When charter-parties specified a voyage 'within or without the Straits', this was generally taken to mean that the charterers could send her wherever they wished. In the case of two ships listed here, however – the *Samaritan* and the *Roebuck* – William Courten and his co-owners argued that this phrase could not reasonably be interpreted to include the East Indies, whereas the charterers argued the contrary (HCA 13/54, fols. 139–40, 308–9, 378). In two cases – those of the *Jeremy* and the *William* – provision was made for a tonnage charter to be continued as a time charter, by which the ship would be hired by the month at a specified rate. Some charter-parties were more detailed and precise than others, and some indicate peculiar concerns. Thus the 1628 charter-party for the *Adventure* reveals that she carried letters of reprisal in her Barbary venture, the merchants to have two thirds and the owners one third of whatever prize might accrue. In several cases the master, and in more than

SHIPS, MONEY AND POLITICS

Appendix C: Table 1: *Time charters where charterers victualled and paid wages*

Ship	Port	T	G	M	M°	£	T/£	T/M	Voyage
Ark	London	340	26	45	12	92	3.7	7.6	Plymouth and WWS
Exchange	London	260	20	40	8	95	2.7	6.5	WWS
Samaritan	London	260	22	52	10	80	3.25	5.0	WWS (East Indies)
Assurance	London	240	14	30	12	64	3.75	8.0	WWS, except Brazil and not beyond Leghorn or Venice
Flower de Luce	Weymouth	240	12	27	8	62.5	3.8	8.9	Virginia or otherwise
Relief	Ipswich	220	10	17	13	31	7.1	12.9	WWS (if S. of Lisbon, extra guns and men)
Adventure	London	200	20	41	6	72.5	2.8	4.9	Barbary (1628)
Adventure	London	200	19	38	7	70	2.9	5.3	WWS
St Francis	London	200	U	14	5	45	4.4	14.3	Archangel
Endeavour	London	170	12	24	6	60	2.8	7.1	WWS, except Barbary, Spain and Portugal
Tristram and Jane	London	160	12	19	8	48	3.3	8.4	Newfoundland and Iberia (5 extra men from N'land)
Gilliflower	London	160	10	22	7	48	3.3	7.3	WWS
Anne and Elizabeth	London	150	14	32	6	55	2.7	4.7	Barbary and Atlantic Is.
William	London	150	10	20	5	45	3.3	7.5	Spain
Suzanna	London	140	4	19	7	40	3.5	7.4	Virginia
Desire	London	90	6	14	4	31	2.9	6.4	Azores, Newfoundland, Ireland or Is. north of 26°
Matthew	London	71	2	10	4.5	20	3.5	7.1	Canaries
Roebuck	London	60	8	17	10	24	2.5	3.5	WWS (East Indies)

T = tons burden
G = pieces of ordnance
M = men, including master and boy
M° = duration of hire in months, excluding extra time allowed
£ = rate of hire per month in £

T/£ = tons per £ per month obtained by charterers
T/M = tons served per man
WWS = within or without the Straits
U = unknown

216

Appendix C: Table 2: Time charters where owners victualled and paid wages

Ship	Port	T	G	M	M°	£	T/£	T/M	Voyage
Anthony	London	240	18	37	8	180	1.4	6.5	Ireland, Iberia, WWS
Bride	London	200	14	31	6	135	1.4	6.5	Portsmouth, Madeira, Canaries (1629)
Faith	London	200	20	39	9	145	1.4	5.1	Canada, Newfoundland, Spain
Rebecca	London	200	U	32	8	150	1.3	6.3	WWS
Salutation	London	200	20	40	5	180	1.1	5.0	Where merchants determine, not beyond Leghorn
Truelove	London	160	12	24	6	120	1.3	6.7	WWS
Lydia	London	130	12	20	5	122.5	1.1	6.5	Biscay, Canaries and another voyage without the Straits
William and Rose	London	120	7	15	9	90	1.3	8.0	WWS, not beyond Malaga
Charles	London	100	6	13	12	80	1.25	7.7	Western Is., France; 2nd voyage Ireland and Atlantic Iberia
Request	London	90	U	16	9	70	1.3	5.6	Canaries
Mayflower	Whitby	68	U	9	8	25	2.7	7.6	Any of Scandinavia, Baltic, Netherlands, France, England or Scotland
Blessing	Falmouth	50	6	U	7	21	2.4	U	Virginia

T = tons burden
G = pieces of ordnance
M = men, including master and boy
M° = duration of hire in months, excluding extra time allowed
£ = rate of hire per month in £

T/£ = tons per £ per month obtained by charterers
T/M = tons served per man
WWS = within or without the Straits
U = unknown

Appendix C: Table 3: *Tonnage charters*

Ship	Port	T	G	M	£/T	T/M	Voyage and cargo
Ambrose and Charles	Ipswich	300	U	12	U	25.0	Norway. 37 shillings per 100 deals
John	Ipswich	300	U	16	1	18.75	Baltic. 41 shillings per last
Exchange	Ipswich	220	U	24	2.75	9.2	Archangel
St George	London	220	22	36	5	6.1	Newfoundland, Spain. Wine, oil, etc.
Elizabeth	London	220	8	24	3	8.3	Archangel
Jeremy	London	200	20	35	4	5.7	Falmouth, Venice. Pilchards. From Venice at £160 per month if charterers desire
Salutation	Yarmouth	200	16	30	3.8	6.7	Malaga. Raisins, etc.
William	London	200	18	31	3	6.5	Middleburg, Genoa/Leghorn. Thence at £150 per month
Ralph Bonaventure	London	190	14	24	5	7.9	Waterford, Spain
Ambrose	London	180	16	30	4.5	6.0	Malaga and Motril
Anne Speedwell	London	160	U	U	U	U	Norway. 41 shillings per 100 deals
Pearl	London	130	10	20	4	6.5	Portugal
Richard and Nathaniel	London	130	10	19	5.5	6.8	San Sebastian, Malaga
Mary Fortune	London	120	8	18	4.75	6.7	La Rochelle, Kinsale, Canaries, Spain
James	Pittenweem	120	10	22	4	5.5	Canaries
Affection	London	110	10	19	4.25	5.8	Sanlúcar
John and Francis	Ipswich	100	U	11	1.25	9.1	Newcastle and Riga. 48–52 shillings per last, depending on type of goods
Jonas	Anstruther	100	U	11	1.4	9.1	Nantes. Wine
Thomas	London	100	8	11	1.8	9.1	Nantes. Wine
Mary	Dover	60	U	6	U	10.0	R. Tees, Rouen. Alum. 16.5 *livres tournois* per ton
Blessing	Falmouth	50	2	9	4	5.6	Tenerife
Hopewell	Shoreham	25	U	6	1.1	4.1	Bristol. Wine. Option of further voyage to Limerick, Dover at 24 shillings per ton on return lading
Mary	Margate	bark	U	6	0.5	U	Poole. For tobacco-pipe clay

T = tons burden

£/T = £ per ton paid on cargo

CHARTER-PARTIES

Appendix C: Table 4: *Lump-sum charters*

Ship	Port	T	G	M	S	£/T	T/M	Voyage and cargo
Mary Constance	London	300	26	42	605	2	7.1	Charlestown or Boston. Passengers and goods
Centurion	London	250	6	18	712.5	2.85	13.9	Archangel
Hopewell	London	100	8	14	200	2	7.1	Dartmouth/Plymouth, Bilbao
Blessing	London	80	4	12	292	3.65	6.7	Tenerife. 3575 *livres tournois* if unladed at Le Havre
Rebecca	London	50	3	8	275	5.5	6.25	Topsham, Le Havre, Canaries, Dover, London/Amsterdam
Content	Colchester	40	U	7	80	2	5.7	Rouen, La Rochelle

T = tons burden
G = pieces of ordnance
M = men, including master and boy
S = lump sum paid by charterers

£/T = £ per ton paid by charterers
T/M = tons served per man
U = unknown

219

one the crew, were allowed a certain interest in the cargo. In the *Blessing* of Falmouth, bound for Virginia, the owner, a mariner, was to sail as master's mate without wages, 'in regard of the said sum of £21 per month paid to him for his freight'. In this vessel cabins were to be provided for the passengers, and in the *Mary Constance*, bound for Charlestown or Boston, 'cabins, stalls and rooms' were to be constructed of boards to be removed on arrival. This ship's company were to share their 'resting rooms', furnaces and oven with the passengers, to assist them with their cattle, to refrain from spoiling or wasting their victuals (viz. taking or consuming them), and to demean themselves well towards them, without offering them 'any disturbance or injury'. Sailors did not often take kindly to passengers of whatever social background. Many charter-parties stated the obligation of the crew to serve the requirements of the merchants or their factors during the voyage. In the case of the *William and Rose* the charterers hired the ship for nine months, but after four months re-chartered her to another merchant for four months at the same rate.

APPENDIX D

THE 1582 AND 1629 RETURNS OF SEAMEN

THE SHIPPING surveys of 1582 (SP12/156) and 1629 (SP16/155/31) included returns of seafaring men. The figures for 1582, summarized in Table 1, though not entirely satisfactory, have some value. Most of the localities classified the men as masters, mariners and fishermen, but some failed to distinguish mariners from fishermen, while Kent made no distinctions at all. In any case it is not clear what such distinctions meant, nor whether all the returning authorities used the same criteria. Some of those listed as mariners were probably fishermen and the total is certainly inflated by large numbers of the latter. The result is a figure of some 15,000 men serving 67,000 tons of shipping, a ratio of 4.5 tons per man. The actual ratio in the merchant service is perhaps better represented by the London figures of approximately 1,300 men serving 12,000 tons – 9 tons per man – but this was probably higher than the national average. Unfortunately the figures for 1629 are too muddled and implausible to be used collectively for national estimates. Most places made some attempt at classification, but in the absence of any consistent terminology the results are baffling. Hampshire, for example, distinguished mariners, seamen and fishermen, while the Isle of Wight divided seamen into masters, mariners, sailors, fishermen and boatmen, and Southwold's return specified 'seamen: masters for Iceland or Castle, 33; sailors or fishermen, 72'. Moreover the totals, being well below those for 1582, are unacceptable. London, however, made a very detailed and seemingly accurate as well as interesting return, which is summarized in Table 2 below. This muster (SP16/135/38) listed the seamen individually, giving their places of abode and the ages of those at home, though not of those at sea. The list is headed by the Elder and Younger Brothers of the Trinity House of Deptford, 31 and 254 in number respectively, and these are added to the rest to make up the total of 3,422 seamen. Since most of them were masters, it is likely that some of them were counted twice, which would have inflated the figure for masters and the total of seamen. Table 2 therefore presents both columns with and without the addition of the Brothers.

The London figures for seamen and shipping show approximately 3,500 men serving 32,000 tons of shipping, a ratio of 9 tons per man – the same as that found for 1582. If we suppose that the national ratio was 7 tons per man and use the estimate of national tonnage for 1629 from Appendix A – 120,000 tons – we reach an estimate of 17,000 seamen for 1629. Using the ratio of 4.5 found in 1582, which was probably based on the inclusion of large numbers of men working the short-distance fisheries, the estimated national total would rise to 26,667. Alternatively we may work from the 1582 figures showing that London had 17 per cent of the national tonnage and 8.67 per cent of the nation's seamen, whereas in 1629 its share of the national tonnage had risen to 27 per cent. We may therefore argue that London's seamen, numbering between 3,000 and 3,500 in 1629, would have made up about 14 per cent of the national total, which would thus be put at 20,000 to 25,000. These are obviously very rough and ready calculations, but they do show a certain convergence and agree with the estimates of Commander Waters in his 'English Pilot'. The growth of the Navy and the merchant marine in the next two decades must have increased the numbers of seamen substantially.

THE 1582 AND 1629 RETURNS OF SEAMEN

Appendix D: Table 1: *Returns of seamen in 1582*

	Mrs	M	F	M/F	Total	Remarks
London	143	986	195		1,324	
Essex	115			578	693	
Norfolk	232			1,438	1,670	
Suffolk	98			1,184	1,282	
Cornwall	108			1,810	1,918	Without Falmouth
Devon	150	1,914	101		2,165	Without Plymouth or Dartmouth
Dorset	85	460	100		645	
Hampshire	46	241	83		370	
Sussex	70	321	302		693	
Kent				243	243	Masters included in total
Cinque Ports	200	604	248		1,052	Most of the mariners belong to small fishing vessels
Bristol and Somerset	48			464	512	
Gloucestershire	17	180	23		220	
Yorkshire	81	292	507		880	
The North	29	372	450		851	East coast north of Yorks
Lincolnshire	20	195	234		449	
Cheshire and Lancashire	35	253	36		324	
Cumberland	12	20	180		212	
Total	1,489	5,838	2,459	5,717	15,503	

Mrs = masters
M = mariners
F = fishermen
M/F = mariners and/or fishermen
This table follows the MS in respect of the order in which the localities are listed.

223

Appendix D: Table 2: *The London return of seamen, watermen and fishermen in 1629*

	Mrs	M	T	H	S	W	F
Greenwich		13	13	8	5	128	14
Deptford	3	37	40	32	8	20	3
Rotherhithe	45	229	274	100	174	47	
Horseydown and St Olaves	22	87	109	47	62	146	11
Tower Wharf and St Katherines	19	241	260	61	199	101	
E. Smithfield and Whitechapel	3	28	31	31			
Shadwell and Wapping Wall	7	141	148	148			
Wapping	35	341	376	143	233	29	
Ratcliffe	73	965	1,038	292	746	34	
Limehouse	25	306	331	131	200		
Poplar	7	77	84	39	45		8
Shipped for East Indies	5	428	433		433		
Gravesend						121	
Erith and Woolwich						19	5
Battle Bridge (Southwark)						25	
Bankside (Southwark)							10
St Saviours (Southwark)						359	
St Saviours Upper Ground						347	8
Lambeth						176	
Battersea, Chelsea and places west to Maidenhead						435	93
Westminster and City						439	
Masters and overseers of watermen						8	
Hobbing							1
Allhallows and St Mary's (Kent)							3
Leigh							3
Barking							41
West Ham							2
TOTAL	244	2,893	3,137	1,032	2,105	2,434	202
Trinity House Brothers	285		285				
TOTAL with Brothers	529	2,893	3,422	1,032	2,105	2,434	202

Mrs = masters
M = mariners
T = total seamen
H = mariners at home
S = mariners at sea
W = watermen
F = fishermen

BIBLIOGRAPHY

The following is a list of the sources and secondary works mentioned in the text and footnotes of this book. Where no place of publication is given this is London.

PRIMARY SOURCES
Manuscript
British Library (BL): Additional MSS, Egerton MSS, Harleian MSS, Lansdowne MSS, Sloane MSS
Public Record Office:
High Court of Admiralty (HCA)
State Papers Domestic, Elizabeth (SP12); James I (SP14); Charles I (SP16)
State Papers Foreign, Barbary States (SP71); France (SP78); Holland (SP84); Portugal (SP89); Spain (SP94); Turkey (SP97); Venice (SP99)
State Papers, Warrants (SP39)
Wills (Prob. 11)

Printed
Andrews, K. R. (ed.), *The Last Voyage of Drake and Hawkins* (1972)
APC: *Acts of the Privy Council*
APC Col: *Acts of the Privy Council, Colonial Series*, 1 (1908)
Aubrey, John, *Brief Lives*, ed. A. Clark (2 vols., Oxford, 1898)
Barlow, Edward, *Journal*, ed. B. Lubbock (2 vols., 1934)
Boxer, C. R. (ed.), *The Journal of Maarten Harpertszoon Tromp, anno 1639* (1930)
Brooks, F. W. (ed.), *A Calendar of the Early Judgements of Trinity House* (1951)
(ed.), *The First Order Book of the Hull Trinity House, 1632–1665* (1942)
Bruce, J. (ed.), *Journal of a Voyage into the Mediterranean by Sir Kenelm Digby, A.D. 1628* (1868)
Burrell, A., *To the Right Honourable, the High Court of Parliament, the Remonstrance of Andrewes Burrell, Gent....* (BL, Thomason Tracts, E.335/6), 1646

BIBLIOGRAPHY

Butler, *Dialogues*: W. G. Perrin (ed.), *Boteler's Dialogues* (1929)
Cal. Muncaster MSS: *The Manuscripts of Lord Muncaster* (Historical Manuscripts Commission, 10th Report, Appendix, vol. IV, 1885)
Carteret, *Barbary Voyage*: B. Penrose (ed.), *The Barbary Voyage of 1638*, by Sir George Carteret (Philadelphia, 1929)
Castries, *Angleterre; France; Pays-Bas*: H. de Castries (ed.), *Sources Inédites de l'Histoire du Maroc* (Paris, 1905–23, etc.)
Cell, G. T. (ed.), *Newfoundland Discovered: English Attempts at Colonisation 1610–1630* (1982)
Clarendon, *History*: W. D. Macray (ed.), *The History of the Rebellion and Civil Wars in England*, by Edward Hyde, Earl of Clarendon (6 vols., Oxford, 1888)
   Life: Edward Hyde, Earl of Clarendon, *The Life of Edward, Earl of Clarendon* (3 vols., Oxford, 1759)
Clarendon *State Papers*: R. Scrope and T. Monkhouse (eds.), *State Papers Collected by Edward, Earl of Clarendon, Commencing from the Year 1621* (3 vols., Oxford, 1767–86)
Commons Journal: Journals of the House of Commons, 1547–1714 (17 vols., 1742, etc.)
Corbett, J. S. (ed.), *State Papers Relating to the Navy During the Spanish War, 1585–1587* (1898)
Cowper MSS: *The Manuscripts of the Earl Cowper* (Historical Manuscripts Commission, 2 vols., 1888–90)
CSPD: *Calendar of State Papers, Domestic Series, James I and Charles I* (27 vols., 1857–97)
CSPI *1633–47*: *Calendar of State Papers Relating to Ireland...* (1901)
CSPI (*Adventurers*): *Calendar of State Papers Relating to Ireland: Adventurers for Land, 1642–1659* (1903)
CSPV: *Calendar of State Papers... Venice* (37 vols., 1864–1939)
Cuningham, Thomas, *The Journal of Thomas Cuningham of Campvere, 1640–1654*, ed. E. J. Courthope (Edinburgh, 1928)
Dan, Père, *Histoire de la Barberie et de ses Corsaires* (2nd edn, Paris, 1649)
Dee, John, *General and Rare Memorials Pertaining to the Perfect Art of Navigation* (1577)
Digby, Sir Kenelm, *Sir Kenelm Digby's Honour Maintained* (1641)
   Private Memoirs of Sir Kenelm Digby... Written by Himself (1827)
Donno, E. S. (ed.), *An Elizabethan in 1582: The Diary of Richard Madox, Fellow of All Souls* (1976)
Drake, Sir Francis (ed.), *Sir Francis Drake Revived* (1628)
Dunton, John, *The true journall of the Sallee Fleet* (1637)
Firth, C. H., and R. S. Rait (eds.), *Acts and Ordinances of the Interregnum, 1642–1660* (3 vols., 1911)
Foster, W. (ed.), *Calendar of the Court Minutes... of the East India Company: 1635–1639* (Oxford, 1907); *1640–1643* (Oxford, 1909)

BIBLIOGRAPHY

Gardiner, S. R. (ed.), *Constitutional Documents of the Puritan Revolution, 1625–1660* (Oxford, 1889)

—— (ed.), *Documents Illustrating the Impeachment of the Duke of Buckingham in 1626* (1889)

Greene, Giles, *The Answer of the Commissioners of the Navie, to a Scandalous Pamphlet...*, BL, Thomason Tracts, E. 340/31 (1646)

A Declaration in Vindication of the Honour of Parliament..., BL, Thomason Tracts, E. 405/8 (1647)

Harlow, V. T. (ed.), *Colonizing Expeditions to the West Indies and Guiana, 1623–1667* (1925)

—— (ed.), *The Voyages of Captain William Jackson (1642–1645)* (1923)

Harris, G. G. (ed.), *Trinity House of Deptford Transactions, 1609–35* (1983)

Jonson, *Works*: C. H. Herford and E. M. Simpson (eds.), *Works of Ben Jonson* (11 vols., Oxford, 1925–52)

Larkin, J. F. (ed.), *Stuart Royal Proclamations, Vol. 2: Royal Proclamations of King Charles I, 1625–1646* (Oxford, 1983)

Laughton, J. K. (ed.), *State Papers Relating to the Defeat of the Spanish Armada* (2 vols., 1895)

Lords' Journal: Journals of the House of Lords, 1578–1714 (19 vols., 1767, etc.)

McGowan, A. P. (ed.), *The Jacobean Commissions of Enquiry, 1608 and 1618* (1971)

Manwaring, G. E., and W. G. Perrin (eds.), *The Life and Works of Sir Henry Mainwaring* (2 vols., 1920–22)

Marsden, R. G. (ed.), *Documents Relating to Law and Custom of the Sea* (2 vols., 1915–16)

Moens, W. J. C. (ed.), *The Registers of the French Church, Threadneedle Street, London* (vol. 1, 1896)

Monson's Tracts: M. Oppenheim (ed.), *The Naval Tracts of Sir William Monson* (5 vols., 1902–14)

Perrin, W. G. (ed.), *The Autobiography of Phineas Pett* (1918)

Powell, J. R. (ed.), *The Letters of Robert Blake* (1937)

Powell, J. R., and E. K. Timings (eds.), *Documents Relating to the Civil War, 1642–1648* (1963)

Richardson, S. (ed.), *Sir Thomas Roe's Negotiations with the Grand Signior* (1740)

Roberts, Lewes, *The Merchants Mappe of Commerce* (1638)

Rushworth, J. (ed.), *Historical Collections* (7 vols., 1659–1701)

Shilton, D. O., and R. Holworthy (eds.), *High Court of Admiralty Examinations, 1637–1638* (1932)

Steckley, G. F., (ed.), *The Letters of John Paige, London Merchant, 1648–1658* (1984)

Stevens, H. (ed.), *The Dawn of British Trade to the East Indies* (1886)

Tanner, J. R. (ed.), *Two Discourses of the Navy, 1638 and 1659, by John Hollond* (1896)

Tawney, R. H., and E. Power (eds.), *Tudor Economic Documents* (3 vols., 1924)

BIBLIOGRAPHY

Twiss, T. (ed.), *The Black Book of the Admiralty* (4 vols., 1871–6)
Wernham, R. B. (ed.), *The Expedition of Sir John Norris and Sir Francis Drake to Spain and Portugal, 1589* (1988)

SECONDARY WORKS

Alcalá-Zamora y Queipo de Llano, José, *España, Flandés y el Mar del Norte (1618–39): la Última Ofensiva Europea de los Austrias Madrileños* (Barcelona, 1975)
Alexander, M. van C., *Charles I's Lord Treasurer: Sir Richard Weston, Earl of Portland, 1577–1635* (1975)
Andrews, C. M., *The Colonial Period of American History* (4 vols., New Haven, 1934)
Andrews, K. R., *Elizabethan Privateering: English Privateering During the Spanish War, 1585–1603* (1964)
  'Sir Robert Cecil and Mediterranean Plunder', *English Historical Review*, 87 (1972), 513–32
  Trade, Plunder and Settlement: Maritime Enterprise and the Genesis of the British Empire, 1480–1630 (1984)
Appleby, J. C., 'An association for the West Indies? English plans for a West India Company, 1621–1629', *Journal of Imperial and Commonwealth History*, 15 (1987), 213–41
  'English privateering during the Spanish and French wars, 1625–1630', 2 vols., Ph.D. thesis, University of Hull, 1983
Ashton, R., *The City and the Court* (1981)
  The Crown and the Money Market, 1603–1640 (Oxford, 1960)
  'The disbursing official under the early Stuarts: the cases of Sir William Russell and Philip Burlamachi', *Bulletin of the Institute of Historical Research*, 30 (1957), 162–74
Aylmer, G. E., 'Attempts at administrative reform, 1625–40', *English Historical Review*, 72 (1957), 229–59
  The King's Servants: The Civil Service of Charles I, 1625–1642 (1961)
Bagwell, R., *Ireland under the Stuarts* (3 vols., 1909–16)
Barbour, V., 'Dutch and English merchant shipping in the seventeenth century', *Economic History Review*, 2 (1929–30), 261–90
  'Marine risks and insurance in the seventeenth century', *Journal of Economic and Business History*, 1 (1929), 561–96
Bard, N. P., 'The earl of Warwick's voyage of 1627', in N. A. M. Rodger (ed.), *The Naval Miscellany* (Navy Records Society, vol. cxxv, 1984), pp. 15–93
Baumber, M. L., 'An East India captain: the early career of Captain Richard Swanley', *Mariner's Mirror*, 53 (1967), 265–79
  'The Navy and the civil war in Ireland, 1641–1643', *Mariner's Mirror*, 57 (1971), 385–97

BIBLIOGRAPHY

Bligh, E. W., *Sir Kenelm Digby and his Venetia* (1932)

Bottigheimer, K. S., *English Money and Irish Land: The 'Adventurers' in the Cromwellian Settlement of Ireland* (Oxford, 1971)

Boxer, C. R., 'English shipping in the Brazil trade, 1640–65', *Mariner's Mirror*, 37 (1951), 197–230

Brenner, R., 'The civil war politics of London's merchant community', *Past and Present*, 58 (1973), 53–107

    'Commercial change and political conflict: the merchant community in civil war London', Ph.D. thesis, University of Princeton, 1970

    'The social basis of English commercial expansion, 1550–1650', *Journal of Economic History*, 32 (1972), 361–84

Brewer, J., *The Sinews of Power: War, Money and the English State, 1688–1783* (1989)

Bridenbaugh, C., *Vexed and Troubled Englishmen, 1590–1642* (Oxford, 1968)

Bridenbaugh, C. and R., *No Peace Beyond the Line: The English in the Caribbean, 1604–1690* (1972)

Brown, A., *The Genesis of the United States* (2 vols., Boston, 1890)

Brulez, W., 'Shipping profits in the early modern period', *Low Countries History Yearbook / Acta Historiae Neerlandicae*, 14 (1981), 65–84

Brunton, D., and D. H. Pennington, *Members of the Long Parliament* (1954)

Capp, B., *Cromwell's Navy: The Fleet and the English Revolution, 1648–1660* (Oxford, 1989)

Cell, G. T., *English Enterprise in Newfoundland, 1577–1660* (1969)

Chaplin, W. R., 'William Rainsborough and his associates of the Trinity House', *Mariner's Mirror*, 31 (1945), 178–97

Chaudhuri, K. N., *The English East India Company: The Study of an Early Joint-Stock Company, 1600–1640* (1965)

Coindreau, R., *Les Corsaires de Salé* (Paris, 1948)

Corbett, J. S., *The Successors of Drake* (1900)

Course, A. G., *A Dictionary of Nautical Terms* (1962)

Craven, W. F., 'The earl of Warwick: a speculator in piracy', *Hispanic American Historical Review*, 10 (1930), 457–79

Croft, P., 'English mariners trading to Spain and Portugal, 1558–1625', *Mariner's Mirror*, 69 (1983), 251–66

Cust, R., and A. Hughes (eds.), *Conflict in Early Stuart England: Studies in Religion and Politics, 1603–1642* (1989)

Davies, C. S. L., 'The administration of the Royal Navy under Henry VIII: the origins of the Navy Board', *English Historical Review*, 80 (1965), 268–88

Davies, G., *The Early Stuarts, 1603–1660* (2nd edn, Oxford, 1959)

Davies, K. G., *The North Atlantic World in the Seventeenth Century* (1974)

Davis, R., 'Earnings of capital in the English shipping industry, 1670–1730', *Journal of Economic History*, 17 (1957), 409–25

    'England and the Mediterranean, 1570–1670', in F. J. Fisher (ed.), *Essays in the Economic and Social History of Tudor and Stuart England* (1961)

'The organization and finance of the English shipping industry in the later seventeenth century', Ph.D, thesis, University of London, 1955
   The Rise of the English Shipping Industry (1962)
   The Trade and Shipping of Hull, 1500–1700 (1964)
Dewar, A. C., 'The naval administration of the Interregnum, 1641–59', *Mariner's Mirror*, 12 (1926), 406–30
Dictionary of National Biography (*DNB*)
Dietz, F. C., *English Public Finance, 1558–1641* (1932)
Dunn, R. S., *Sugar and Slaves: The Rise of the Planter Class in the English West Indies, 1624–1713* (1973)
Edmundson, G., *Anglo-Dutch Rivalry During the First Half of the Seventeenth Century* (Oxford, 1911)
Farnell, J. E., 'The navigation act of 1651, the first Dutch war, and the London merchant community', *Economic History Review*, 2nd Series, 16 (1964), 439–54
Firth, C. H., 'Sailors in the civil war', *Mariner's Mirror*, 12 (1926), 237–59
Fisher, S. (ed.), *Innovation in Shipping and Trade* (Exeter Maritime Studies, no. 6) (Exeter, 1989)
Friis, A., *Alderman Cockayne's Project and the Cloth Trade* (1927)
Fulton, T. W., *The Sovereignty of the Sea* (1911)
Gabrieli, V., *Sir Kenelm Digby: un'Inglese Italianato nell'età della Controriforma* (Rome, 1957)
Gardiner, S. R., *History of England from the Accession of James I to the Outbreak of the Civil War, 1603–1642* (10 vols., 1883–4)
Gordon, M. D., 'The collection of ship-money in the reign of Charles I', *Transactions of the Royal Historical Society*, 3rd Series, 4 (1910), 141–62
Grant, A., 'John Delbridge of Barnstaple, merchant, 1564–1639', in Fisher, *Innovation*, pp. 91–109
Groenveld, S., 'The English civil wars as a cause of the first Anglo-Dutch war, 1640–52', *Historical Journal*, 30 (1987), 541–66
   Verlopend Getij: De Nederlandse Republiek en de Engelse Burgeroorlog, 1640–1646 (Dieren, 1984)
Hannay, D. *Naval Courts Martial* (Cambridge, 1914)
Harlow, V. T., *A History of Barbados* (Oxford, 1926)
Harris, G. G., *Trinity House of Deptford, 1514–1660* (1969)
Havran, M. J., *Caroline Courtier: The Life of Lord Cottington* (1973)
Hillier, S. E., 'The trade of the Virginia colony, 1606 to 1660', Ph.D. thesis, University of Liverpool, 1971
Horn, J., 'Servant migration to the Chesapeake in the seventeenth century', in T. W. Tate and D. L. Ammerman (eds.), *The Chesapeake in the Seventeenth Century* (1979)
Israel, J., *The Dutch Republic and the Hispanic World, 1606–1661* (Oxford, 1982)
Johns, A. W., 'The *Constant Warwick*', *Mariner's Mirror*, 18 (1932), 254–66
   'The Principal Officers of the Navy', *Mariner's Mirror*, 14 (1928), 32–54

Julien, Ch.-A., *History of North Africa: Tunisia, Algeria, Morocco from the Arab Conquest to 1830* (1970, translated from the French edn of 1961)

Junge, H.-C., *Flottenpolitik und revolution. Die Entstehung der Englischen Seemacht während der Herrschaft Cromwells* (Stuttgart, 1980)

Keeler, M. F., *The Long Parliament, 1640–1641: A Biographical Study of the Members* (Philadelphia, 1954)

Kennedy, D. E., 'The English naval revolt of 1648', *English Historical Review*, 77 (1962), 247–56

'The establishment and settlement of Parliament's Admiralty, 1642–1648', *Mariner's Mirror*, 48 (1962), 276–91

'Naval captains at the outbreak of the English civil war', *Mariner's Mirror*, 46 (1960), 181–98

Kepler, J. S., *The Exchange of Christendom: the International Entrepôt at Dover, 1622–1651* (Leicester, 1976)

'Fiscal aspects of the English carrying trade during the Thirty Years War', *Economic History Review*, 2nd Series, 25 (1972), 261–83

'The value of ships gained and lost by the English shipping industry during the wars with Spain and France, 1624–1630', *Mariner's Mirror*, 59 (1973), 218–21

Kippis, A., *Biographia Britannica*, vol. IV (1789)

Kirke, H., *The First English Conquest of Canada* (2nd edn, 1908)

Lang, R. G., 'The greater merchants of London in the early seventeenth century', D.Phil. thesis, Oxford University, 1963

Lewis, A. H., *A Study of Elizabethan Ship-Money, 1588–1603* (Philadelphia, 1928)

Lockyer, R., *Buckingham. The Life and Political Career of George Villiers, First Duke of Buckingham, 1592–1628* (1981)

MacCarthy-Morrogh, M., *The Munster Plantation: English Migration to Southern Ireland, 1583–1641* (Oxford, 1986)

MacCormack, J. R., 'The Irish adventurers and the English civil war', *Irish Historical Studies*, 10 (1956), 21–58

McGrath, P. V., 'Merchant shipping in the seventeenth century', *Mariner's Mirror*, 40 (1954), 282–93; 41 (1955), 23–37

'The Merchant Venturers and Bristol shipping in the early seventeenth century', *Mariner's Mirror*, 36 (1950), 69–80

Mahan, A. T., *The Influence of Sea Power upon History, 1660–1783* (Boston, Mass., 1890; London, 1965 edn)

Manship, H., *The History of Great Yarmouth*, ed. C. J. Palmer (Great Yarmouth, 1854)

Nef, J. U., *The Rise of the British Coal Industry, 1550–1700* (2 vols., 1932)

Newton, A. P., *The Colonising Activities of the English Puritans* (New Haven, 1914)

Oppenheim, M., *A History of the Administration of the Royal Navy and of Merchant Shipping in Relation to the Navy, 1509–1660* (1896)

The Maritime History of Devon, ed. W. E. Minchinton (Exeter, 1968)
Pearl, V., *London and the Outbreak of the Puritan Revolution: City Government and National Politics, 1625–1643* (1961)
   'London's counter-revolution', in G. E. Aylmer (ed.), *The Interregnum: The Quest for Settlement, 1646–1660* (1972)
Penn, C. D., *The Navy under the Early Stuarts* (1920)
Petersson, R. T., *Sir Kenelm Digby: The Ornament of England, 1603–1668* (Cambridge, Mass., 1956)
Porter, R., 'The Crispe family and the African trade in the seventeenth century', *Journal of African History*, 9 (1968), 57–77
Powell, J. R., *The Navy in the English Civil War* (Hamden, Conn., 1962)
   Robert Blake, General at Sea (1972)
Powell, J. W. D., *Bristol Privateers and Ships of War* (1930)
Prestwich, M., *Cranfield: Politics and Profits under the Early Stuarts* (Oxford, 1966)
Pullan, B., (ed.), *Crisis and Change in the Venetian Economy in the Sixteenth and Seventeenth Centuries* (1968)
Quinn, D. B., and A. N. Ryan, *England's Sea Empire, 1550–1642* (1983)
Rabb, T. K., *Enterprise and Empire* (Cambridge, Mass., 1967)
Rediker, M., *Between the Devil and the Deep Blue Sea: Merchant Seamen, Pirates, and the Anglo-American Maritime World, 1700–1750* (1987)
Rediker, M. et al., 'Roundtable', *International Journal of Maritime History*, 1, no. 2 (Dec. 1989), 311–57
Rodger, N. A. M., *The Wooden World. An Anatomy of the Georgian Navy* (1986)
Rose-Troup, F., *The Massachusetts Bay Company and its Predecessors* (New York, 1930)
Rowe, V. A., *Sir Henry Vane the Younger* (1970)
Salisbury, W., 'Early tonnage measurement in England', *Mariner's Mirror*, 52 (1966), 41–51
Scammell, G. V., 'Manning the English merchant service in the sixteenth century', *Mariner's Mirror*, 56 (1970), 131–54
   'Shipowning in the economy and politics of early modern England', *Historical Journal*, 15 (1972), 385–407
   'The sinews of war: manning and provisioning English fighting ships c. 1550–1650', *Mariner's Mirror*, 73 (1987), 351–67
Senior, C. M., *A Nation of Pirates: English Piracy in its Heyday* (1976)
Senior, W., *Naval History in the Law Courts* (1927)
Smith, A. E., *Colonists in Bondage: White Servitude and Convict Labour in America, 1607–1776* (Chapel Hill, NC, 1947)
Stearns, R. P., *The Strenuous Puritan: Hugh Peter, 1598–1660* (Urbana, 1954)
Stone, L., *The Crisis of the Aristocracy, 1558–1641* (Oxford, 1965)
Strachan, M., *Sir Thomas Roe, 1581–1644: A Life* (1989)

Stradling, R. A., 'Catastrophe and recovery: the defeat of Spain, 1639–43', *History*, 64 (1979), 205–19
  'The Spanish Dunkirkers, 1621–1648: a record of plunder and destruction', *Tijdschrift voor Geschiedenis*, 93 (1980), 541–58
Swales, R. J. W., 'The ship money levy of 1628', *Bulletin of the Institute of Historical Research*, 50 (1977), 164–75
Taylor, H. W., 'Trade, neutrality and the "English Road", 1630–1648', *Economic History Review*, 2nd Series, 25 (1972), 236–60
Tenenti, A., *Piracy and the Decline of Venice, 1580–1615* (1967)
Thompson, C., 'The origins of the politics of the parliamentary middle group, 1625–1629', *Transactions of the Royal Historical Society*, 5th Series, 22 (1972), 71–86
Thompson, I. A. A., *War and Government in Habsburg Spain, 1560–1620* (1976)
Tomlinson, H. (ed.), *Before the Civil War: Essays in Early Stuart Politics and Government* (1983)
Waters, D. W., *The Art of Navigation in England in Elizabethan and Early Stuart Times* (1958)
  'The English Pilot: English sailing directions and charts and the rise of English shipping, 16th to 18th centuries', *Journal of Navigation*, 42 (1989), 317–54
Wiggs, J. L., 'The seaborne trade of Southampton in the second half of the sixteenth century', M.A. thesis, University of Southampton, 1955
Wildes, H. E., *William Penn: A Biography* (1974)
Willan, T. S., *The English Coasting Trade, 1600–1750* (1938)
  Studies in Elizabethan Foreign Trade (1959)
Wood, A. C., *A History of the Levant Company* (1935)
Woodward, D. M., 'Ships, masters and shipowners of the Wirral, 1550–1650', *Mariner's Mirror*, 63 (1977), 233–47
  The Trade of Elizabethan Chester (Hull, 1970)
Wren, M. C., 'London and the twenty ships, 1626–27', *American Historical Review*, 55 (1949–50), 321–35
Young, M. B., *Servility and Service: The Life and Work of Sir John Coke* (1986)

LATE ITEMS

The following came to my notice too late to be used in this work:
Baumber, M. L., 'The Navy and the civil war in Ireland, 1643–1646', *Mariner's Mirror*, 75 (1989), 255–68
Milford, E., 'The Navy at peace: the activities of the early Jacobean Navy, 1603–1618, *Mariner's Mirror*, 76 (1990), 23–36
Ohlmeyer, J. H., 'Irish privateers during the civil war, 1642–1650', *Mariner's Mirror*, 76 (1990), 119–33
Quintrell, B., 'Charles I and his Navy in the 1630s', *The Seventeenth Century*, III (1988), 159–79

INDEX

Abbott, Sir Morris, 50
Abdy, Sir Anthony, 50
Abell, William, 50
Adams, Robert, 163
Admiralty, 13, 67, 110–11, 153, 188–9, 199;
   High Court of, 14, 42, 47–8, 63–4, 67–9,
   70–4, 84, 105, 111, 118, 126–7, 136, 196;
   see also Marten, Sir Henry
Al-Ayachi, Sidi, 167–72, 176–81
Aldeburgh, 24–5, 46, 49, 86, 173
Aldworth, Robert, 50
Aleppo, 120–2, 125–6
Alexandretta, see Scanderoon
Algiers, 116–17, 161–3, 171, 177, 181
Al-Mansur, Mulay Ahmed, 167
Amsterdam, 52, 103
Andrewes, Thomas, 58–9, 91, 198, 201
Andrews, Henry, 50
Andrews, Jonathan, 201
Andrews, Peter, 42, 47, 60, 190, 193
Anthony, Thomas, 13, 84–105
Archangel, 28, 60
Ascue, Thomas, 36
Ashley, Thomas, 197
Ashman, Jeromie Williams, 103–4
average, 43, 76
Avery, Samuel, 198

Badiley, William, 201
Bagg, Sir James, 36
Baltic Sea, 4, 19, 23–4, 28
Barbados I., 52, 60, 72, 86, 92, 100–4, 114
Barbary Company, 51, 167, 182–3
Barbary Corsairs, 5, 19–20, 27, 62, 115–17,
   131, 135, 160–83
Barbary trade, 27–8, 51, 56, 114, 182–3, 215
Barker, John, 89–90
Barker, Thomas, 25
Barlow, Edward, 83
Barlow, George, 189
Barnstaple, 20, 50

Batten William, 37, 44, 46, 81–2, 186–7,
   189–90, 195, 201
Bayning, Sir Paul, 141–2
Beane, Edmund, 42
Bence, family of, 13, 49, 60
Bence, Alexander, 12, 46–9, 188–9, 193, 201
Bence, Squire, 44, 46–9, 117, 173, 182,
   188–9, 193
Berkeley, William, 201
Berkshire, Thomas Howard, earl of, 40
Bermuda Is., see Somers Is.
Best, Thomas, 47
Biscayners, 133–5, 155
Blackman, Jeremy, 42
Blackwall, 25, 49
Blake, Admiral Robert, 89, 178
Blake, Robert (senior), 178, 182–3
Blake, Robert (junior), 183
Blyth, Richard, 187
Bonnell, Samuel, 41–2, 52, 114
Borough, Stephen, 59–60
Borough, William, 60
Boroughs, Sir John, 136
bottomry, 72
Bowyer, George, 99, 101
Bradshaw, Edmund, 170, 182
Brames, Arnold, 50
Brazil trade, 22, 43, 56, 85–90
Bridgwater, 20, 84, 88, 90
Briggs, Thomas, 182
Bright, John, 25
Brissenden, William, 177
Bristol, 19–21, 34–5, 48, 55, 85, 87, 89–90,
   171, 209
Bristol, Sir John Digby, earl of, 109
Broad, —, 174
Brokhaven, John, 102, 197
Browning, Thomas, 25
Buckingham, George Villiers, duke of, 2, 6,
   7, 68, 109–11, 144–8, 162, 164, 168
Burley, John, 186–7

234

INDEX

Burrell, Andrewes, 192–4, 198
Burrell, William, 148
Bushell, family of, 47
Bushell, Browne, 72
Butler, Nathaniel, 29, 62–3, 78–9, 131, 165

Cadiz, 1–2, 8, 23, 36, 62, 68, 78, 145–7, 164, 167
Canada, 57
Canary Is., 18, 56, 86–7, 193
Caribbean, *see* West Indies
Carlisle, James Hay, earl of, 37, 86
Carteret, George, 153, 174, 177, 179–81, 187–9
Castle, William, 25
Cecil, Sir Robert, 115
Cephalonia I., 113, 118, 124
Chamberlain, Abraham, 198
Chamberlain, Thomas, 198
Charles I, King: and domestic politics, 3, 8–12, 15, 79, 103, 111, 126–7, 146, 158–9, 184, 187–8; and foreign policy, 8–12, 79, 109, 116–17, 125–7, 132–4, 138–9, 154–8, 167–71, 181–2; and Royal Navy, 11–12, 80–1, 145–59, 184–8; and ship money, 11–12, 128–59
charter-parties, 28–9, 33, 35, 42–3, 71, 215–20
Chester, 48
Clarendon, Edward Hyde, earl of, 12, 80, 106–8, 122, 130, 138, 184–5, 188
Cleborne, William, 57
Clement, Gregory, 46, 54, 57, 60, 194–6
Clement, Robert, 53
Cloberry, Oliver, 183
Cloberry, William (senior), 18, 23, 51, 56–7, 178, 183
Cloberry, William (junior), 183
Coachman, Gervase, 193
coal trade, 5, 19, 28, 38, 40, 48, 75
Cockayne, William, 58, 90
Coke, Sir John, 8, 78–80, 85, 131, 133–5, 144–6, 154, 183
Colchester, 24–5
Cole, John, Jeremy and Robert, 25
Colston, Thomas, 35
Colthurst, Thomas, 92
Compaen, Claes Gerritz, 163
Constable, Robert, 197
Constantinople, 73, 116, 121
Contarini, Alvise, 125–7
Conway, Sir Edward, 125
Cordell, Sir John, 50
Coruña, 23
Cottington, Lord Francis, 132–4, 139
Courten, family of, 51–2

Courten, Peter, 51–2, 182
Courten, Sir William, 51–2, 57–8, 85, 88–9, 114, 182, 200
Courten, William, 41–2, 51, 114, 183, 215
Courts martial, 66–9, 110–11
Cowes, 99, 100, 102
Coytmore, Rowland, 173
Cradock, Damaris, 91
Cradock, Matthew, 58–60, 85, 89–104, 112, 197
Cranfield, Lionel, 8, 143–4
Cranley, Benjamin, 190, 193
Cranley, Richard, 12, 44, 46–7, 114, 189–90, 193–4, 198, 201
Crispe, Ellis, 183
Crispe, Sir Nicholas, 18, 23, 51, 56–7, 112, 195
Crispe, Samuel, 183
Cromwell, Oliver, 57–8, 60, 108, 139, 159, 173
Cumberland, George Clifford, earl of, 110
Cuningham, Thomas, 197–8
currants trade, 6, 113, 118, 124

Danke, Henry, 25
Dartmouth, 19–21, 35
Deane, Richard, 201
Dearsley, John, 25, 53
Dee, John, 136
Delabarr, John, 53, 57, 92
Delabarr, Robert and Vincent, 53
Delbridge, John, 50
Delphos I., 123
Deptford, 25, 53
Dethick, Thomas, 198
Dick, Louis, 197
Digby, Sir Kenelm, 13, 59, 63, 106–27, 154
Digges, Sir Dudley, 146
Dike, John, 182
Docks, Captain, 198
Dorset, 20–2, 35, 161–4, 209
Dover, 22, 37, 50, 92, 196
Drake, Sir Francis, 7, 63
Drake, Sir John, 36
Drew, Elias, 193
Driver, Charles, 35, 117, 124, 182
Dunkirkers, 5, 7, 19–20, 57, 133, 137, 140, 155, 157
Dunscombe, George, 47
Dunton, John, 175–6
Duppa, James, 54–5

East India Company, 4, 18, 27, 36, 49, 51–2, 56, 58–60, 90, 112–13, 200
East Indies trade, 5–6, 27–8, 45, 215
Edisbury, Kenrick, 79

235

Elbridge, Giles, 35, 50
Elizabeth I, Queen, and naval power, 5–8, 139–43, 149
Emery, Thomas, 72
Estwick, Stephen, 58, 201
Exeter, 19, 35

Fairborne, John, 42, 72
Falmouth, 20
Felgate, Tobias, 42, 44
Ferrars, Thomas, 182
Figgott, Matthew, 25
fisheries: Newfoundland, 5, 19–21, 53, 75, 162–4, 172; North Sea, 134–6, 155–6
Fletcher, George, John and Thomas, 183
Foard, Zephonias, 25
Fogge, Richard, 186–7
Forbes, Alexander, Lord, 196–7
Fowke, John, 59, 92
Fox, Robert, 186–7
France: naval power of, 7, 22, 137; ships loaned to, 79–80
Freeman, Sir Ralph, 50–1, 92
Freeman, William, 50–1
Frizell, James, 117

Garway, William, 50
Geere, William, 183
Gifford, Richard, 1, 131, 148–9
Gilson, John, 37
Girling, Richard, 72
Goddard, Henry, 42
Goddard, William, 41–2, 54
Gonning, John, 35
Goodlad, family of, 45, 48
Goodlad, John, 70
Goodlad, Nathaniel, 44–5, 86
Goodlad, William, 45
Gosnold, Ralph, 114
Gosport, 38
Graves, John, 25, 175
Graves, Matthew, 25
Gray, Lady Ruthven, 42
Great Yarmouth, 18–19, 24–5, 48
Greene, Giles, 188–94, 199, 201
Greene, William, 42, 53–5, 114
Griggs, Thomas, 194
Guevara, Dom Francisco de, 86–8
Guinea, 6, 18, 27, 51, 56–8, 60, 112

Haddock, Richard, 190
Haies, John, 99
Halyburtoun, William, 198
Hardwyn, Grace, 92
Hardy, Andrew, 92–104
Harrison, Brian, 174, 187, 190, 198

Harrison, John, 167–70, 182
Hatch, George, 44, 174, 187, 190
Hawes, Joseph, 59
Hawes, Nathaniel, 59
Hawkins, Sir John, 7, 193
Hawkins, Sir Richard, 63
Hawkins, Thomas, 25
Hawley, Henry, 101
Hay, Peter, 100, 102
Henrietta Maria, Queen, 108
Hill, Captain, 186
Hill, John, 198
Hill, Richard, 46–7, 58, 114, 195–6, 201
Hippisley, Sir John, 36–7
Hodges, William, 197–8
Hogg, John, 175
Holland, *see* United Provinces
Hollond, John, 85, 189–94, 198, 201
Hooke, James, 92, 101–2
Hopton, Sir Arthur, 132–4
Horseydown, 25, 53
Hosier, John, 198
Hudson, Henry, 68
Hugesson, Abraham, 92
Hull, 19, 35, 39, 43, 45, 64, 76, 203, 209, 210
Humble, Thomas, 42
Humfry, John, 196
Hurdidge, Francis, 73
Hutchinson, Richard, 201

Ipswich, 16, 19, 24–5, 28, 48
Ireland, 87, 161, 194–200; *see also* Kinsale, Munster
Iskenderum, *see* Scanderoon

Jackson, William, 57
Janson, Sir Brian, 178
Jansz, Jan, 163
Jephson, Major, 193
Jessop, William, 37, 195
Johnson, family of, 49
Johnson, Bence, 44, 49, 79
Jonson, Ben, 106
Jordan, family of, 47, 190
Jordan, Elias, 193, 197
Jordan, Joseph, 82
Jourdain, Captain, 42

Kent, I., 57
Kettleby, Thomas, 186–7
King's Lynn, 24, 48
Kinsale, 73, 86, 93–9
Kipp, John, 53
Kirke, Gervase, 57
Kirke, Lewis, 177

INDEX

Knightsbridge, William, 197
Knott, Nathaniel, 62, 131, 164
Kynaston, Thomas, 52

Langley, John, 201
La Rochelle, 62, 68, 79, 145, 147, 150, 164
Leghorn, 41, 73, 113–14, 176
Leigh, 24, 45
Levant Company, 50, 56, 58–60, 112–15, 120–7
Levant trade, 27, 113–14
Limehouse, 25, 47, 54, 88
Lindsey, Robert Bertie, earl of, 11, 67, 128, 131, 150–1, 154–5, 173
Lisbon, 23, 29, 73, 87
Love, Sir Thomas, 36
Lucas, Nicholas, 37
Lyme, 35

Maddock, John, 73, 169, 182
Mainwaring, Sir Henry, 63, 131, 153, 168–9, 187
Mainwaring, Randall, 59, 91
Mamora, 167, 172, 178
Man, John, 198
Mansell, Sir Robert, 144, 171
Mansfeld, Count, 146
March, Henry, 42
Marten, George, 193
Marten, Henry, 188, 193
Marten, Sir Henry, 63, 67, 111, 115, 126–7, 168; *see also* Admiralty, High Court of
Massachusetts Bay Company, 60, 90–1, 112
masters, 14, 38–48, 63–5, 67, 69–73, 78–9, 89, 92, 103–4, *et passim*
Mennes, Sir John, 186–7
merchants, 35–7, 48–61, 112 *et passim*
Meredith, Edward, 92, 99
Mervyn, Sir Henry, 68–9
Methold, William, 198
Middleburg, 92, 103–4
Mikonos I., 123
Milbourne, Peter, 112
Milos I., 123–4
Monson, Sir William, 29, 63, 131, 143
Morris, John, 44, 46–7, 189–90, 193, 198, 201
Moulton, Robert, 37, 44, 52, 89, 91, 190, 194–5, 201
Moyer, family of, 48
Moyer, James, 44–5
Moyer, Samuel, 45, 58, 91, 195–6, 201
Munster, 93–9
Murray, Sir David, 187
Muscovy Company, 59
Muscovy trade, 17, 51
mutiny, 9, 13–15, 62–83, 100, 118–19

Navigation Acts, 29
Navy Commissioners, 46–7, 68, 173, 189–95, 198, 201–2
Navy, Parliamentary, 12–13, 44–7, 80–1, 152, 184–202
Navy, Royal, 5–12, 62–3, 65–9, 128–88; captains in, 2, 36, 66–9, 78–80, 117, 153–4, 172–4, 176–7, 186–8; commissions of inquiry into, 7–8, 143–5, 148, 151–3, 165, 200; corruption in, 140, 144–5, 152–3; manning of, 1, 62, 75, 78, 147, 153; Principal Officers of, 78, 107, 148, 151, 188–91; victualling of, 68, 145, 152, 172, 183, 191–2, 200; *see also* Navy Commissioners, ship money, ships (royal)
Newcastle, 19, 28, 35, 38, 40, 48
Nicholas, Edward, 21, 67, 78, 111, 154, 177
Northumberland, Algernon Percy, earl of, 11, 75, 151–7, 173, 179, 184–5, 188, 190
Nottingham, Charles Howard, earl of, 110, 115, 144
Noy, William, 128–9

Onby, Humphrey, 182
Oquendo, Antonio de, 137, 157–8

Page, John, 25
Palmer, Sir Henry, 185, 189
Partridge, Captain, 198
Pasajes, 86–8
Patras, 118, 124
Payne, Edward, 88, 90, 102
Penn, Giles, 170–3, 175, 180, 182
Penneye, William, 92, 99
Pennington, Isaac, 36, 91
Pennington, Sir John, 1, 36, 85, 137, 147, 151–4, 156–8, 174, 177, 184–5, 187–8
Pennoyer, Samuel, 58, 201
Pennoyer, William, 58, 92, 195–6, 201–2
Pepys, Samuel, 65
Perry, Thomas, 193
Peter, Benjamin, 196
Peter, Hugh, 197–9
Pett, Peter, 25, 36, 37, 53, 195, 201–2
Pett, Phineas, 25, 38, 53–4, 143, 189–90, 202
piracy, 14, 27, 71, 113–14, 130–1, 142, 155, 160–83
Plumleigh, Richard, 137
Plunkett, Thomas, 193–4
Plymouth, 20–1, 35, 69, 203
Poole, 20, 35
portage, 42–3, 71, 102
Porter, Endymion, 107
Portland, Richard Weston, earl of, 128–9, 132, 139
Portsmouth, 38

237

Potton, Thomas, 121
Powell, Henry, 41, 52, 114
Powell, John, 52
Price, Thomas, 187
primage, 43, 76
privateering, 4–6, 8, 13, 20, 27, 30–2, 36–7, 46, 57, 59, 63, 66, 74, 86, 92, 106–27, 139–43, 146–9, 192, 194–8
Privy Council, 27–8, 31–2, 67–9, 70, 77–8, 115, 117, 125, 129, 131, 133–4, 140–2, 149–50, 161–2
prizes, 25, 74, 88, 109, 117–18, 124–7, 147, 149–50, 152, 189, 194–9
Providence Company, 6, 37, 62, 146
Pulman, William, 54
Pye, Sir Robert, 188
Pym, John, 60, 146, 186

Rainborowe, Thomas, *see* Rainsborough
Rainborowe, William, 1, 11, 27, 44, 45, 49, 80, 131, 154–5, 159–83, 187
Rainie (or Rany), Andrew, 104, 197
Rainsborough, Thomas, 81–2, 190, 195–6
Ralegh, Sir Walter, 6, 36, 54
Ratcliffe, 25, 59
Reynardson, Abraham, 47, 112, 121
Reynolds, —, 193
Rich, Sir Nathaniel, 146
Richaut, Sir Peter, 52, 85–6
Roberts, Lewes, 23
Roe, Sir Thomas, 24, 116, 118, 122, 181
Rolle, John, 188–9
Rookes, George, 117
Rotherhithe, 40
Royden, Sir Marmaduke, 37, 51, 85–6, 89
Rudyerd, Sir Benjamin, 146
Russell, Anna, 59
Russell, Edward, 183
Russell, James, 58, 201
Russell, Sir William, 41–2, 51, 75, 189

St Kitts I., 57, 95–9, 101–2
St Saviour's, 25
Sallee, 1, 11, 80, 154, 160–83
Salmon, family of, 45, 48
Salmon, Robert, 44, 45
São Tomé I., 53
Scanderoon, 1, 106–27
Seaman, Edmund, 174, 194
seamen, 13–15, 220; ages of, 13, 48; health of, 13, 104–5, 115–16; losses of, 161–4, 170; numbers of, 75, 221–4; pressing of, 9, 13, 75, 78; punishment of, 13, 62–5, 67, 69–73; religion and politics of, 78–83, 182–8; wages of, 14–15, 65, 72–7, 82, 87,
89, 100, 103, 153, 199; *see also* masters, mutiny, portage
sea power, 3–4, 7, 10, 124, 137–8, 156–9; English, 1, 5–10, 130, 137–40, 142–59
Selden, John, 136
servants trade, 42, 93–105
Setúbal, 24, 73, 88
Seymour, Sir Edward, 36
Shafto, Thomas, 193
Shield, Samuel, 40
shipbuilding, 24–9, 42, 53–4, 89, 92, 143–5, 148–52, 165, 172, 174–5, 195, 210–14
ship money, 9–12, 128–59
shipowning, 29–61, 78–9, 85–6, 91–2, 192–4 *et passim*
shipping industry, 16–33, 203–24; bounties, 27–9; losses, 19–21, 27, 140, 147, 161–4; profitability, 29–33, 88, 104, 127, 172, 196–8
ships, merchant: accounts of, 30–1, 35, 53, 60, 84–105; ages of, 32, 193–4, 208, 209; assurance of, 33, 54; manning of, 26–9, 75, 83, 221–4; prices of, 33; purchase of abroad, 22, 25, 36, 210; state hire of, 7, 9, 28–9, 31–2, 62, 67–8, 75, 78–9, 143, 145–7, 149–50, 154, 190–8; tonnage of, 45, 209
ships, merchant, by name: *Abraham* (renamed *William*), 35, 90–105, 197; *Achilles*, 198; *Adventure*, 117, 215, 216; *Aeneas*, 41–2, 54; *Affection*, 53–4, 218; *Ambrose*, 91, 218; *Ambrose and Charles*, 218; *Amity*, 72; *Angel*, 50; *Angel*, 193; *Anne*, 54; *Anne and Elizabeth*, 54, 216; *Anne Percy*, 193; *Anne Speedwell*, 218; *Anthony*, 91, 217; *Ark*, 18, 216; *Assurance*, 44, 49, 51, 117, 216; *Barbara Constance*, 50; *Bark Andever*, 35, 40; *Beaver*, 91; *Black Dog*, 92; *Blessing* (of Falmouth), 42, 217, 218, 220; *Blessing* (of London), 51; *Blessing* (of London), 44, 46, 193; *Blessing* (of London), 219; *Bride*, 217; *Centurion*, 53, 54, 219; *Charles*, 44; *Charles*, 217; *Clement and Job*, 44, 46; *Concord*, 59; *Confidence*, 173; *Confident*, 44; *Constant Warwick*, 36, 37, 53, 89, 194–5, 200; *Content*, 219; *Costly*, 92; *Crispiana*, 18; *Defiance*, 194; *Delight*, 51; *Desire*, 54, 216; *Destiny*, 54; *Diamond*, 35, 54; *Discovery*, 46, 57, 74, 194, 197; *Dolphin*, 103; *Dove*, 90; *Dragon*, 73; *Eagle*, 51, 112, 118; *Edward and George*, 103; *Edward and Sarah*, 35–6; *Elizabeth* (of Aldeburgh), 49; *Elizabeth* (of London), 42, 72; *Elizabeth* (of London), 59; *Elizabeth* (of London), 218; *Elizabeth and Susan*, 54; *Employment*, 91, 197; *Endeavour* (of Bideford), 42; *Endeavour* (of London), 216; *Esperance*, 67; *Exchange* (of Ipswich), 218; *Exchange* (of

INDEX

London), 44; *Exchange* (of London), 91, 216; *Expedition*, 60; *Faith*, 217; *Flower de Luce*, 216; *Four Sisters*, 53; *Freeman*, 51, 91; *Friendship*, 44; *George*, 36; *George* (or *St George*), 44, 89; *George*, 53, 218; *George and Elizabeth*, 112, 118; *George Bonaventure* (or *Lesser George*), 44, 47, 197; *Gilliflower*, 216; *Golden Cock*, 59, 92; *Golden Fleece*, 50; *Golden Lion*, 197; *Greenfield*, 35, 41–2, 52–3, 114; *Greyhound*, 72; *Guist*, 197; *Hector*, 51; *Hercules*, 174–6, 179; *Hester*, 182; *Honour*, 194; *Hope*, 72; *Hopewell* (of Dover), 92; *Hopewell* (of London), 197; *Hopewell* (of London), 219; *Hopewell* (of Shoreham), 218; *Hunter*, 92; *Increase*, 53; *James* (of London), 53, 59; *James* (of Pittenweem), 218; *Jeremy*, 53, 215, 218; *Jewel*, 92; *John*, 218; *John and Dorothy*, 59; *John and Francis*, 218; *John and James*, 85; *Jonas*, 218; *Jonas* (prize), 124–7; *Joseph*, 53; *Josias*, 53; *Katherine*, 89; *Levant Merchant*, 50, 59; *Lion's Whelp*, 59, 91; *Little David*, 175; *London Merchant*, 50; *Lorne*, 197–8; *Love*, 50; *Lucy*, 193; *Lydia*, 53–4, 217; *Lyon*, 118; *Magdalen*, 198; *Marigold*, 198; *Marten*, 193; *Mary* (of Dover), 218; *Mary* (of London), 50; *Mary* (of London), 54; *Mary* (of London), 91; *Mary* (of London), 173–6; *Mary and John*, 49; *Mary Anne*, 72; *Mary Constance*, 53–4, 91, 219, 220; *Mary Fortune*, 218; *Matthew*, 53, 216; *Mayflower* (of London), 60, 193; *Mayflower* (of Whitby), 217; *Merchant Bonaventure*, 51, 85–8; *Mercury*, 50; *Mermaid*, 194; *Messenger*, 193; *Nathaniel*, 59; *Negro Merchant*, 18; *Pearl*, 218; *Pelican*, 53; *Pennington*, 197; *Peter*, 182, 197; *Peter and Andrew*, 44, 86–8; *Pleasure*, 44; *President*, 194; *Priscilla*, 36; *Protection*, 53; *Providence*, 54, 193; *Rainbow*, 47; *Ralph Bonaventure*, 218; *Rebecca*, 92, 217; *Rebecca*, 219; *Reformation*, 59; *Relief*, 28–9, 216; *Request*, 217; *Resistance*, 53; *Richard and Nathaniel*, 218; *Richard Bonaventure*, 46–7, 114; *Robert Bonaventure*, 57; *Roebuck*, 52, 215, 216; *Royal Merchant*, 44–5, 50; *Ruth*, 197; *Safety*, 59; *St Francis*, 216; *St Michael*, 124–7; *St Peter*, 36; *Salutation*, 44, 217, 218; *Samaritan*, 52–4, 215, 216; *Sampson*, 27, 44–5, 50, 173; *Samuel*, 59; *Samuel*, 193; *Scipio*, 174; *Scout*, 198; *Shipwright*, 42; *Society*, 91; *Spy*, 92; *Star*, 36; *Sun*, 200; *Susan*, 44; *Susan*, 53; *Susan and Mary*, 38, 101; *Suzanna*, 216; *Swallow*, 118, 125; *Talbot*, 51; *Thistle*, 198; *Thomas*, 53, 218; *Thomas*, 60; *Trial*, 51; *Tristram and Jane*, 53–4, 101, 216; *Truelove*, 102; *Truelove*, 193; *Truelove*, 217; *Tryall*, 87; *Unicorn*, 92; *Vintage*, 86; *Whale*, 59, 92; *William*, 36, 86; *William*, 74; *William*, 215, 216; *William*, 218; *William and John*, 54, 73, 169; *William and John*, 44; *William and Ralph*, 27, 44, 51, 53; *William and Rose*, 217, 220; *William and Thomas*, 50

ships, royal, by name: *Antelope*, 175–6, 179; *Assurance*, 67, 151; *Bonaventure*, 186; *Charles*, 152; *Convertive*, 181; *Defiance*, 151; *Dreadnought*, 151; *Due Repulse*, 151; *Entrance*, 153; *Expedition*, 152, 174–5, 181; *Fifth Whelp*, 177; *Golden Lion*, 63; *Greyhound*, 152; *Guardland*, 81; *James*, 186; *Leopard*, 175–6; *Lion*, 186; *Lion's Whelps*, 7, 150–2, 165; *Mary Rose*, 174, 177, 179; *Merhonour*, 151; *Nicodemus*, 152; *Prince Royal*, 143; *Providence*, 152, 174–5, 177, 184; *Roebuck*, 152, 174, 179; *Sovereign of the Sea*, 144, 152; *Swallow*, 186; *Swan*, 152; *Tenth Whelp*, 186; *Unicorn*, 152–3; *Venguard*, 79

Shoreham, 25
Shute, Richard, 58, 195, 201
Slany, family of, 56
Slany, John, 51
Slany, Humphrey (senior), 18, 23, 51, 55, 183
Slany, Humphrey (junior), 183
slaves, 57–8, 60
Slingsby, Robert, 186–7
Smith, Thomas (Admiralty secretary), 153, 156–8, 188–9, 198
Smith, Thomas (Navy Commissioner), 188–90, 193–4, 201–2
Smith, William, 200
Smythe, John, 55
Somers Is., 6, 37, 50–1, 57, 62
South, Robert, 57
Southampton, 48
Southwark, 69
sovereignty of the sea, 134–7, 155–6, 158
Spain; naval power of, 1, 6, 22–4, 137, 156–8; negotiations with, 132–4, 139; trade with, 18, 22–3; war with, 6–7, 13, 18, 139–40, 145–50; *see also* Biscayners, Dunkirkers
Spenser, Thomas, 90
Spenser, William, 37
Stanley, Venetia, 108–9
Stephens, William, 25
Stepney, 53
Stevens, John, 85–6
Stevens, William, 36
Stewart, Sir Francis, 162

239

Stigg, Thomas, 92, 96, 99
Stradling, Edward, 112, 117
Stradling, Henry, 78, 117, 186–7
Strode, Sir George, 47, 112
Strong, Peter, 197
Swanley, family of, 13, 47, 187, 190
Swanley, George, 193
Swanley, Richard, 37, 195, 199–200
Swanley, William, 193
Symonds, Thomas, 36

Tayler, John, 198
Taylor, John, 25
Thierry, James, John and Stephen, 52
Thompson, George, 58, 195
Thompson, Maurice, 13, 45, 57–61, 91–2, 194–9, 201–2
Thompson, Robert, 58, 201
Thompson, William, 195
Titfall, Thomas, 25
tobacco, 1, 6, 23, 33, 42, 57, 59, 91, 95, 100–4
Totten, John, 47
Tranckmore, Robert, 25, 175
Trenchfield, Thomas, 12, 27, 44–6, 54, 124, 174, 177, 187, 190
Trenyman, Ben, 193
Trevor, Sir John, 144
Trevor, Sir Sackville, 67
Trinity House of Deptford, 13, 24–5, 31, 36, 38, 43–9, 58, 64, 69–73, 78, 80, 83, 88, 162, 168, 173–5, 177, 187, 190, 192, 200–1, 221; certificates of, 24–5, 34–5, 39, 46, 48, 71, 91–2, 210–14
Trinity House of Hull, 64, 69–70
Tromp, Maarten Harpertszoon, 1, 137, 156–8
Tryon, Francis, 42
Tucker, William, 57
Turgis, Simon, 57
Turner, Thomas, 37, 195
Turvile, Edmund, 42, 54
Tutchin, Anthony, 47
Twiddy, Roger, 12, 44, 46–8, 189–90, 193, 198, 201

United Provinces, 65; merchant shipping of, 25–6, 29, 30; naval power of, 7, 135, 137, 155–8; and North Sea fishery, 135, 155–6

Vane, Sir Henry (senior), 188
Vane, Sir Henry (junior), 78, 91, 176, 188–90
Vassall, John, 59
Vassall, Samuel, 12, 49, 59–61, 91, 176, 188–9, 193, 201

Vassall, William, 60
vessels, types of: argosies (Ragusans), 112, 124; *bertoni*, 5, 112–13; brigantines, 112; caramusals, 112, 123; caravels, 163; colliers, 5, 19, 148; feluccas, 112; fluits, 26; flyboats, 26, 117; frigates, 112, 194–5, 197; galeots, 112; galleasses, 112, 119–20; galleons, 112, 119–20; galleys, 112; hoys, 26; ketches, 26; pinnaces, 148–9, 152, 172, 174–5; saettias, 112, 117–19; shallops, 172, 196; tartans, 112, 148
Venice, 41, 113–14, 118–27
Vincent, Thomas, 195
Virginia, 42, 57, 60, 90–100, 104, 220
Virginia Company, 51, 56, 60

Wake, Baldwin, 186–7
Wake, Sir Isaac, 125
Wapping, 25, 53, 173
Waring, Richard, 195
Warwick, Robert Rich, earl of, 62, 89; as Lord High Admiral, 6, 13, 44, 82, 188–202; as privateering promoter, 111, 117, 194–5; and sea war with Spain, 6–7, 109–10; as shipowner, 36, 37, 53, 89, 194–5, 200; *see also* Providence Company
Watts, Sir John, 36
Weddell, John, 52, 200
West India Company, 6, 146
West Indies, 6, 37–8, 56–7, 146
Weymouth, 20–1, 35
whaling, 51, 59
Whetcombe, Simon, 93
Whetcombe, Tristram, 93, 97, 99
White, Thomas, 174
Williams, Sidrach, 46
Willoughby, William, 195, 201
Windebank, Sir Francis, 132–4, 139, 156, 179
wine trade, 18, 33, 86
Winthrop, John, 91
Wirral, the, 39
Wood, John, 23, 56–7, 183, 196
Wood Matthew, 193
Woodbridge, 24–5
Wright, Nathan, 59
Wright, Nathaniel, 59, 91–2, 112
Wright, Thomas (of Bristol), 35
Wright, Thomas (of Ipswich), 25
Wyche, Sir Peter, 121–2
Wye, William, 182

Zante I., 41, 113, 118, 124
Zidan, Mulay, 165–82